$\mathcal{A}$ SWINDLER'S PROGRESS

Nobles and Convicts in the Age of Liberty

Kirsten McKenzie

Harvard University Press
Cambridge, Massachusetts
London, England
2010

For my parents, who took me on their journeys.

First published in 2009 in Australia by the University of New South Wales Press

This work was published with the assistance of a grant from the Australian
Academy of the Humanities

Library of Congress Cataloging-in-Publication Data
McKenzie, Kirsten, 1970–
A swindler's progress : nobles and convicts in the age of liberty / Kirsten McKenzie.
    p.   cm.
Includes bibliographical references and index.
ISBN 978-0-674-05278-9 (cloth : alk. paper)
1. Impostors and imposture—Case studies.   2. Social status—Case studies.   I. Title.
HV6751.M35   2010
364.16'3—dc22   2009043797

CONTENTS

SIMPLIFIED LASCELLES FAMILY TREE

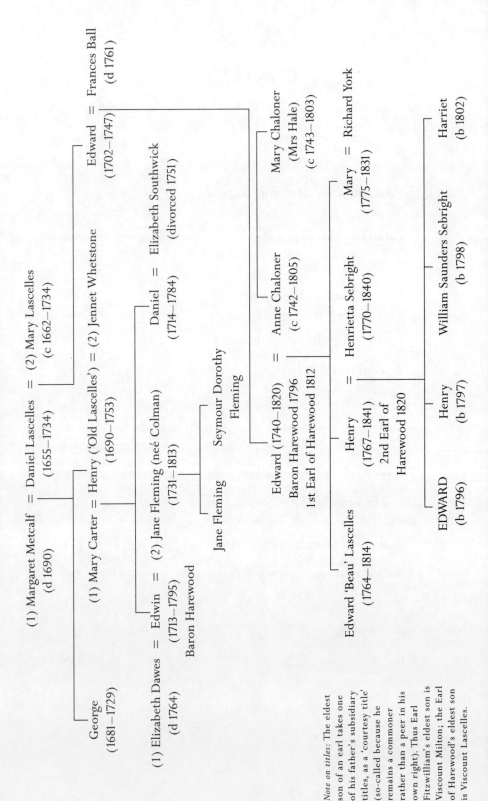

Note on titles: The eldest son of an earl takes one of his father's subsidiary titles, as a 'courtesy title' (so-called because he remains a commoner rather than a peer in his own right). Thus Earl Fitzwilliam's eldest son is Viscount Milton; the Earl of Harewood's eldest son is Viscount Lascelles.

(1) Margaret Metcalf (d 1690) = Daniel Lascelles (1655–1734) = (2) Mary Lascelles (c 1662–1734)

George (1681–1729)

Edward (1702–1747) = Frances Ball (d 1761)

(1) Mary Carter = Henry ('Old Lascelles') (1690–1753) = (2) Jennet Whetstone

Daniel (1714–1784) = Elizabeth Southwick (divorced 1751)

(1) Elizabeth Dawes (d 1764) = Edwin (1713–1795) Baron Harewood = (2) Jane Fleming (neé Colman) (1731–1813)

Jane Fleming   Seymour Dorothy Fleming

Mary Chaloner (Mrs Hale) (c 1743–1803)

Anne Chaloner (c 1742–1805) = Edward (1740–1820) Baron Harewood 1796 1st Earl of Harewood 1812

Mary (1775–1831) = Richard York

Edward 'Beau' Lascelles (1764–1814)

Henry (1767–1841) 2nd Earl of Harewood 1820 = Henrietta Sebright (1770–1840)

EDWARD (b 1796)

Henry (b 1797)

William Saunders Sebright (b 1798)

Harriet (b 1802)

PROLOGUE:
HIS LORDSHIP ON TRIAL

'But, Huck, dese kings o' ourn is reglar rapscallions;
dat's jist what dey is; dey's reglar rapscallions.'
'Well, that's what I'm a-saying; all kings is mostly
rapscallions, as fur as I can make out.'

Mark Twain, *The Adventures of Huckleberry Finn*, 1884

James Roberts, a settler of Blacktown in New South Wales, was confident he could recognise the signs of rank. When a man decked out in gold chains, accompanied by a deferential servant and calling himself Edward, Viscount Lascelles, arrived in January 1834 wanting to buy some horses, Roberts saw opportunity knocking. Roberts freely admitted that he wasn't much of a reader, though he could write a little. In any event he would have had to wait a little more than fifty years to profit from the warnings of Huckleberry Finn: 'kings is mostly rapscallions'.

As it was, the servant picked out three likely animals from Roberts's stable, the master selected some brandy, tack and snuff from his stores, and a promissory note for £50 duly changed hands. The note, a legally binding IOU, would entitle Roberts to claim the money from his lordship's bank within one month. He thought his customer's title and appearance were sufficient guarantee for payment, but before the month was up Roberts began to have his doubts. The servant had been most punctilious in addressing his master as 'my lord' and 'your lordship' during the transactions. But later the pair were seen upon the public road, laughing, joking and 'making very free together'. This was not, considered Roberts, 'the way in which Lords usually conduct themselves towards their menial servants, and [I] began to think that all was not right'.[1]

Francis Prendergast had been similarly disillusioned by his brush with the British aristocracy. A former convict, Prendergast had worked out his sentence and now farmed in a small way in the Hawkesbury district.[2] Late one night a mysterious visitor arrived at his house near Windsor. The newcomer had met Prendergast's wife at the lodging-house of one of her friends in Sydney, and he asked if he might stay for a few days. In the heat of a Sydney summer he had 'come to that part of the country for the benefit of his health'. Prendergast even loaned him a horse until such time as he could be purchase his own from Roberts. Some three or four days after his arrival the visitor admitted his identity, acknowledging that he was 'Lord Viscount Lascelles … a Peer of England and a Member of Parliament, and was shortly going to his estate in Yorkshire'.

By purchase, rent and government grant the Prendergasts laid claim to some 100 acres (40 hectares) of land, worked by convict servants assigned to them by the colonial government. They were clawing their way out of their own convict servitude onto the lower rungs of the colony's landed class. But to their illustrious guest they were objects of disdain: 'He always dined by himself in the parlour', remembered Prendergast, 'and after he had taken what he thought proper, he sent the remainder out to me and my wife and servants into the kitchen'. The visitor sent to Sydney for gallons of wine, and committed startling depredations upon the poultry yard. More than a dozen of Mrs Prendergast's finest turkeys, as well as 'innumerable geese, ducks, fowls &c', fell victim to an aristocratic appetite over the course of the next two weeks.[3]

Roberts duly visited the Bank of New South Wales to claim his money. He was told they had no account held in the name of Lascelles. Beginning to be anxious, his lordship's creditor went on to the lodging-house in Prince Street to which the viscount had now returned, having also left his bill at the Prendergasts' unpaid. When asked for the money, Lascelles pulled out his pocket-book but claimed to be £10 short. Roberts was persuaded to return on the morrow. When the unlucky horse-dealer did so, his lordship had vanished, leaving the landlord without payment for nine months' board. Apparently his creditors in the surrounds of Sydney were becoming overly pressing.

Some six months later, in the winter of 1834, the *Monitor* newspaper in Sydney carried a letter from 'A Subscriber' dated 'Argyle, July 24th' complaining of a 'mysterious personage' travelling around the interior who 'goes by the different appellations of Lord Viscount Lascelles, and "Commissioner of Enquiry," and also "Government Spy!"' He was accompanied by a manservant 'who carries an oblong square tin case, containing writing materials, &c'. Lord Lascelles was said to be busily investigating the conditions of assigned convicts, entering their huts, asking them questions about their treatment by their masters, and committing questions and answers to paper. Having 'obtained such information as he requires at one farm, he then departs for another'.[4]

The time was certainly ripe for such an investigation. Nine

months earlier, a convict mutiny had occurred on the 'Castle Forbes' estate on the Hunter River, property of local magistrate James Mudie. The rebels had declared they preferred death to life under Mudie, and implored the government to institute an inquiry into their treatment.[5] To the outrage of the jittery masters of the neighbourhood, the authorities had complied. In the usual manner of such reports, however, the outcome pleased no-one. There was outrage from some, and calls for the tyrannous Mudie to be dismissed from the bench. There were petitions from others about the need for tighter control of the convict population, and scare-mongering about the prospect of widespread revolt. The rebellion began a prolonged afterlife as a stick with which the embattled political factions of New South Wales delighted in beating their opponents. A conservative rural oligarchy of settlers (of which Mudie was a vocal member) claimed that the rebellion was a symptom of the overly liberal policies of Governor Richard Bourke. Their rivals spat back that the Hunter Valley magnates were a tyrannical jumped-up aristocracy with no respect for the rule of law. The colony's press was still deep in this protracted mud-slinging over the issue of convict discipline when news began to filter through of a travelling investigator by the name of Viscount Lascelles.

The *Monitor*'s editor was inclined to think that 'A Subscriber's letter complaining of the 'Government Spy' was a hoax; 'a specimen of Argyle wit, which this bracing weather has elicited from the fertile invention of the writer'. But he was wrong. The very same day appeared in the *New South Wales Government Gazette* a warning from the Colonial Secretary. Alexander McLeay gave notice against 'a person calling himself Lord Lascelles' who was making his way through the interior, falsely claiming to be 'a

Commissioner appointed to receive and transmit to His Majesty the complaints of Assigned Servants'.

The Sydney papers were soon awash with speculations: 'Lord Lascelles seems to be coming into greater note than ever'; 'Who and what is this man?' Opinions canvassed varied: the self-proclaimed commissioner was a spy (both the government and the Hunterian party were suggested as spymasters); he was part of Mudie's faction; he was in league with convict agitators; he was a 'travelling speculator', a former convict from Van Diemen's Land (Tasmania); he was the victim of 'monomania', a mad-man inspired by the continued settler calls for a government investigation into convict discipline. Intrigue also mounted about the visitor's ever-present but ostentatiously locked 'tin box and its mysterious contents'. Masters of assigned servants called for the arrest of the 'Grand Inquisitor', whose promises to redress the grievances of convicts were bound to cause trouble in a tense political situation.

It would be six months before the *Herald* was able to break the news of 'the safe arrival of this *nobleman* at the Penrith Gaol'. In April, the press reported, 'That most *distinguished* individual, "Lord Viscount Lascelles," arrived in town ... with his honors (double irons) thick upon him'. The *Herald* fed the thwarted curiosity of readers by ending its report with the tantalising information that 'his Lordship' was 'bearing the mystic "tinbox"'.[6]

The following month, May 1835, a slight, prematurely balding man appeared before Sydney's Supreme Court. The dignity of the law was somewhat compromised by the building's dilapidated state. Its walls were shored up with poles, and bureaucrats housed in second-floor offices lived in peril of falling through the ceiling of the courtrooms below.[7] The prisoner at the bar was charged with forging the promissory note to James Roberts under the name Edward Lascelles. Indicted under the name 'John Dow', he refused to plead, claiming he was 'improperly described'. And so began, before a noisy and appreciative capacity crowd, a meticulous investigation into the prisoner's identity. 'I have sworn before my God', the prisoner urged, 'that I am Edward, Lord Viscount Lascelles, the eldest son of the Earl of Harewood, and heir apparent to that illustrious name'.[8] 'Gentlemen', the defendant reminded the court, 'the son of the Earl of Harewood is well known to have disappeared from England in 1825':

> I have been in Van Dieman's Land since that period. What proof have you had today that he has been seen, or indeed heard of, in any country since that period, save Van Diemen's Land? Does it not forcibly carry conviction to your minds, that if that nobleman had existed in any country under the canopy of heaven, except Van Diemen's Land, he would have been frequently announced in the London and other Journals? Will it be believed, Gentlemen, that a Peer, and the son of a Peer, would remain in a state of absolute obscurity, through a series of ten years? Could his exact residence – in fact, his every movement, have remained a secret to the enquiring eye, the unceasing industry of public report? Gentlemen, it is absurd.

The viscount's family had done all they could to keep the mystery from being discovered. Now, claimed the prisoner, the sensational truth would out. Under sentence of transportation, he had taken the fictitious name of John Dow 'in order that the spotless honor of my family might not be sullied by my disgrace'. He had appealed repeatedly to his powerful father for

A Swindler's Progress

help, but in vain. And thus 'through the malignity of my parent, the being of all others, to whom I naturally looked for clemency', was he 'thrown, a stranger and destitute of the ordinary comforts of life' onto the shores of a far and savage country.[9]

The impassioned defence seems, to our ears, lifted direct from a convict melodrama. After all, that stellar example of the genre, Marcus Clarke's *For the Term of His Natural Life* (1874), included a chapter entitled 'The Lost Heir'. But the events that lay behind the prisoner's claim are no less dramatic than the courtroom rhetoric they inspired. For Edward Lascelles, heir to the house of Harewood, had indeed disappeared. And his fate was bound up in much larger global events, a struggle in which the heirs to power across the British empire were lost and found also.

In the midst of what I have called the 'age of liberty', British and colonial societies were intertwined in debates over what it meant to be free. The industrial revolution was transforming Britain's economy and population. With the rise of a new American republic, the empire had lost half its possessions in the Atlantic, but was expanding into new regions in Africa, Asia and the Pacific. Europe was convulsed by the French Revolution and its aftermath. As the tide of public opinion turned against them, British slavery and convict transportation were abolished. The franchise was expanded to encompass increasing numbers of men. What was it like to be buffeted by such forces? To follow the tale of Edward Lascelles from Britain to Australia is to feel the possibilities and losses unleashed on those unwittingly caught up in these tumults.

The trial in Sydney took place in a colony whose inhabitants were desperately trying to assert their social respectability.

They were wracked with doubts about the proper definition of status, about who had the right to exercise authority in a colony where most men and women had arrived as convicted criminals. Almost everyone – bond or free – was trying to scrabble their way up a slippery social ladder. Former convicts were becoming wealthy, but would their wealth translate into political authority? To act as magistrate, as Mudie did, to sit on juries (indeed for trial by jury to exist at all), or to vote for future legislative bodies: this was to wield power in New South Wales. Were these privileges to be confined to that small number of settlers who had come free to the antipodes, and who held themselves aloof from the vast majority who had not? A trial about whether a man was a viscount or a convict impostor was bound to touch a collective nerve in a society where all were on the make.

The benchmark against which these claims to social standing and political power were measured was of course Britain itself. Both sides of antipodean politics held it up as the model of proper society and governance, whether as a contrast to the tyranny of local officials, or as a place where rank and status were properly respected. Yet this ideal, where all knew their place and kept to it, was an image as powerful as it was false. Britain too was embroiled in debates about social status and political authority.

At the very moment that criticism mounted against morally suspect wealth, especially the wealth gained through imperial rapacity, the Lascelles were clawing their way up through society's ranks. Funded by a West Indian fortune, they were as much imperial opportunists as were the Prendergasts or the Mudies of Australia, albeit on a vastly inflated scale. In seeking the highest honours, the Lascelles family would be forced to face the question of who had the right to represent the British people and to direct their destiny. It would take them almost one hundred years of social and political manoeuvring. It would culminate in a desperate gamble to win over the country's most prestigious electorate. But the Lascelles would stare down their critics. In the midst of industrial upheaval, global expansion and struggles over the meaning of liberty for both blacks and whites, they finally reached into the heights of the peerage. In 1812 Edward Lascelles's grandfather Edward was created 1st Earl of Harewood. Four short years later, the heir to this hard-won title would cast his family's careful planning to the winds. His recklessness would not only bring ruin and disgrace on himself. It would endanger his entire lineage.

We come to that dingy Sydney courtroom, then, through a tragedy of dynastic ambition: the rise and threatened fall of a family caught up in the birth pangs of a new vision of empire, attacked as West Indian adventurers just as they were re-inventing themselves as British aristocrats. And so the tale of Edward Lascelles's disappearance is a story of social climbing as much as it is of falling; of the bids for political dominion taking place on both the farthest edge of the British empire and at its very centre; of men and women who risked all to cast themselves in a new image, and by so doing transformed their world.

PART ONE

Arcadia

The Author ... must confess, that when he has visited some of our capital seats, their seemingly interminable length of lawn, broken only by a few gloomy woods, has worn, to him, an air of melancholy solitude and idle waste, that was far from being agreeable ... What then must be the case, when these fashionable decorations are acquired by immediate rapine, extortion, or oppression; by the plunder of Hindoos, and the slavery of Negroes? One is ready to ask if it be possible to enjoy them.

John Scott, *Critical Essays on Some of the Poems of Several English Poets*, London, 1785

Harewood House, Yorkshire, 1802

William Wilberforce. Icon of the anti-slavery movement. Tireless campaigner to reform the manners and morals of the British people. No-one could accuse him of lacking vision – but it could make him something of a liability as a house guest. As landscape gardener Humphry Repton observed, Wilberforce was frequently lost in his own reflections; he would abruptly leave the company 'and retire to his own apartment'. His 'health was generally supposed to be the reason for this', but Repton thought otherwise:

> I could not help fancying, that although he paid the
> strictest attention to the duties of life, he had been in the
> constant habit of meditating on another – and without any
> abatement from the calm enjoyment of Society, he never
> lost sight of that Being who solaced his private moments,
> and made solitude delightful.

Wilberforce had always been a sociable man, and continued so after his dramatic religious conversion. But on occasion he clearly preferred the company of his God. All well and good, but a potentially disastrous source of distraction when combined with his child-like enthusiasm for trying new things. 'Every thing appeared delightful to him', remembered Repton, 'Yet his admiration was so blended with abstract thoughts, and unlooked for reflections, that it was uncertain whether he was observing what he did see, or thinking of what he did not see'.[1] None of this boded well when Wilberforce persuaded Repton to let him take the reins of the carriage as they surveyed the grounds of Harewood House, seat of the Lascelles family in Yorkshire.

It was in the year of Edward, future Viscount Lascelles's birth, 1796, that his father Henry first joined William Wilberforce as one of the two members of parliament for Yorkshire. They were on good personal terms for the ten years they represented the county together, and Wilberforce became a regular visitor at Harewood House. It was, he described to his wife Barbara:

> one not only of the most magnificent, but of the finest
> places in England. Great natural beauty, vast woods,
> expanses of water, a river winding through a valley
> portioned into innumerable enclosures. Within the
> house, perfect ease and great good-humour without the
> smallest mixture of pomp and parade, except in the rooms
> themselves, which are too gaudy for my taste.[2]

Arriving with Henry Lascelles after the rigours of a successful joint canvass in the election of 1802, Wilberforce found that the house party included Repton, the well-known 'layer out of ground'.[3] Repton was at Harewood investigating the possibilities of improvements to a landscape laid out some thirty years earlier by a group of designers that included his still more illustrious predecessor, Lancelot 'Capability' Brown.

For Repton, inveterate snob that he was, the chance to partake in family life at Harewood was a high treat. As he boasted in his unpublished memoirs, the 'elegance and splendour of Harewood House' might be well known to the common 'crowd of *felicity hunters* who swarm over the house and gardens' on public days. But 'of its comforts as an *English Home* those only can speak, who like my self have been permitted to share them'. Three generations of the family, headed by young Edward's grandfather, Lord Harewood, were established there: 'A Palace of Peace and Love! And a magnificent receptacle of domestic harmony', claimed Repton.[4]

Repton clearly wasn't privy to the currents then swirling below the family surface, for Edward's aunt had recently eloped in order to marry against her family's wishes. What harmony there was at Harewood, though, was apparently as much musical as domestic. Evening concerts involved family, visitors and servants. Lord Harewood was a noted lover of music, kept his own band of musicians and maintained the organist of Harewood Church virtually as a member of his own household.[5] Repton modestly (or prudently) failed to reminisce about his own performance, but in one of several anecdotes about meeting Wilberforce at Harewood, Repton described how the latter's 'seraphic' tenor voice soared above the other singers when moved by the spirit of his God.

During their 1802 visit, Wilberforce and Repton narrowly escaped joining the seraphim *en permanence*. As the one surveyed the grounds, the other was continually getting under foot. His youthful enthusiasm ('In wit a man, simplicity a child', quoted Repton) was apt to endanger his tolerant companions, whether rowing on the lake (Henry Lascelles prudently took one oar himself) or driving in the lanes. Joining Repton in a 'low fourwheeld carriage', Wilberforce asked to be instructed with the reins. Repton was dubious, but Wilberforce 'seemed delighted with his newly acquired art'. All went well until they reached the new entrance arch being constructed near the village. Wilberforce airily waved aside his passenger's navigational concerns, and the inevitable occurred.

The histories of abolitionism and English landscape gardening alike almost took an unexpected turn. Wilberforce, in his 'anxiety to pull the *right* rein ... pulled the *wrong* one'.

Arcadia

The carriage went 'bouncing against an ionic capital' and its two occupants were almost upset. Repton drew a sigh of relief and, as 'the novelty began to wear off', Wilberforce agreed to return the reins and to read aloud from William Cowper, that bard of the evangelical middle classes, instead.[6] Neither man could know that five years later, overcome with ill health and surrounded by rumours of his demise, Wilberforce would be turning to the same poet for succour during a rancorous election campaign fought against his one-time host and ally Henry Lascelles.[7]

On this same 1802 visit, Wilberforce and Repton less eventfully toured Harewood's 'celebrated' glasshouses. These supplied pineapples and other exotic fruit to the house, and included two granadillas which seemed as much at home – 'as if they were in the island of Jamaica'.[8] Repton later recounted how they had also been shown:

> an evolved leaf of the most beautiful tender green – just rising out of a garden plot. I caught Wilberforce's attention by its beauty – and when the gardener told him it was a *young sugar cane plant* he seemed lost in admiration, and we could read in his glistening eye, all the complicated train of thought which had called forth his extraordinary energy and engaged his deep attention for so many years!

'Providence', continued Repton's reminiscences, 'has been pleased to allow the reward of his labours in the abolition of the Slave Trade – and has permitted him to live to *see* the success of his exertions'.[9]

It was, of course, not unusual for the hothouses of Britain's elite to play host to exotica from throughout the empire. But there are tactful omissions in Repton's tale of Wilberforce and the Lascelles's sugarcane. In the midst of his protracted campaign to end the slave trade, Wilberforce was enjoying the hospitality of a house whose palatial surrounds — Ionic capitals, glasshouses and all — had been paid for by the bitter profits of sugar plantations worked by African slaves. The Lascelles's West Indian fortune had brought forth Palladian splendour in the Yorkshire countryside. Now, in the first decade of the nineteenth century, it was about to become a political liability.

Arcadia

1

ET IN ARCADIA EGO

Sir Walter Elliot, of Kellynch-hall, in Somersetshire, was a
man who, for his own amusement, never took up any book
but the Baronetage; there he found occupation for an idle
hour, and consolation in a distressed one; there his faculties
were roused into admiration and respect, by contemplating
the limited remnant of the earliest patents; there any
unwelcome sensations, arising from domestic affairs,
changed naturally into pity and contempt, as he turned over
the almost endless creations of the last century.

Jane Austen, *Persuasion*, 1818

Et in Arcadia ego. In the paintings of French classicist Nicolas
Poussin, shepherds from antiquity contemplate Virgil's phrase
carved upon a tomb. Its richly ambiguous meaning has provided inspiration for countless artists since, from Evelyn
Waugh's *Brideshead Revisited* to Tom Stoppard's *Arcadia*. For who
is the 'I' of the motto? Is it not Death itself? 'Even in Arcadia,
there am I!'

In the grounds of Harewood House, the Lascelles had bent

nature to the fashionable conception of Divine will. The vision was intended to evoke the classical images of French painters like Poussin or Claude, an aesthetic irony sometimes lost on those who admire it today as quintessentially English. When Wilberforce and Repton made figures in the Harewood landscape, the latter had been brought in (to quote Stoppard's play) 'to bring God up to date'.[1] And in this, the Lascelles were spectacularly successful. 'What taste and judgment crown the vast design?' proclaimed an 1822 guidebook. 'The gods themselves might think Elysium here.'[2] It was a setting perhaps as far as it is possible to imagine from a crumbling Sydney courtroom and a colony made up of the sweepings of Britain's criminal refuse.

If the Antipodes is the world turned upside-down, is Arcadia then the paradise of order? In the progress we are tracing from one to the other, death is present right at the start, be it the 'death' of social disgrace, of exile, or of bondage. To learn how Edward Lascelles came to vanish we need to go back in time. We need to follow the Lascelles as they battled their way into the upper ranks of British society. Only then can we understand what haunted the pastoral idyll in which Repton and Wilberforce contemplated that young sugarcane. Only then can we learn how Edward's name came to be invoked on the furthest side of the world.

The bitter fruits of empire

Connections between the Lascelles family and the West Indies go back to the 1680s. Various branches of the family made at least three attempts to secure a fortune there. Only the last of these was sufficiently successful to transfer across the generations and to transform their status. In the monumental election battle that would sweep up Henry Lascelles and William Wilberforce in 1807, the opponents of the house of Harewood would work hard to prove them parvenu colonial upstarts, descended from 'a Family Nobody knows'.[3] In fact, as the nineteenth-century tour guides to Harewood House were at pains to demonstrate, the Lascelles were of Norman descent, settling in Yorkshire around the time of the Conquest, and establishing themselves amongst the local gentry. They had deep roots in Yorkshire, and it was to Yorkshire that they would return with their West Indian fortune.

The efforts of an earlier Henry Lascelles (1690–1753), and to a lesser extent his two brothers, secured the fabulous wealth necessary to catapult the family into the ranks of the peerage. Henry Lascelles (or 'Old Mr Lascelles' as he was sometimes known, to distinguish him from all the Henrys and Edwards who followed) joined his elder brother George on the island of Barbados in 1711 or 1712. Half-brother Edward followed. All three were the sons of Daniel Lascelles, MP for Northallerton, and the grandsons of Francis Lascelles of Stank Hall, Kirby Sigston, who had been MP for Thirsk, the North Riding of Yorkshire, and for Northallerton. Francis had served as a colonel in the Parliamentary army during the English Civil War and numbered amongst the commissioners who tried Charles I for high treason, although he prudently failed to vote on the question of execution and did not sign the royal death warrant.[4]

Shortly after his arrival in Barbados, Henry married Mary, the daughter of Edwin Carter, a local merchant, planter, slave-trader and deputy collector of customs. It was a fortunate match, as slave-trading was a key interest for Henry in these years. In 1715, around which time George returned to England, Henry was appointed collector of customs in Barbados, a post

Et in Arcadia ego

he would hold for some two decades until replaced by his half-brother Edward. Both would face accusations of corruption and improper conduct during their times as collectors, and they certainly profited from their position. The charges levelled against them have to be seen in the context of highly partisan factional conflicts and commercial rivalries in both Britain and Barbados. Charges of fraud were habitually brought for political effect amongst men who were often all under investigation for similar offences. The Lascelles brothers do not appear to have differed too much from their contemporaries at a time when the standards of public accountability were very different from our own. The Lascelles were able to escape prosecution through their political connections and by judiciously purchasing political office.

In the 1720s and 1730s, Henry moved between England and Barbados. Mary died in 1721, and was buried in Yorkshire. He married his second wife, Jennet Whetstone, in Barbados in 1731. By then, Henry was established as a leading West Indian merchant with business interests in several key areas. The three brothers had founded a London commission house, known from 1743 as 'Lascelles and Maxwell' after the addition of George Maxwell as partner. The core activities were receipt and sale of cargoes of sugar and rum, but the enterprise was also involved in commissions somewhat less familiar to a modern importing business. It was responsible for looking after the children of West Indian clients, dealing with schoolboys expelled and undergraduates disgraced. Two such had to be shipped back to Barbados after living it up at Oxford.[5] This was part and parcel of the world of the eighteenth-century West Indian elite inhabited by the Lascelles and their ilk, one that stretched across the Atlantic from the North American colonies to the coast of Africa.

The commission house, however, was a relatively small part of Old Lascelles's activities. Even more lucrative were government contracts to provision the armed forces during the protracted wars between the British and the French which convulsed the eighteenth-century Caribbean.[6] Henry further diversified his business interests into slave-trading (creating a syndicate of merchants to establish a 'floating factory' to process slaves off the Guinea coast), shipping and money-lending. He might have been up to his neck in the human misery that sustained the West Indian slave economy, but the Lascelles did not start out as classic absentee sugar planters. It was only at the end of the eighteenth century, as their business foreclosed on an extensive series of loans to mortgaged estates, that the Lascelles family became substantial plantation owners in their own right.

For the last twenty years of his life, Henry directed his gargantuan business operations without leaving England, for his last visit to Barbados seems to have been around the time of his second marriage in 1731. Historian Simon Smith uses the term 'gentry capitalism' to explain the activities of men such as Henry Lascelles and his peers. Unlike other kinds of imperial adventurers, who were escaping poverty and degradation in Britain, such men came from families of the British landed gentry and were already respectable and well connected. But colonial trade allowed them to greatly increase their wealth and influence, building on a series of pre-existing networks, and combining government patronage and the pursuit of private profit to emerge as immensely powerful figures in the Atlantic world.

In a pattern that would extend into the following century, the 'people-based networks' upon which such gentry capital-

Et in Arcadia ego

ists relied helped to reduce financial risk by tying their members into mutually reliant relationships. Political influence and patronage were vital to success. In 1745, the year in which the accusations of corruption against the Lascelles brothers were coming to a crisis, Henry Lascelles ensured that he and his second son Daniel were returned as MPs for Northallerton and Scarborough. Henry's eldest son Edwin took part in repelling an invasion by Britain's ousted royal dynasty, the Jacobites, and Henry himself wisely provided financial assistance to the Hanoverian crown. Later that year, the Treasury ordered the corruption proceedings against the Lascelles to be dropped.[7] Northallerton became the accustomed Lascelles family parliamentary seat.

'Old Lascelles' had married twice in Barbados, his three surviving children were all born there, and the seeds of his fortune was sown there. But he had long-range ambitions for that fortune, and they lay not in the West Indies but in the place of his birth. Henry was founding a dynasty, and a dynasty needs ancestral roots. Stank Hall, the family seat near Northallerton, was too modest for his purpose. Shared family lineage as well as geographical association dictated the choice of purchase. In 1739 Henry bought the estates of Gawthorpe and Harewood, between Leeds and Harrogate, for £63 827. The lands, sold by the Boulter family to clear their debts, had previously been owned by the Gascoignes, with whom the Lascelles were distantly connected. By 1748, son Edwin was already installed as lord of the manor (Henry preferred London) and lived with his family in the Old Hall of Gawthorpe. Although the location was excellent (even including a suitably decayed and picturesque ruin nearby in the form of Harewood Castle) the aging edifice could not fulfil the grand plans of its new owners. The southern slope rising behind the Old Hall, with a series of suitable vistas already to hand, would be the eventual site of Harewood House.

Shortly before work on the mansion and its surrounding landscape began, the man whose money lay behind it met his demise. When Old Lascelles died in 1753 his exact worth was unclear, for he had transferred property to his sons prior to his death, but he was without doubt one of the richest men in England. He was also the last to expire of the three brothers who had departed for Barbados. Henry's funeral in Northallerton was a public affair of great magnificence but this did not quiet murmurs about 'the Tragical end of Harry Lasceles', who was rumoured to have committed suicide by cutting his own throat.[8] The exact circumstances of Henry's death remain mysterious. We are left to speculate on what private demons were conjured by a life spent in relentless pursuit of such extraordinary wealth by such ruthless means. We should not be too quick to speculate, though, on torments of conscience about the scores of lives destroyed, directly or indirectly, by the Lascelles's business. Henry was of a time which still largely accepted the horrors of slavery. It would be very different for his namesake some fifty years later.

Old Lascelles's death, just two years before the first major building works at Harewood began, created one degree of remove between the family's aristocratic setting and the source of their wealth. The Lascelles brothers had come from solid local gentry stock before they left Yorkshire for Barbados. But the sudden acquisition of their wealth, and its West Indian origins, seems to have attached an air of the upstart to Henry's generation, at least in the eyes of some contemporaries. Forty years later, gossip about Old Lascelles, his wealth and his suspicious death was still making the rounds. The artist and diarist

Et in Arcadia ego

Joseph Farington (whose waspishness was legend) was meticulous about recording what he called 'the floating opinions' of the day. In 1796 he visited a fellow artist and met 'Old Mr Carr of York, the Architect', the man largely responsible for the design of Harewood House, who had come 'to sit for a profile'. We can imagine the architect regaling the two painters with the latest local *on dit*, for the next section of Farington's diary is full of Yorkshire gossip: financial scandals, an elopement with a grocer, rumours of insanity amongst a prominent family. In a jumble of facts, Farington records the word on the street about the Lascelles:

> Mr Lascelles, the Father of the late Lord Harewood, of
> Daniel Lascelles, and of General Lascelles killed himself,
> by opening the veins in his wrist. He had been in the West
> Indies & been guilty of extortion. The present Mr. Lascelles,
> (now Lord Lascelles) was a 7th or 8th cousin only of the
> late Lord, but preferred in the will of his Lordship, on
> acct. of general Lascelles having married Miss Catley. The
> grand father of the present Ld. Harewood, though a distant
> relation, was a servant at that time in the Lascelles Family.[9]

The information Farington records is somewhat mixed in its accuracy. Simon Smith has attempted to trace the origins of the rumour about the grandfather being a servant, yet its importance lies rather in its vague and unsubstantiated quality.[10] By 1796, the year of young Edward Lascelles's birth, there was a sense, however unjustified, that the Lascelles family had emerged from humble origins. It was a popular perception that would be employed to brilliant political effect a decade later.

'The first in the north': building Harewood House

It was Edwin, son of Old Lascelles, university educated, polished on the Grand Tour and purged of the unsavoury associations of his father (both in life and in death), who would build Harewood House. One of the established jokes of the second half of the eighteenth century was the errors of taste made by the retired businessman when he purchased or built his '"bran-new" country seat'. For a society concerned about the explosion of new wealth, such vulgarities illustrated the 'excesses of the upstart, his bad taste, and his idle pretension'.[11] Edwin, however, did not put a foot wrong. With a certain unerring instinct for posterity, he employed the luminaries of the age, not only gossiping architect John Carr of York, but also three of the usual suspects of eighteenth-century country house design: Robert Adam, Thomas Chippendale and Capability Brown.

Edwin's plans, so grand they had to be continued by his cousin and successor Edward, encompassed as complete a reinvention of his physical surrounds as befitted a family who had accumulated such astonishing wealth. Even nearby Harewood village received a series of fresh buildings and amenities along 'model village' lines.[12] The new drive and gateway to the park (on which Wilberforce and Repton almost came to grief) was built in 1801. Judiciously re-housing various tenants, and diverting the course of the Leeds–Harrogate road, removed the house from public view. It was a scheme of improvement very much in the spirit of its time. The country house of the eighteenth century was more often than not physically separated from the wider community and surrounded by a park emptied of all but picturesque figures. This gave the owner free rein to show off his erudition and sophistication to an appreciative audience.

Et in Arcadia ego

It took Edwin considerable time to decide upon an architect. William Chambers and John Carr of York, who had begun work on a new stable block to the west of the Old Hall in 1755, drew up the plans. In 1758 Edwin Lascelles met Robert Adam, who was already becoming a celebrated figure in British aesthetic life. Lascelles eventually settled upon Adam's adaptation of Carr's designs (although he later abandoned many of Adam's suggestions) and the foundation stone of the house was laid in 1759. In also choosing the increasingly fashionable Adam for the interior decoration of his house, Edwin ensured the interest and curiosity of the *beau monde*. By 1767 the house was sufficiently complete for Chippendale, similarly at the height of his reputation as furnisher to the elite, to begin a survey for the work which now constitutes one of the greatest surviving collections of his art. Amongst the more lavish of his masterpieces was the gilt and brocade state bed. A purpose-built state bedroom, ostensibly reserved for visiting royalty, served Edwin Lascelles's more immediate purpose of providing a status symbol essential to the country house of the day. The requisite family portraits would find a place in the long gallery, with its carved and painted *trompe-l'oeil* pelmet, again by Chippendale. The grand public rooms that dominated the ground floor provided the spaces necessary for the house to perform its function as a nerve-center of social and political power.

By 1771 Harewood House was habitable, the family moved in, and the Old Hall was demolished. Edwin, a great admirer of the French classical style evoked by Capability Brown, turned his attention to the grounds. He was less impressed that Brown's transformation came in at three times the original budget — before the costs of planting had even been added. Nor was he pleased that the lake, which Brown had constructed on the

Arcadia

site of the Old Hall by damming Stank Beck, persisted in leaking.[13] Edwin Lascelles used excuses about the quality of Brown's workmanship to delay settling his accounts. Both Brown and Chippendale reached the point of desperation trying to expedite payment from their patron, lending unintended irony to the confidence later shown by antipodean creditors James Roberts and Francis Prendergast that aristocrats would surely pay up. Brown had to call twice on Edwin personally to pressure him for payment, and Chippendale's unpaid bills reached such proportions that the craftsman downed tools in protest.

But with his surrounds suitably transformed, Edwin could now begin using Harewood for one of the express purposes for which such houses were built: staging entertainments of fitting magnificence. These would broadcast a family's status, wealth and good taste to an envious and admiring world. Edwin's first wife, Elizabeth Dawes, a wealthy Yorkshire heiress, had died in 1764. His second wife, Lady Fleming, came with two eligible daughters who had inherited an impressive fortune from their late father, and the new house was conveniently finished in time to launch them into society.[14]

Things did not quite turn out as planned. In 1778, Edwin played unwilling host to one of the most notorious parties in Harewood's history, and the chief culprit was none other than his own step-daughter, Seymour Dorothy, wife to Sir Richard Worsley. Seymour was already possessed of a scandalous reputation: the previous summer she had attracted attention as one of a cohort of glamorous fashionables, including the famous 5th Duchess of Devonshire, who were cavorting with the officers at the military camp of Coxheath.

When Harewood was thrown open to party-goers during the Christmas and New Year period of 1778–1779, news about

Et in Arcadia ego

the occasion soon spread its way around the country, but it was not of the sort for which Edwin might have wished.[15] 'There has been great masquerading this Christmas at Harewood', wrote one correspondent:

> & all the rooms both ladies & gentlemen were thrown
> open & made *common*. Lady Worsley & the two Miss
> Cramers threw most of the gentlemen's Cloaths out of the
> window particularly their *Breeches* thinking them I suppose
> unnecessary.

In retaliation, the trees in Harewood's park ended up festooned with Lady Worsley's caps and bandboxes. 'You see', joked another writer, reporting 'the amusements that have been going on' in the generally less fashionable northern counties, 'that we enter into the follies of the age and make ourselves as ridiculous as they do in the South'.[16]

Before long the 'follies' spilled out of the gates. Two weeks into the new year, the girls begged Edwin Lascelles to lend them his coach to visit Leeds. When her step-father refused, Seymour and her cronies rode themselves to town on the estate cart horses, stopped at an inn *en route*, and broke into a room used as the sanctum of the local militia. There they defaced the colours, setting them alight with red hot pokers. 'How do you think they quenched the flame their own fair selves had caused? They did not call water! Water!, it was more at hand. They fairly _____ it out.' A respectable Leeds worthy, sent for by the Harewood truants, and 'thinking it right to wait upon the ladies in form', had his best coat, wig and waistcoat ruined as they ambushed him with a dish of water and a bag of soot.

Several days of 'pranks' and rioting around the countryside followed, providing ample gossip about 'the wit and courage of the Belles of Harewood'. Edwin was horrified by their wild behaviour, not least because it had destroyed his glassware and furniture to the value of £500. 'I fancy', commented one who had heard the gossip from a bemused guest, 'there will be an end of all Xmas meeting at Harewood as soon as Miss Fleming [Seymour's sister, Jane] is married'. Three years later Sir Richard Worsley brought a divorce action against Seymour and a ruinous case of damages against the lover with whom she had eloped. As the most intimate and shocking details of the Worsleys' marriage were shaken out and aired, both were pilloried before the public and immortalised in the satirical print shops of a deliciously scandalised London.

There may have been mutterings about nefarious goings on at Harewood House, but by 1790, when Edwin was created 1st Baron Harewood, his title had the appropriate setting. In this, the Lascelles were not alone. Some 209 peerages appeared between 1776 and 1830 in the United Kingdom.[17] The new creations were a widely recognised if not always welcome phenomenon (sneered at, for example, by Sir Walter Elliot in the opening passage of Jane Austen's *Persuasion*). By the end of the process, rank and wealth were more closely aligned. Along with their titles, the newly ennobled competed with one another to build splendid edifices befitting their station, and to amass fabulous collections of art. These trappings of wealth and the pursuit of honours allowed what was in fact novel to be presented as timeless and secure. While on the one hand the aristocracy was promoting itself as standing for stability in troubled times, that self-same landed class was busily remaking itself.

Edwin Lascelles had spent at least £50 000, around £20 000 more than he had planned,[18] but the grandeur of Harewood House and its surroundings, and the impeccable taste with

Et in Arcadia ego

which these were laid out, were already being celebrated. Indeed, Harewood House was fast becoming a tourist destination. Respectable visitors, carefully vetted by the domestic staff, would be admitted to the house and grounds. The finely calculated balance between privacy and publicity was vital for any country house owner who had cultured pretensions. If the house were to perform one of its key functions – asserting its owner's status through taste – then its owner had to make sure it was just accessible enough for word to get out.[19] Despite his earlier gawking interest in Old Lascelles's rumoured suicide, in 1801 Joseph Farington visited Harewood House as part of a journey to the Lake District and Scotland, and he was favourably impressed.[20]

John Jewell, a porter at Harewood House who filled his spare time (and supplemented his income) in conducting visitors around the estate, published the first guidebook to 'The magnificent and princely residence of the Right Honourable the Earl of Harewood' in 1822. The house, he claimed, was 'so justly celebrated for its beauty, grandeur of style, elegance of decoration and finishing, both externally and internally, that it is deservedly ranked with the first buildings of the kingdom'. The grounds 'have long and deservedly been celebrated as the first in the north of England'.[21] The 'Ode to Harewood' that opens the book bears witness to the fulfillment of Edwin's idyllic vision, asserting 'The gods themselves might think Elysium here'.

The real Elysium received Edwin in 1795, or so we might hope. Dying at Harewood House, aged 82, he had enjoyed the title of Baron Harewood for only five years. His father, Old Lascelles, had split his estate between his sons, but, foreshadowing the tragedy of the 'Lost Heir' enacted in Sydney, the dynasty was proving far harder to sustain in lineage than it was in finance. All of Old Lascelles's sons had died without leaving sons of their own to inherit. The lion's share of the fortune was therefore reunited in 1795 under the control of one of Edwin's cousins, Edward, the Barbadian-born son of Old Lascelles's younger half-brother (and fellow customs collector) Edward.[22] The title of Baron Harewood was similarly revived for cousin Edward in 1796. He was then fifty-five years old, and father to two sons, who seemed to secure the succession at last. The eldest, yet another Edward, known as 'Beau' Lascelles, was unmarried. But the second son – yet another Henry, and Wilberforce's future colleague – and his wife provided a grandson for the newly minted Lord Harewood that very year. A second grandson would follow a year later. (Unsurprisingly, these two boys were christened Edward and Henry respectively.)

So when Edward Lascelles, the mysterious viscount whose credit was dishonoured in dusty New South Wales, was born in Yorkshire in 1796, his birthplace was, in historian Mark Girouard's memorable phrase, literally a 'power house' as much as it was home to three generations of the Lascelles family.[23] Harewood was a vital stronghold in a particular sphere of political alliance and influence. It was as part of this alliance that Henry Lascelles, Edward's father, would fight one of the most celebrated election campaigns of the period. The Lascelles were prominent members of a grouping from which Britain's Tory party, as we know it today, would emerge. So far, so familiar, but the politics of Edward's childhood can sometimes feel immeasurably alien, not only from our own time, but even from that of the Victorians just a generation hence. Such is the transformation that would take place over the course of Edward's life.

Et in Arcadia ego

The Lascelles were about to be swept up in three of the most important forces of their day: the abolition of slavery, industrialisation, and the connection between social status and political power. To follow the Lascelles into the audacious gamble they took in the 1807 election is to show how profound was the change taking place in their world.

'All politics is local'

Politics in Yorkshire was not for the faint-hearted. It demanded a combination of personal ability, social influence, and the confidence to bully an opponent into backing down. It also required money. At a time when electioneering was openly acknowledged as a rich man's pastime, the costs of mounting an election in the county were liable to make even the wealthiest flinch. When Edward's father Henry fought his monumental battle in 1807, it had been more than sixty years since a Yorkshire county election had even been fought to poll: one party had always withdrawn rather than risk the staggering expense. Yet the potential rewards were seductive. Containing more than 10 per cent of the nation's electorate, and with a strong tradition of political independence, Yorkshire was the largest English constituency of its day. Holding one of the two seats that represented 'proud Yorkshire'[24] in the House of Commons was always prestigious; to do so in open contest would command the attention of the whole country. For the Lascelles, then on the hunt for a peerage, there was an added incentive in the form of royal patronage. In the first decade of the nineteenth century, relations between George III and his ministers were increasingly vexed over the issue of Catholic emancipation. (Catholics still suffered restrictions on their civil and political rights in this period. Dynastic and political struggles in the seventeenth and eighteenth centuries made it an emotive issue that remained hotly, and sometimes violently debated.) At this fractious constitutional moment, binding Yorkshire to the King's interest was an act of political loyalty that would surely bring suitable reward.

When Henry died, thirty-four years after the event, he was still remembered for fighting that 'memorable contest' of 1807. It was perhaps the Lascelles's most prominent moment on the national political stage. 'The Yorkshire Election', reported *The Times* in the midst of the titanic struggle, 'is still contested with an obstinacy that keeps that large County in an uproar, and threatens the fortunes of the rival Candidates with ruin'.[25] The Lascelles and their Whig rivals each spent the sum of around £100 000 on the campaign (roughly £6.2 million today, or almost as much as Old Lascelles and Edwin had spent on the entire Harewood estate, house and grounds). It was a figure that stunned observers: 'I hear Mr. Lascelles says he wishes his Father would give him the money instead of the seat'.[26]

'All politics is local', declared US House of Representatives Speaker, Thomas 'Tip' O'Neill. O'Neill died in 1994, but he could equally have been speaking of the Lascelles and their world. General elections were usually a host of separate contests fought across the country on completely different issues. Only rarely did a national question take prominence. When changes in government took place, it was mostly because of new coalitions in Whitehall or because royal patronage had shifted, not because of a grassroots swing amongst the voters. Political influence was exerted primarily within one's own backyard. When the Lascelles returned to Britain with their West Indian money, then, the politics on their mind was that belonging to Yorkshire.

Et in Arcadia ego

The three brothers who went to Barbados were the sons of a Northallerton MP, and Old Lascelles took on this role after his return, as would Edwin. The market town remained the family's parliamentary seat from the middle of the eighteenth century until its abolition in 1832. As new generations were born, and as Harewood House rose white and shining from the ashes of the Gawthorpe estate, the Lascelles took up a commensurate place in the Yorkshire political landscape. In the elections of 1761, 1768 and 1774, Edwin carried the prestige of being returned, along with Sir George Savile, as member for the county of York. Savile stood on the other side of the period's broad political divide, member of a faction known as the Rockingham Whigs for their leader Charles Watson-Wentworth, 2nd Marquess of Rockingham. The expense of contesting a seat like Yorkshire, and the social turmoil it could potentially unleash, meant that coming to a gentleman's agreement to split the county between the two main political spheres of influence was not uncommon.

The two-party system along the lines of Britain today was not yet cemented. There had been self-described 'Whigs' and 'Tories' in the early eighteenth century and there would be so again. But in the years around the turn of the nineteenth century there was something of an interregnum. 'Whig' was a label used by many politicians across a broad political spectrum, while 'Tory' usually figured as an insult (and it was used as such against the Lascelles in 1807). 'Tory' was directed in particular at those men who allied themselves with the King's party and with Prime Minister William Pitt 'the younger'. Only later would the Tories appropriate the label to themselves. In any event, personal alliance was often far more characteristic of parliamentary politics than party uniformity, making men who stood as independents a real political force. Political factions also coalesced around individuals, hence 'Pitt's friends' or 'Pittites' opposed the 'Foxite Whigs', led by Charles James Fox. In retrospect, the 1807 election lay on the cusp of a new two-party system, though this was not always obvious at the time. Since it was from the Lascelles and their allies that the modern Tory party would emerge, their rivals in 1807 are more conveniently labelled 'Whigs'. To avoid confusion, this is what I have chosen to call them.

Before 1807, even Wilberforce – then the most celebrated MP in the Commons – had avoided an all-out contest in Yorkshire over a career spanning almost three decades. He was first elected in 1780 to the borough of Hull, a seat that could be won with comparative ease. He made his move, and his national reputation, four years later in the tumultuous general election of 1784. The loss of the American colonies had been a traumatic blow to the establishment. Rockingham, first lord of the treasury (the office which evolved into that of prime minister), had died in office two years earlier. Now a faction of the Whigs under Fox, who had strenuously opposed the American war, made an unexpected alliance with a former opponent, Lord North. Together they mounted an audacious challenge to the power of George III through the East India Bill. This would have placed the East India Company, and so British imperial expansion in the subcontinent, under the direct control of their own ministry. For many, though, the issue was more the power struggle at home.

Fox's enemies declared themselves scandalised by the Whigs' ambition. At issue, quipped Dr Johnson to his biographer James Boswell, was 'whether the nation would be ruled by the sceptre of George III or the tongue of Fox'.[27] In outrage,

Et in Arcadia ego

the King engineered the fall of the Fox-North coalition and on 19 December 1783 he appointed William Pitt the younger, Wilberforce's close friend and exact contemporary, as prime minister. It was a risky (and arguably unconstitutional) gambit on the part of the monarch. Pitt was fighting for his political life when Wilberforce, MP for Hull, hastened up to Yorkshire to speak at a public meeting on the King's actions.

In 1784 the county was dominated by some of the greatest Whig dynasties in the land, and they were out in force to denounce Pitt that freezing day in March. As Wilberforce mounted the platform erected in the York Castle yard, a crowd of over four thousand had endured hours of weak, inaudible speeches in blasting wind and hail. Slight of frame, and standing only five foot four inches (162 centimetres) tall, it seemed to one eyewitness that he must be blown off his feet. Yet Wilberforce was about to show both his physical endurance and his mastery of political rhetoric. Raising his voice against the gale, he attacked the Whigs as a self-interested oligarchy who sought tyranny over King, Commons and people. 'I saw', wrote Boswell, in the audience that day, 'what seemed a mere shrimp mount upon the table; but, as I listened, he grew and grew until the shrimp became a whale'.[28]

It was in this moment that Wilberforce took the decisive step towards realising an ambition he had not dared to confide even to Pitt: garnering the support needed to represent the county of Yorkshire. In the manoeuvring that immediately followed, the Whigs were routed and withdrew from the contest rather than risk a poll. 'We were beat by the ragamuffins', fumed Rockingham's nephew, Earl Fitzwilliam. In fact Fox, that most compulsive of gamblers, had overplayed his hand. Across the whole country, support had poured in for the King and his new prime minister. Pitt's 'mince pie administration', so called because few considered it would last past Christmas, had not only survived, but secured a decisive majority. Wilberforce had won national fame and arguably the most prestigious county seat in the House of Commons. Both he and Pitt were only twenty-four years old.[29]

It was this history that effectively made the celebrated election of 1807 a grudge match. Three candidates would contest the two county seats. Wilberforce, hailed as a national hero for abolishing the slave trade just months earlier, stood as an independent. In the King's interest was Lord Harewood; 'ready', wrote Wilberforce in his diary, 'to spend in it his whole Barbados property'.[30] Henry Lascelles and Wilberforce had represented Yorkshire together since the year of Edward's birth, 1796. The two seem unlikely political bedfellows, one a committed abolitionist, the other the son of a sugar planter. Yet on other important issues of the day, such as support for Pitt and the King against the Foxite Whigs and opposition to Catholic emancipation, they were natural allies. Over ten years as joint members, relations between them were cordial, as Repton's reminiscences of Wilberforce's visit to Harewood House make plain. Recently they had been working even more closely together as they drafted recommendations on the industrialisation of the wool industry. This would prove a vital issue in the two general elections held in punishingly quick succession: that of October 1806, which in Yorkshire was not taken to poll, and that fought to the finish in the spring of 1807. Ironically it was the weavers of Yorkshire rather than the slaves of the West Indies who would shortly tear the two men asunder.

If the Pittite Lascelles were resolute, opposition from the Whig side of politics was equally so. The Lascelles commanded

Et in Arcadia ego

West Indian money, but William Wentworth-Fitzwilliam, 2nd Earl Fitzwilliam, was heir to an equally vast fortune.[31] As Rockingham's nephew, he had inherited both his uncle's estate and his revered political lineage. Fitzwilliam owned more than 100 000 acres of England and Ireland, and his principal seat, Rockingham's Wentworth House, sat bang on top of one of the richest seams of coal in the nation.[32] The scale of Wentworth is almost unimaginable, dwarfing even the glories created at Harewood. Its grandeur was born not only of the usual social ambitions but also of a building spree egged on by bitter jealousy between two rival heirs to the family name and fortune.[33] Wentworth remains the largest privately owned dwelling in Britain, with an east façade twice the length of Buckingham Palace. At house parties in later years, guests would be given silver caskets of confetti to mark the route from their bedrooms to the dining room, so that they might find their way back through the labyrinthine corridors afterwards.[34] Until the 1784 upset, it was from Wentworth that the Rockingham Whigs had dominated Yorkshire county politics. Fitzwilliam was determined, 'having so lately rescued the county out of hands so hostile to us' in 1806, to 'take the tremendous step of entering into a contest, such as must be that of the county of York'.[35]

Over fifteen days of polling, the campaign convulsed the entire country with its nail-bitingly close result and the vast sums of money risked to secure victory. 'There is no earthly thing talk'd of or thought of but duels and the Yorkshire Election' complained Fitzwilliam's sister, Lady Bessborough:

> if its consequence is measur'd by its cost, no wonder, for they say it will far exceed the original stake of 100 thousand a piece. It seems to me like madness, for what does it prove? Not that the person is either the most meritorious, or

the most belov'd. If Elections really were the voice of the people, and if the people really had judgement enough to *chuse* from merit, not from accidental bias, then it would be an honour, and worth any thing; but like any thing worth having, it could not then be bought.[36]

Lady Bessborough was right to baulk at the cost, but she was wrong on at least one count: the drama, the expense and the close result of the 1807 contest lay precisely in the fact that in Yorkshire the voice of the people was unusually powerful.

'Proud Yorkshire' and the spirit of the age

English politics prior to the 1832 Reform Act was a bewildering maze of eccentric voting rights. At the broadest level there were two kinds of parliamentary seats: county seats (where all adult men could vote if they owned land worth more than 40 shillings) and borough seats (where the franchise varied). The so-called 'rotten' boroughs were throw-back constituencies representing populations long departed. The most notorious, Old Sarum, near Salisbury, had two MPs but only seven voters. 'Pocket' boroughs were controlled by wealthy landowners, and could be bought and sold (an average one would set you back some £4000). In a 'freeman' borough, such as Wilberforce's initial seat of Hull, the vote was enjoyed by hereditary descent. Elsewhere again, the franchise might attach to buildings rather than to their inhabitants. Sometimes these buildings had also vanished long ago, so that natural features of the landscape might be surprised to find themselves possessed of a vote.[37] In the county of Yorkshire, the 40-shilling freehold rule – the property qualification to the franchise – was broadly interpreted. It included assets like leases, mortgages, offices and

Et in Arcadia ego

annuities as well as freehold land. So Yorkshire's diverse electorate included a large landed interest in the North and East Ridings; the iron, steel and cutlery industries of the Sheffield area; the worsted and woollen weaving industries of the West Riding; and the rapidly expanding industrial town of Leeds. In the 1807 contest, the candidates would have to meet head-on a bitter debate over who possessed the right status credentials to represent this cross-section of the British nation.

There is more to our following the 1807 election than the Lascelles's personal fate. Unusually for the highly localised politics of the period, Yorkshire was an acknowledged barometer of national sentiment – a 'bell wether' seat as they are now called. It was Britain in miniature: the characters who took up their parts in the 1807 electoral drama – the aristocratic power-brokers, the artisans, the industrial middle classes, the evangelical reformers, the provincial journalists, the slave-trade abolitionists – these are a heady mix of the most significant players of the period. To show them in action is to distil some of the key struggles by which Britain was transformed across the age of liberty.

The county of Yorkshire possessed two parliamentary seats. The region also sent representatives from its 'boroughs', amongst them the market towns of Northallerton (the Lascelles 'pocket' borough) and Malton (Fitzwilliam's equivalent) as well as the ancient city of York. However, the spread of seats across the electorate reflected a political geography that was centuries out of date – and was the target of increasing resentment. Industrialisation was changing the social and economic fabric of the whole country, but political rights had not kept pace. Like other parts of the centre and north of England, the imbalance in Yorkshire was particularly stark. Leeds was a relatively new regional powerhouse. Its inhabitants increased four-fold in number in the fifty years after 1780, to reach 120 000 by the 1830s when parliamentary reforms would finally rectify the matter. Back in the early 1800s, however, Leeds had a pop-ulation of over 50 000, more than five times that of North-allerton, but it had no borough MPs.[38] In the early nineteenth century, the wool trade was still the town's prime source of income. Wool merchants dominated the town 'corporation', its municipal council, forming a self-perpetuating oligarchy that had been running things for two hundred years. Their politics was Anglican and 'Tory', defending existing institutions and resisting change from below. They were staunch allies of the Lascelles against Whig peers like Fitzwilliam.

The Leeds merchant community was not an entirely closed shop, however. It was unusual, though not impossible, to rise into their ranks. Richard York was one such example. In 1807 the Yorks were at the heart of the merchant elite and close political allies of the Lascelles. But though Richard's father had twice been mayor of Leeds, the family were of yeoman stock. They had recently changed their surname from a far less regal 'Sheepshanks'. And while political alliance was one thing, social alliance was quite another. Henry Lascelles might have been 'the darling of Leeds corporation',[39] but this did not mean his family wished to *marry* amongst them. In 1801, Henry's sister Mary Lascelles took it into her head to disagree.

Corpulence, opined Jane Austen, contemplating a charac-ter's 'large fat sighings' in *Persuasion*, should not be considered a barrier to sentiment. Nevertheless, Mary Hale, whose sister had married Henry's father, took an acerbic view of her niece's cross-class romance:

Et in Arcadia ego

Miss Lascelles, of famous fat memory, has thought proper
to elope with a young man who was either enamoured with
her extensive person, or more probably with her prospective
fortune. His name was formerly Sheepshanks, now Yorke;
his father is a merchant at Leeds, who has grown rich by his
own industry and had settled £800 a year on his son, who I
hear has been well educated.

Luckily the intrepid Mary (whose portrait by Hoppner only
confirms Mrs Hale's snide remarks) did not have far to go. The
Lascelles's town-house was just across the square from one of
London's most famous churches. Nor, sensibly, did she risk the
rope ladder so beloved of romance fiction. As Mrs Hale told it:

Miss Lascelles left her Father's house very early in the
morning, and herself opened the door into the Street with
a bundle of Cloathes under her arm and was married at
St George's Church from whence the happy couple went
to Swansea, where they still remain. I hear Lord and Lady
Harewood are more composed than they were, and for my
part I think it may be all for the best, for she was most
certainly a great Plague to them all, and as a Husband has
long been her aim, she may in future be more placid.

The Lascelles were eventually reconciled to the marriage,
although Wilberforce's faint praise of Richard York during his
and Repton's 1802 visit – 'a very pleasant well behav'd young
man, to whom they [the Lascelles] behave extremely well' – perhaps suggests that his presumption was never quite forgotten.[40]

Mr Baines and the Leeds Mercury

The merchants and their corporation might be running Leeds, but the town was also home to another increasingly vocal group nipping at their heels. At a broader level, they were attacking the electoral inequalities that kept them from what they considered was their rightful place in national affairs. They were nearly always Foxite Whigs and later Liberals. Often religious dissenters, they were engineers, machine-makers, and small-time tradesmen and manufacturers. In short, they were the middle class. And as their towns rose in strength and wealth around them, they increasingly saw that their moment was at hand.

Amongst these men was one Edward Baines, the editor of the *Leeds Mercury* newspaper. In later years, Baines would see his own story as that of the rise of merit over hereditary privilege; he was a symbol of the coming man.[41] 'There was', wrote his son:

> a remarkable correspondence between the spirit of
> Mr. Baines and the spirit of the age. It was the spirit of
> improvement. Active, inquiring, enterprising, humane,
> just and popular, the age witnessed a series of reforms
> unequalled in any previous period of the like duration.

In boyhood, claimed Edward Baines the younger, his father was fired by the example of Benjamin Franklin. Later he would be 'called, not without reason, "the Franklin of Leeds".[42] Baines is the first of the crusading newspaper editors who will cross these pages. Like him, they will all, with some justification, see their own reflection in the changing times.

Baines was born in 1774. Of farming stock, his father had

Et in Arcadia ego

entered into the grocery trade, but fell foul of the local corporation since he was not a member of the guild. It was a lesson in vested privilege that helped shape the family's political views. Baines was educated at a variety of grammar schools – his schoolmates included William Wordsworth – until the age of sixteen when he was apprenticed to a printer. In 1795 he moved to Leeds to complete his apprenticeship with a firm of printers and booksellers who were also proprietors of the *Leeds Mercury*.

In 1798 Baines married Charlotte Talbot, sister of a fellow member of the reform-minded club known as the 'Reasoning Society' and the daughter of religious dissenters. These were dangerous times for such gatherings, even for groups as innocuous as this. In the wake of the French Revolution, radical and pro-reform organisations were springing up all over Britain. Thomas Paine published his *Rights of Man* in 1791 and 1792, calling for government that protected mankind's natural and civil rights rather than hereditary privilege. In May 1792, with tensions between revolutionary France and Britain rising, Pitt issued a Royal Proclamation outlawing seditious meetings and writings. In 1793, before cheering crowds of citizens, Louis XVI lost his head beneath the blade of the guillotine, and France declared war on Britain a month later. By the following year, the war was going badly, and rumours of invasion were rife. Pitt's administration came down even harder on civil liberties, increasing penalties for criticising the government, suspending *habeas corpus* (thus allowing for detention without trial), and restricting public meetings to no more than 50 people in specially licensed premises. Parliamentary reform was set back by decades, and the consequences for Edward Baines were as much personal as they were political. His engagement was almost broken off by Charlotte's father, who feared that his prospective son-in-law risked arrest for his membership of the Leeds Reasoning Society. Talbot's alarms were persuaded away, but Baines's courtship troubles would gain an ironic significance some twenty years later. As we shall see, his investigative journalism in the midst of another debate over the suspension of *habeas corpus* would turn the editor and his newspaper into household names.

By marrying Charlotte, whose father was a prosperous Leeds leather manufacturer, Baines had improved his fortunes. In 1801, with financial backing, he was able to buy the *Leeds Mercury*, and he transformed it into one of the most influential provincial newspapers in the country. Baines's backers were a group of like-minded individuals compelled to do something about 'the defenceless position of the Reformers in Leeds'.[43] He would not disappoint them. Under his editorship, the *Mercury* became the kind of paper seldom, until then, seen outside London, a harbinger of the growing power of the industrial north and its emergent middle class. It spoke with their voice, it acquired its own leading articles and political news, and it would prove a worthy adversary for the *Leeds Intelligencer*. The *Intelligencer*'s proprietors had a seat on the Leeds corporation, and it was regarded as in the pay of the Tory Anglican merchant community.[44] The *Mercury* became known for its moderate social and political reform. As his backers had intended, Baines and the *Mercury* channelled the general dissatisfaction felt by the new dissenting manufacturers with the Leeds status quo and focused their political energies on bringing down the merchant oligarchy. It would prove a formidable weapon in the election arsenal of 1807.

Et in Arcadia ego

Risking the voice of the people

Elections, as Hogarth's popular cycle of paintings on this theme shows, were rumbustious affairs of high drama. Candidates needed to be tough to survive what was a gruelling process. Even victory could be hazardous, traditionally celebrated by carrying the candidate on a chair through the town. 'They would chair me to the inn', wrote Wilberforce in 1806:

> One man threw something which hit me on the forehead, happily not hard, and I kept watching afterwards. Amazing squeeze, and a very awkward operation. Taken to the Talbot. Bad, especially going through the gorges of the gates and narrow streets.[45]

The elaborate rituals and festivities that marked both canvassing and elections involved the whole community, who could enjoy the spectacle regardless of whether they had the vote. These rituals were intended to channel the energy of public opinion in appropriate ways. During elections, the hierarchical bonds of patronage and loyalty were generally reinforced, but these bonds were also open to renegotiation. By placing the leaders of society as supplicants to the people, however limited that definition might be, elections licensed their own world turned upside-down, one with which candidates had perforce to play along.[46] As such they were viewed from above with some trepidation, as a threat to the natural order of things. Apart from cost, this undercurrent of potential disorder was an added incentive for candidates to come to some kind of arrangement rather than risk an open contest.

Voting was public, and poll books were published so that any dependant or tenant, regardless of what kind of electoral division he lived in, had to weigh up the consequences of how he voted. Landed proprietors openly required their tenants to vote in their interest, and most tenants largely regarded this as natural and expected. Employees, tradesmen or others who relied on the patronage that was such a ubiquitous force in this society were in a similar position. These relationships were generally as much personal as they were economic, and they worked both ways. Neglected dependants could sometimes deliver their patrons a salutary lesson. Fitzwilliam lost the pocket borough of Malton in the 1807 election, though some 450 out of 500 votes belonged directly or indirectly to his tenants, in part because he was distracted by the wider Yorkshire county contest, but also because he failed to treat these voters sufficiently well. Malton was swiftly regained for Fitzwilliam by accusing his rivals of corruption, by pressuring his tenants, and by purchasing more property in his interest.[47] But such instances of bald intimidation were comparatively rare, and the pre-Reform electorate was not as easily controlled as we might expect. Elites had to treat their voters carefully and cultivate them assiduously, or they suffered the consequences. Elections were therefore a dialogue between patrons and community, rather than an expression of either outright autocracy or open democracy. They were part of a broader culture of paternalism and deference, but by 1807 it was a system in which cracks were starting to appear.

The cost of mounting a campaign in a county election was formidable. 'No man', commented one observer in 1820, 'ought to engage in such an undertaking who is afraid of his Money'.[48] If this were true of county elections in general, it was a particular problem in Yorkshire. Candidates were expected to bear the costs of transporting their voters to the hustings. This meant

Et in Arcadia ego

transporting the main part of some twenty to thirty thousand freeholders, some from as far away as London, to the poll in York. Getting them safely to poll could be a challenge. One Lascelles agent, trying to get his voters through hostile territory in 1807, lost his punctuation in the heat of the moment:

> I myself may safely say that we was in danger of our Lives, if there is not some meathod taken there will be some of Mr Lascelles Friends Lame'd if not something more serious I thought it my duty to inform you that some meathod might be taken to prevent it on my Opinion the best way would be of you or the Landlords in Harewood to tell them that called at Harewood to take the Tickets out of their Hats when coming through Otley the Cry in Otley is Milton forever Lascelles down River with a Knife in is Heart and a Fork in is Liver, by those expressions you may Judge their disposition.[49]

Logistics were key, for while voters were waiting to cast their vote they also expected to be housed, fed, entertained and protected from the blandishments and intimidation of the other side. During the 1807 campaign the *Leeds Intelligencer* reckoned that around two thousand men at any one moment were passing through York, a swarm of locusts that consumed daily what the city might otherwise have lived on for a year.[50] Agents for candidates had to ensure a quick turnaround as voting could not go on for more than fifteen days, and they needed to get as many through the hustings and back out of York as possible. Every voter was significant in an election contest which, by the very fact that it had gone beyond a canvass, indicated that the poll would be a close one.

As freeholders possessed two votes apiece, tactical voting

and alliances between candidates were frequent strategies. Wilberforce was attacked repeatedly in 1807 for entering into a secret alliance with Lascelles against the Whigs:

> What a base *Coalition* has lately ta'en place
> Twixt the Driver of Slaves, and the Preacher of Grace![51]

Despite legislation against bribery, what was known as 'treating' voters was universal, as the verse accompanying Hogarth's *Election* series points out:

> So at *Elections* 'tis discreet
> Still first of all to have a *Treat*;
> The Pulse of ev'ry Man to try,
> And learn what Votes they needs must *buy*;
> No Freeman well can tell his Side,
> Unless his Belly's satisfy'd.[52]

Voters expected public recognition of their privileged status. Many required payment to compensate them for the loss of time, labour and income that making the journey to vote undoubtedly did entail. Food, alcohol and accommodation had to be provided both to keep them happy and to keep the peace. To refuse to do so was to invite violence and social disorder. Quite apart from the needs of voters, election largesse – the food, the lodging, the music, the decorations, the publications, and especially the drink – provided employment and boosted incomes for a large proportion of the population. Every tavern in the town would be appropriated by the campaign, decked out in blue for the Pittites or orange for the Whigs, and assigned to one or another of the candidates. The Lascelles campaign in 1807 had its headquarters at the George Inn, where their bill came to almost £2000, including items for broken furniture

Et in Arcadia ego

and smashed windows.[53]

As an alternative to the expense of fighting an election, canvassing could determine the likely outcome, and candidates would generally withdraw unless they were confident of victory. A cat's cradle of correspondence was woven across every possible point of personal influence in the electorate, in order both to gauge the chances of winning and to intimidate the opposition into withdrawing. Those with votes, and influence over other voters, had to be persuaded both to make the effort to attend (one Yorkshire landowner responded to Henry Lascelles that he 'did not mean to take any Part in the Bustle of an Election') and to give their support to the candidate's cause. Canvassing was, in effect, a quasi-election, though much less costly than a real poll. It involved active campaigning and personal visits by the candidate and his agents, and endless circular letters seeking support. When a high-spirited friend of Henry Lascelles received one of these polite supplications in 1806 he couldn't resist a tease: 'Dear Henry, I have received so formal an Epistle from you beginning "My Dear Sir, &c" that if I thought it was designed at first for me I would go to the north on purpose to vote against you'. 'I am so glad to have an opportunity of making a Member of Parlt. pay postage', he concluded, 'that I have separate[d] the sheet in the hope you will pay double'.[54]

Wilberforce was well-known for both his tardiness and his slapdash business methods, but even he was organised enough to instruct his election agents to record detailed notes on his supporters' wealth and social influence, connections, likes and dislikes, 'whether he likes the leg or wing of a fowl best, that when one dines with him one may win his heart by helping him, and not be taken in by his "just which you please, sir"'.[55]

Insults and irritations to voters were a real danger. The social diversity of the Yorkshire electorate comes across vividly in two letters responding to Henry Lascelles's canvass of 1806. First we have the coarse paper, eccentric orthography (even for its day) and pugnacious tones of Charles Holmes of York Street, Leeds:

> Sir, In 1796 I was Called upon By Mr Hull & Mr Cookson for my Voate for you and I Gave it them thay Towld Me all My Expences would Be paid I Got a Horse and went to York and stayd Till Mr Fawkes Gav it up and never Got nothing It Cost Me £3. 8s. 0d. Now I am Calld upon a Gain for My Voate But I shall Not Give it Till I Get Paid the Last Expences.

Next, 'H Cholmley Esq' of Howsham, who expressed his chagrin in more genteel but no less heart-felt terms:

> Sir, When I read over the Letter you wrote me, I very much doubted whether it was not intended for another Mr Cholmley, that you should condescend to write to me, to ask my attendance to your Nomination, when for the last five years you have hardly deigned to Honor me with a Nod, and that that coldness should extend to your Lady, who neither returned my Wife's card on her call the last winter in London. I shall neither attend your Nomination or your Election.[56]

The Saints come marching in

The timing of the 1807 election, only months after the Bill abolishing the slave trade had finally become law, Wilberforce's heroic stature in that cause, and the fact that Henry Lascelles was financed by his father's West Indian fortune all meant that

Et in Arcadia ego

slavery would play a prominent part in the Yorkshire campaign.

Those who now know the name of William Wilberforce do so mostly for his battle for abolition. It was not always so. The Yorkshireman first made his name as an ardent supporter of William Pitt in the first anxious months of the 'mince pie administration'. The two men were contemporaries at Cambridge – Pitt, with typical precociousness, had gone up aged fourteen, Wilberforce three years later – but it was as novice MPs that the two men became inseparable. They were an odd couple: one nearly a foot taller than the other; one shy and aloof in public ('stiff to everyone but women', was the sly insinuation made of the seemingly asexual Pitt), the other warm and gregarious.[57] They were at the heart of the drinking, gambling and generally licentious fashionable political set of London's 1780s. In the aftermath of the 1784 election, it must have seemed to the young prime minister that the member for Yorkshire represented a bastion of unquestioned personal and political support. The very next year, however, a letter arrived that shocked him profoundly. Wilberforce was weathering the most profound crisis of his life. In common with many of his contemporaries, he had experienced a religious conversion.

As Wilberforce turned towards the principles of Christian evangelicalism, beliefs that would dictate the actions of the rest of his life, he began to doubt his choice of career. In a letter that has not survived, he wrote explaining his dilemma to Pitt: did his faith demand that he withdraw from the world? From Downing Street, the prime minister replied in a long letter dated 2 December 1785. He would call on Wilberforce the very next day to talk it over: 'open yourself fully and without reserve to one, who, believe me, does not know how to separate your happiness from his own'. Pitt's letter exerted all his considerable powers of persuasion to change his friend's mind. 'Surely', went one of its most famous sentences, 'the principles as well as the practices of Christianity are simple, and lead not to meditation only but to action'.[58] His was one of several voices urging Wilberforce to turn his religious conversion to practical account. Another belonged to John Newton, former slaver turned evangelical preacher, who had penned the hymn *Amazing Grace*. Wilberforce took the decision to stay in parliament. As part of a group of activists ridiculed by their opponents as the 'Saints', he would further God's work on earth.

The slave trade had not only made the fortunes of individual families like the Lascelles, it was throughout the eighteenth century absolutely central to Britain's economy and wealth. All those sweet puddings and cups of tea were impossible without it. Cities like Liverpool and Bristol depended upon it. Before the 1780s, if people thought critically of the slave trade at all, they mostly saw it as an unfortunate necessity of life. It was a rare (often Quaker) voice that called for its abolition. Yet in 1787 the Society for Effecting the Abolition of the African Slave Trade was established, and twenty years later the Bill outlawing the trade became law. In 1834, slavery itself would be abolished across the British empire.

Scholars have long tried to understand the complexities of this shift. For the first historians of abolition (often the activists themselves or their children) it was the heroic battle of the Saints that had brought it about. Such hagiographers largely ignored the struggles that slaves had themselves made to end their torment, notably in the Haitian revolution of 1791. Eric Williams, pioneering author of *Capitalism and Slavery* (1944) and prime minister of the newly decolonised Trinidad and Tobago, was one of the first to see the cause of abolition in the demands

Et in Arcadia ego

of an industrialising economy rather than the pricks of conscience. For him, ending slavery and promoting free labour was self-interested rather than altruistic. The debate between the demands of British economics and the forces of British morality has raged ever since. Williams's figures about industrialisation and the decline of West Indian sugar production have been largely disproven. (The latter seems to have been rather the effect than the cause of slavery's end.) But he is rightly credited with bringing about a more balanced view of the Saints, and of providing a much-needed economic basis to the changes that brought about the end of slavery. Free trade and free labour benefitted a country that had so rapidly industrialised but which could no longer feed itself, so that it looked to all corners of the world for raw materials, foodstuffs and markets.[59]

What historians do not dispute is the grassroots support that the campaign for abolition achieved. It was arguably the first mass movement of Britain's modern political era. Consumer boycotts, popular rallies and, above all, the deluge of petitions which it rained down on parliament, swept up countless numbers of people with no formal political rights, including women and workers. The campaign's fortunes waxed and waned between the time Wilberforce took up the cause and the abolition of the trade in 1807. The lowest point came in the 1790s, when Britain seemed about to succumb to the unstoppable forces of revolution. As Edward Baines knew to his cost, war with France provoked a backlash against all mass movements and reform activism, antislavery amongst them. Having weathered that storm, however, abolition gained pace again in the first decade of the nineteenth century, ironically reinvigorated by the very force that had once threatened it.

Britons facing the French revolutionary juggernaut tended

to think of themselves as 'unusually and distinctively free'.[60] Disregarding the crackdowns of the 1790s, they boasted of a constitution that guaranteed them freedom from despotic or arbitrary power. It is easy, suggests historian James Walvin, to dismiss this as propaganda, but it was no less powerful for that. In the midst of apocalyptic fears over industrial upheaval at home and revolutionary war abroad, many wondered whether the horrors of slavery had brought divine judgement upon a sinning nation. Was it not their responsibility to extend the benefits of British freedom to those suffering under slavery's yoke? The 'rights of freeborn Englishmen', as the concept was often expressed, was as powerful as it was nebulous, a 'marvellous mixture of delusion and promise'.[61] As Napoleon reintroduced slavery across the enemy empire, abolition could be affirmed as an emblem of national virtue in the battle against French tyranny.[62]

One of the most recent salvos in the long debate over the forces of British abolition argues that, for all the genuine abhorrence the Saints had for the slave trade, it was also a 'Trojan horse' for men like Wilberforce who had far broader (and less popular) moral reforms in mind. It was far 'less threatening', for example, 'than asking the public to reconsider how they spent their Sunday afternoons'.[63] But however we may explain its causes, abolition was a hugely emotive and popular issue. And, as such, it was the perfect wagon to which a political campaign could be hitched. In Yorkshire, the burning question of the Lascelles's 1807 election was not, in fact, abolition. It was the manufacture of woollen cloth. But the election was fought in the midst of the high emotion attendant on finally bringing the slave trade to an end. Slavery and industrialisation were about to prove a potent mixture.

Et in Arcadia ego

The 'spoiled child of English manufactures'

Industrial factory production was only just beginning to establish a toehold in the Yorkshire woollen cloth industry. Cotton would later become a far more important engine of Britain's industrial revolution, but the struggle over wool was a sign of things to come. It was all the more bitter for arising in a sector of the economy steeped in historic traditions and protective legislation that stretched back beyond the Middle Ages. Wool, as Williams put it in the 1940s, 'was the spoiled child of English manufactures'.[64]

For the most part, woollen cloth was still made in Yorkshire as it has been for centuries. What was known as the 'domestic system' dominated the region: small-scale production by a master weaver assisted by his family and apprentices. Cloth was made at home, and brought on horseback on market day to be sold at the cloth halls of Leeds and Huddersfield. Even in the first decade of the nineteenth century, wool production was still the domain of the skilled artisan who owned his own tools and raw materials, and who supplemented his income by subsistence farming. The overheads of small-scale producers were minimal, and their farms kept them afloat when demand for wool was low. This arrangement also gave the artisan clothier enough freehold land to qualify him as a voter in the county election.

Yet new technologies were slowly being introduced. The most significant of these were gig mills and shearing frames, devices that raised and trimmed the nap of the undressed cloth. Both machines were necessary for large-scale production. The gig mill allowed three men to dress woollen cloth in the same time it took twenty-four to do the job by hand. Scores of cloth workers, it was rightly feared, would be 'thrown out of work by this fatal machine'.[65] The merchants in centres like Leeds began to invest in these new technologies and branch into large-scale production, but to do so they needed to dispense with centuries-old laws that forbade the use of machines and insisted upon rigorous apprenticeships. The artisan clothiers knew that if the law were changed, then merchants would turn to factory manufacture and the domestic system of cloth production would be annihilated. Operating, as historian EP Thompson's classic account would have it, in 'a twilight world of semi-legality',[66] the cloth dressers used early forms of trade unionism to enforce apprenticeship laws. Through their organisation, the Yorkshire Institution, they threatened strike action if operators employed journeymen who had not served a full apprenticeship or who were not members of the Institution.

It would be another half century or so before wool in Yorkshire caught up with the dark satanic mills of Lancashire cotton production. There were still some 10 000 hand looms in the Leeds cloth producing districts in 1840.[67] Nevertheless, the writing was on the wall. Violent protests began against mechanisation. Large-scale manufacturers and merchants sought to overturn the laws dating from the Tudor period that restricted the use of machinery in the wool industry, and that laid down the rules governing apprenticeship. War with France and the continental blockade, that pressed hard upon British manufacturers, gave these debates a sharper edge. As an interim measure, parliament suspended the regulations, and there were various attempts to pass a Bill ending the restrictions. Petitions and protests on the part of both small-scale clothiers and would-be manufacturers traded arguments based on the writings of Montesquieu and Adam Smith.[68] As tempers flared, and unrest

Et in Arcadia ego

began to break out in the woollen manufacturing districts, the House of Commons hastily summoned a Select Committee to investigate.

The Select Committee on the Woollen Manufacture of England worked fast, beginning its deliberations in March 1806, calling its first witnesses a month later and delivering its report to Parliament at the beginning of July. As the incumbent members for Yorkshire, Lascelles and Wilberforce both sat on the committee, and Wilberforce himself drafted the report. The Select Committee heard evidence from all sides, but its composition was avowedly anti-clothier and it came down decisively on the side of repealing the restrictions on both mechanisation and labour.[69] Lascelles and Wilberforce were as one in dismissing the concerns of the clothiers, and their report claimed (incorrectly, although the effects were not immediate) that the end of the regulations would not cause the demise of the domestic system. Even though the process was not completed until the middle of the nineteenth century, the 1806 report saw the first steps taken towards the tyranny of the factory system. Several committee members had direct links to the cloth merchant interest, and Henry Lascelles was well known for his political (and now, through his determined sister, familial) alliance with the merchant corporation of Leeds. In 1804, as the debate over woollen cloth production raged on the floor of the House of Commons, Henry was burnt in effigy across half a dozen villages in Yorkshire.[70]

Within a year of the Select Committee's report, not one but two general elections would be fought. The timing was unfortunate, at least for some. Members of parliament might hail

Arcadia

from the most powerful and wealthy stratum in the land, but in elections they were supplicants. Candidates' *faux pas*, social and otherwise, could be political liabilities. It was this that made the Harewood decision to fight the 1807 election such a gamble. To make matters worse, Henry Lascelles was about to commit a social solecism of dangerous proportions.

Et in Arcadia ego

2

THE PRICE OF THE COUNTY

There is no stage of inertness and don't-carishness from
which an Englishman may not be roused by the stimulus of
politics; and a contested election is perhaps one of the finest
remedies that can be applied to a confirmed languor, either
of mind or body.

Emily Eden, *The Semi-Attached Couple*, 1860

As the members of the Select Committee presented their report
to Parliament, it was to a political landscape being swept away
before their eyes. 'Oh, my country! How I leave my country!'
were the last reported words of William Pitt, killed by alcohol and overwork aged forty-six. Pitt's appetite for port was
legendary, even in a hard-drinking age. Faulty medical advice
about the strengthening properties of alcohol, received in his
teens and acted upon with alacrity, was at least partly to blame.
By the time Wilberforce heard of the seriousness of Pitt's last
bout of illness, it was too late for him to say a final farewell.

Over the course of twenty years, their friendship had
weathered a variety of personal and political storms. Amongst

the most serious breaches was that in 1798, when Pitt chose to fight a duel with a political opponent – and on a Sunday at that. For Wilberforce, it was a crime against God to sport with one's own life; an added outrage for a prime minister to do so in time of national emergency and threatened invasion. He came within a whisker of bringing a motion of censure against Pitt in the Commons. Neither of the combatants was harmed, though there was a lot of talk, not all of it serious. Contrasting physiques, claimed the wits, made the contest manifestly unfair. Pitt's lanky outline should have been chalked upon the rotund body of his opponent; any hits outside the mark to be disallowed.[1]

Now, in the summer of 1806, Wilberforce mourned his friend and saw the cause of his death in the strain of over a decade of war. 'Pitt killed by the enemy as much as Nelson', he noted in his diary.[2] The country had lost the prime minister of all but three of the previous twenty-two years. In alliance with William Grenville, Charles Fox was back in power for the first time since George III had ejected him in 1783. Yet by bitter irony, it was as if he could not survive without the rivalry that had defined his career. Within months of Pitt's demise, Fox too was stricken, and he died on 13 September. The era of the Pittites and the Foxites, of eighteenth-century politics, was ending. From the ashes of these factions would rise the Whigs and the Tories of the nineteenth century, and the modern Liberal and Conservative parties.

With the death of Fox, Grenville called a general election to fortify his position. For the sitting members for Yorkshire, Wilberforce and Lascelles, it was a dangerous time. Feeling against them both ran high in the cloth districts, and the Whigs had been reinvigorated by their return to power. Yet for all the

The price of the county

apparent dreaminess described by Humphry Repton, and the tardiness complained of by Pitt, Wilberforce was a shrewd political operator. He would hardly have been so successful as an activist had things been otherwise.

Wool and the 1806 election campaign

With its extended history and artisan traditions, the woollen cloth industry was strongly connected in the mind of the public with ideas about the proper conduct of labour, good government, and the relations between masters and men. Debates over its regulation were shot through with the language of liberty and patriotism. Those advocating its modernisation had to tread carefully. And so, in drafting the Select Committee's report, Wilberforce took care to praise the 'habits and virtues' and the 'health and morals' of the domestic system, and to describe the clothiers as 'a very respectable class of Petitioners'.[3] Lascelles was less tactful (or less disingenuous) with both the cloth workers and their representatives, and his hasty remarks and manner on the committee would come back to haunt him.

The Lascelles family was already at a disadvantage in a time of widespread anti-slavery sentiment, for the West Indian origins of their wealth were well known. In the symbolically charged atmosphere of the debates over wool, Henry Lascelles now compounded their difficulties by opening himself up to accusations that he was dismissive of the rights and dignities of British freemen. As the trustees of the Cloth Hall of Leeds complained, 'he treated the whole Body of Clothiers, in the Persons of their Delegates, with Partiality, Rudeness, and even with Insult'. As the *Leeds Mercury*, organ of the dissenting

Edward Baines, reported:

> It is impossible clearly to describe the general Conduct of
> Mr Lascelles, when the Evidences in favour of the Domestic
> System were before the Committee. To puzzle them with
> intricate Questions, and, by cross Examination, to take
> Advantage of their simple and undesigning Evidence,
> appeared to be his constant Aim; and a significant Shrug, a
> doubting Look, and an unbelieving Sneer, he had ever ready
> at Command when a Clothier was under Examination;
> but when a Factory Owner, or a Man of large Property or
> Influence, appeared, he was all Candour, Complacency and
> Civility.[4]

Lascelles had 'had the Imprudence to say, to 19 000 Yorkshire
Clothiers in the Persons of their Representatives, "You may hoot
me, or scout me, or do what you please, I don't give a d____n
for you all."' They did not 'call in Question the Right of Mr
Lascelles to Speak and Vote according to his Conscience; but
we complain of being treated in a rude and very unwarrantable
Manner'. 'Against Mr Wilberforce', continued an address during
the 1807 election, 'they have no Hostility; on the contrary, they
are his warm and ardent Friends, *when he stands alone*, and their
Individual and Collective Endeavours shall not be wanting to
return him to Parliament along with another Gentlemen, who
they are confident will treat them with Respect'. Lascelles's
alleged behaviour and language during the committee hear-
ings was flung in his face at every turn: 'you will recollect, Sir',
thundered 'An Elector' in the pages of the *Leeds Mercury*:

> that when a petition to Parliament signed by 19 800
> manufacturers in the West Riding was made the subject of

The price of the county

conversation, that you had the confidence to say of these humble, but worthy people, '*that you did not regard their signatures, they would sign anything for a tankard of ale!*' Was this decent, Sir? Was this suitable language to be held by a Member of Parliament to any part of his Constituents?[5]

While the wool issue hurt Wilberforce, it was Lascelles who drew the main fire, for his demeanour as much as for his views. As one Lascelles supporter wrote bitterly, 'an intemperate expression, said to have been uttered by [him], has been retailed and aggravated, and re-echoed from one part of this vast county to the other'. A private letter to Lascelles from a canvasser in 1806 advised:

Mr Wilb had preserved the good will of the people about Huddersfield by some speeches in favour of the Domestic System of Manufacturing whilst the more Manly part acted by you has exposed you to the ill will of a numerous sett of freeholders whose enthusiasm in this cause cannot be corrected at present by any means possible.

Although the two men canvassed together early in the 1806 campaign, Wilberforce was advised by his agents of the political necessity of guarding against any perceived connection with Lascelles: 'I am extremely sorry for Mr. Lascelles; yet self-preservation, as far as is compatible with friendship to him, is a fair principle'. Wilberforce's supporters took fright that their candidate might be harmed, and Lascelles was warned that 'every effort will be made to induce every friend of Mr Wilberforce to forsake your cause entirely'.[6]

In general, Wilberforce had managed the wool debate far more cannily than had Lascelles. In addition, the success of the campaign for abolition of the slave trade had cast a kind of political armour around him. As *The Times* put it in 1806:

> In the annals of County Elections there is not to be found,
> perhaps, such a display of ardent and general affection
> [as] has attended [Wilberforce] during his canvass ... he
> has passed in a kind of triumphant procession, preceded
> by bands of music, his carriage drawn by multitudes of
> the populace, and great numbers of gentlemen of the first
> respectability in carriages, and on horseback, attending their
> old and beloved Representative, whenever he appeared.

The 'Representative' was duly grateful, for it had been an anxious time: 'How truly may I say that Goodness & Mercy follow me all the days of my life', he confided to his diary:

> It is really astonishing ... to be so popular among all ye
> common people, clothiers & all ... It is only to be ascribed
> to ye overruling Providence of God, who turned the Hearts
> of Men at will. O what a less[on] is this to put our trust in
> God & I humbly hope I have been enabled to see him in all
> these Events.[7]

Wilberforce, then, survived the criticisms of 1806 and was duly returned. Lascelles took the prudent course and withdrew a week before nomination day. Local landholder Walter Fawkes (backed by Earl Fitzwilliam) was elected as the second candidate.

The 'memorable contest' of 1807

For the moment, Wilberforce was safe, but the new ministry, which formed a government in the autumn of 1806 and presided over the final abolition of the slave trade the follow-

The price of the county

ing February, soon came to grief over the question of Catholic emancipation. The King's dismissal of this ministry forced another election in just over four months, ending the shortest-lived British administration in modern times. It soon became clear that the daunting task of mounting a full-scale election in Yorkshire loomed. Notwithstanding the continued sentiment amongst the clothiers, the Lascelles family was now determined to fight to the finish.

The King signed the dissolution of Parliament on 29 April 1807. There was but scant time to prepare for such a massive contest before polling opened on 20 May. Hustings and poll booths were hastily erected in front of the courts of justice in York, facing the castle yard. Deer customarily grazed there; by the end of the campaign not a blade of grass would remain. For the Wilberforce camp, a battle of some twenty years standing had finally been won in February 1807 with the passage of the Slave Trade Act. The prospect of another exhausting and costly campaign made news of the dissolution of parliament 'a most unwelcome intelligence'. Wilberforce himself felt 'sickened at a contest'; 'No one could foresee the result of such a collision'. 'Whatever was its issue', wrote Wilberforce's sons in their father's biography, 'the contest must be ruinous to any man of ordinary fortune'.[8]

Even those at Wentworth and Harewood were anxious. Lord Harewood, who was of course funding his son Henry's campaign, 'had just bought the Wike estate in this Parish of Mr Ingram for [£]30 000', remembered Richard Hale, Harewood vicar (and Henry Lascelles's cousin) in his memoirs:

> and at the commencement of the Contest [he] brought the money to pay for it in his carriage from London and on entering the Hall where I & his two sons were sitting, told

us so, pointing to a small box under his arm the candidate quietly said 'we want half for the Leeds Bank and half for the York Bank tomorrow, to set the thing agoing.' It made the old man stagger.[9]

As the two great families stood eyeball to eyeball, there were evidently hopes that the other fellow might blink. 'The advertisement [of intention to stand] published by Lascelles seems a little faint & hesitating', wrote one supporter to Fitzwilliam. 'Most anxiously do I hope that his courage may fail him.'[10]

The prospect of an open contest quickly proved too rich for the blood of Fawkes, elected just months previously. At the last minute he withdrew, throwing the Wentworth camp into acute anxiety as to whom to put forward. After decades in the Yorkshire county political wilderness, the furore over the wool issue had at last prised open a chink in the Lascelles armour and the Pittites looked vulnerable. It was too good a chance to pass over. For Fitzwilliam, left without a candidate, a 'more vexatious event could not have been imagined, being one that all circumstances considered placed me in the most awkward situation, & involv'd me in the greatest perplexities'. There was no time for consultation. A snap decision was needed. Against Lascelles and Wilberforce, both experienced political veterans, the Whigs decided to run Charles William Wentworth-Fitzwilliam, styled Viscount Milton, eldest son and heir to Fitzwilliam himself.

The 'most ungainly young man I ever saw': enter Lord Milton

A slight and boyish figure with red hair and a decided resemblance to the younger Pitt (this last surely a matter of regret to the Foxite Whigs), Milton would celebrate his twenty-first

The price of the county

birthday on 4 May, gaining his legal majority just days before the election campaign began. The occasion called for celebrations of a fitting magnificence. Two oxen and twelve sheep were roasted and 'given to the populace', while invited guests consumed (to make but a selection from the bill of fare) some 54 fowls, 555 eggs, countless dishes of mutton, beef, lamb, calf's head hash, pigeon pies, 72 hogsheads of ale and six of small beer, and 473 bottles of wine.[11] 'A large fat Ox, with his head crowned with garlands and his horns tipped with gold, was commodiously roasted, and attracted particular attention and admiration.' At 20, Milton was already both a husband and an MP, with a reputation for probity: 'To see a young Nobleman of the 18th century abstain from fashionable dissipation, enter at an early age into married life, and give his mind to politics, is a pleasing spectacle', fawned *The Times*.[12]

Fitzwilliam had introduced his son to politics early. In the wake of the Regency crisis, when a temporary bout of madness in the King had exposed the greedily unfilial ambitions of his son, the dissolute Prince of Wales went on a conciliatory trip to Yorkshire in September 1789. By holding a three-year-old Milton in his arms before the crowds assembled at Wentworth, the Prince had 'charmed the people within and without the House'.[13] The boy barely grown, Milton entered the Commons in 1806, standing for his father's pocket borough of Malton. Technically, parliamentarians were required to be of age, though most turned a blind eye (as with the case with Fox, aged nineteen) so long as an under-age member refrained from voting until his majority. A quarter of the members who sat between 1734 and 1832 first entered the house before reaching the age of 25, and a further quarter before the age of 33.[14]

This cohort of youthful precedents didn't stop his opponents harping on Milton's age and inexperience, which for a prestigious county seat *was* extreme: 'the baby', the 'boy with red hair', the 'sickly *Jacobin* Lad' and the 'little Lord' were just a few of their jibes. Milton countered by describing himself as taking up 'a regular Apprenticeship' in standing for Yorkshire – language well calculated to appeal amidst the emotive labour issue.[15] For all his youth, his supporters gambled that, as heir to the political mantle of the Rockingham Whigs, and with Fitz-william's formidable electoral machine behind him, Milton would punch above his weight. An *Ode* published to celebrate his birth in 1786 (the author surely hoping that party loyalty would make up for art) made these expectations quite clear:

> Yes, Melton, yes, the fire who gave thee birth
> High in the patriot constellation shines;
> Great heir of Rockingham's exalted worth,
> Whose mind like his each manly grace combines …
> Thus parented, not long in tame repose
> Shall rest, bright babe, thy mind's inherent pow'rs;
> But soon the germs of lineal worth disclose
> A golden promise of maturer hours.[16]

Needless to say, the *Ode* did not mention another reason for the family's rejoicing. Milton had been born sixteen years after his parents' marriage, and would prove to be an only child. If the incumbents of Harewood House had found their lineage diffi-cult to sustain, those at Wentworth must have been even more anxious. Had Fitzwilliam died without a surviving son (and Milton had come through a serious illness as recently as 1806) the estates would have reverted to the progeny of his moth-er's sister, Lady Harriet Wentworth, who had made a runaway match with a footman.[17]

The price of the county

Like his father, Milton never quite attained the heights of brilliance hoped for by a family in whose firmament the star of Rockingham had shone so brightly. His somewhat awkward physical appearance and manner were cause for repeated comment. Georgiana, 5th Duchess of Devonshire and a relation by marriage, found him very 'odd in person', yet also 'both clever and amiable' and 'so good natured, one cannot help liking him'. One Fitzwilliam supporter, dutifully travelling up to York to cast his vote for Milton in 1807, called the candidate 'one of the most ungainly looking young men I ever saw'. Henry Lascelles, whose handsome appearance provoked some wryly admiring comments from Queen Charlotte herself, was perhaps the only one of the three candidates in 1807 who actually looked the part.[18]

Despite Milton's odd person, his young wife Mary was widely acknowledged as a woman of great humour and charm. The artist Joseph Farington described her as 'delightfully easy & pleasant', and MP Thomas Creevey relied upon her to enliven his visits to the Fitzwilliams'.[19] In public, Milton could appear a serious-minded young man, his mind 'plodding about business'. He looked 'like a Methodist, – so formal; lank Hair and Buckles in His shoes', claimed one observer to Farington; his 'appearance & carriage has something puritanical in it', reported another.[20] Yet visitors to house parties at Wentworth might find Milton and his children 'without their coats playing at cricket with the servants just in front of the house'. In letters to his family he also showed a lighter side, once comforting his mother that her visit to a group of tiresomely garrulous ladies would prevent any danger of 'consumptive habit'. Since she wouldn't be able get a word in edgeways, her lungs must surely be preserved.[21]

The polls are opened

On 13 May, in the pouring rain, the presiding officials held formal nominations in the York Castle yard. His Majesty's writ was read and so too (with, one hopes, a commendably straight face) was 'the act for the better prevention of bribery and corruption'.[22] The traditional 'show of hands' followed. Milton's supporters were strategically placed, so he got a good showing. Wilberforce's campaigners were caught on the hop, scattered around and to the back of the crowd. They saw the show of hands go against him, which meant that Wilberforce, as the man with the least showing, had to demand the poll. This always put a campaign on the back foot.[23]

The prophets of doom were croaking that night, advising his resignation. Wilberforce could not compete financially against the vast resources marshalled by both Fitzwilliam and Harewood. His capital lay in his personal reputation. His supporters hoped that this would be enough to garner sufficient funds by subscription to pay his election expenses, despite the accepted wisdom that the scale of a county election in Yorkshire was simply beyond what any subscription could hope to sustain. Wilberforce urged his voters as far as possible to cover their own expenses to save the campaign money. (In the event, more than £64 000 was collected, and so many voters paid up themselves that almost half the money was returned.[24]) As the candidates gave their nomination speeches, the public was just impatient to get it all over with, 'the more so as many were standing in pools of water'.[25] Polling would begin one week later.

The hustings (from which candidates made their speeches, and where voting took place in specially constructed booths) held around a hundred persons 'conveniently', though up to

The price of the county

double that number occasionally managed to squeeze in. Tumult turned to tragedy when two men lost their lives in the crush.[26] Regulations set down the number of poll booths, and the 'wapentakes' (electoral subdivisions) had to be split between them. This caused problems for wapentakes with larger populations as it created major blockages while officials checked the eligibility of voters. This was a particular hazard for Milton, whose adherants were concentrated in a few electorates. Some hundreds of Milton's voters were in fact sent home unpolled at the end of the campaign.[27]

Candidates' names were printed on cards that supporters stuck jauntily in their hat bands, as can be seen in James Gillray's 1809 print 'Orange Jumper', commissioned to celebrate one of Milton's most ardent supporters. So far as they could, the crowds decked themselves out in the campaign's signature colour, which made the opposition easy to spot. Edward Baines traded the sign and counter-sign of 'Blue!' and 'Orange!' with a group of Leeds magistrates and merchants on the streets of York, later complaining in his paper of their 'hissings and hootings' that outraged 'decency and decorum'. With the merchant corporation at loggerheads with the clothiers, tension on the streets of Leeds ran high, and the Riot Act (which authorised dispersal by armed force) was read. Later that day, described the *Mercury*:

> A little boy parading the streets on Tuesday night, with
> one of Lord Milton's Orange-coloured cards in his hat, was
> pursued by a soldier on horse back with his drawn sword, a
> woman cried out to him as he passed, 'take the colour out,
> thou little fool.' 'No I won't take it out for any of them,'
> said the lad, 'they shall kill me first; Milton for ever –
> huzza.' The soldier, like a generous fellow, was pleased with

the lad's firmness, and left him to enjoy his favourite cry without further molestation.[28]

Excited, partisan crowds, rowdy with free meat and drink, trembled constantly on the brink of anarchy. Jostling and frustration were endemic on the hustings, as more than one hundred constables tried to keep order. (By law, the army was not allowed within two miles of the place of election until the day after polling was over.[29]) The costs of keeping order was yet another expense for the campaigners.

If the candidates were exhausted, so too were the voters:

> Considering the intense heat of the weather during the first days of the election; that hundreds of persons were violently pressing and struggling for admission, while only one at once could be passed through the booth; and that the crowd of persons attempting to poll at one booth, was often sufficient to have supplied that booth with voters for two days at least; no wonder that numbers were exhausted, and obliged to give up the attempt after many hours exertion.

Those unable to stand the strenuous conditions could apply for a 'certificate of infirmity' to allow them to vote at a separate time and place for an hour each day, though the under-sheriff drily remarked that 'the agility with which the *aged and infirm* climbed over seats and tables to procure tickets, was astonishing'.[30]

The campaign is launched

Historians have noted the professionalism of the Fitzwilliam electioneering machine, but he was also ably served by enthusiastic amateurs. Prominent amongst these was the formida-

The price of the county

ble Mrs Jane Osbaldeston of Hutton Bushell, mother of the celebrated local sporting fanatic 'Squire' Osbaldeston. George Osbaldeston greatly admired his mother, a widow since her son was six years old, although he was clearly in awe of her: 'None of her children', he frankly admitted, 'have inherited half her intellect'. Squire Osbaldeston was of an age with Milton, and although his memoirs show a touching confusion as to the political affiliations of the candidates in 1807 (he found political life 'a great bore') he well remembered his mother as 'a most enthusiastic politician' in the campaign. She 'came out as a strenuous and devoted supporter of Lord Milton. She actually canvassed in person every voter within 20 or 25 miles of Hutton Bushell ... Perhaps no lady ever performed such a feat, or even attempted it.'[31] Mary Milton reported to her mother-in-law that Mrs Osbaldeston was 'exerting herself to the utmost for both the country and the city'.[32] The Fitzwilliam election records bear this out, with countless 'plumpers' (single votes) for Milton in the area canvassed by Mrs Osbaldeston, despite the fact that it covered a Lascelles stronghold. As for the Squire, he left well alone, hastening out of the way to the Knavesmire race meeting during the campaign, to avoid 'interfer[ing] with my mother's labours'.[33]

Mary Milton was herself heavily pregnant and did not join her husband in the tumult of York. The couple's first child, Charlotte ('Kitten', as Milton called her), would be born just five weeks after the end of the campaign.[34] Mary was nonetheless busily canvassing for her husband in London. She treasured every scrap of news about the campaign, and was relieved to hear reports that Milton's voice had held up well against the other candidates in the nomination speeches. In fact, it had been pouring so hard with rain that the press had found it difficult to take down the particulars of any of the candidates' speeches.[35] Audibility was always a significant challenge, as Wilberforce had proven in 1784, but perhaps especially for Milton with his youth and inexperience. Mary Milton reported with glee the words of an eye-witness: 'they told us he was a boy, but this is not the voice of a boy & he don't speak like one'.[36]

The Fitzwilliam campaign also made strategic use of less delicate assistance, 'men of strong fists and Stentorian throats, who have latterly taken care that neither Mr Wilberforce nor Mr Lascelles should have a hearing'. Sometimes the belligerence of these 'fighting cocks' could get out of hand. Two of Milton's supporters, Martin Hawke (younger son of Lord Hawke and stalwart, like Squire Osbaldeston, of the fashionable Four-in-Hand Club) and Colonel Henry Mellish (the notorious buck, gambler and crony of the Prince of Wales) had a falling out that led to 'a few rounds with the fist' and a duel with pistols the next morning. The two combatants, bosom friends before their dispute, survived with relatively minor injuries and were later reconciled. Mellish was the acknowledged leader of Milton's hecklers, though his wild reputation could be a liability: 'Mr. Mellish used to endeavour to harangue from the Hustings; but the cry of "Why don't you pay your debts?" was so loud, on one or two occasions, that, after that time, he used to address the people from his own window'.[37]

Candidates needed to be physically and mentally robust, able to make themselves heard against the rabble-rousers of the opposition, and able to turn a hostile situation to their advantage with skilful repartee. The best election orators were those who played up to the crowd and made them feel included in the election spectacle. Despite his small size and feeble frame, Wilberforce was a past master at this:

75

The price of the county

After the first few days it was only by great skill in
managing a most unruly audience, that he could ever gain
a hearing. 'While Wilberforce was speaking the other
day,' writes Mr. Thornton, 'the mob of Milton interrupted
him: he was attempting to explain a point which had been
misrepresented; he endeavoured to be heard again and
again, but the cry against him always revived. 'Print, print'
cried a friend of Wilberforce in the crowd, 'print what you
have to say in a hand-bill, and let them read it, since they
will not hear you.' 'They read indeed,' cried Wilberforce,
'what, do you suppose that men who make such a noise as
those fellows can read?' holding up both his hands; 'no men
that make such noises as those can read, I'll promise you.
They must hear me now, or they'll know nothing about the
matter.' Immediately there was a fine Yorkshire grin over
some thousand friendly faces.[38]

For all Wilberforce's joke, sufficient voters could read (or be
read to) to leave Yorkshire awash in paper. Arguments in favour
and against the three candidates were continually printed in
handbills, mock playbills, squibs, poems and ballads – most
then reproduced in the press. That reform-minded dissenter,
Edwards Baines, had of course nailed his colours firmly to the
Whig mast. He proved himself a worthy lieutenant of the Fitzwilliam campaign, putting the considerable forces of the *Leeds
Mercury* at Milton's command, and squaring off against the Pittite Leeds merchants and their *Leeds Intelligencer*.

The street literature of elections made political rhetoric
accessible and familiar.[39] It was filled with in-jokes about the
candidates, often framed as mock playbills or racing announce-
ments:

Arcadia

YORK SPRING MEETING, 1807

A list of the Horses, and their Riders, entered to run for the county plates.

Earl F——w——m's chestnut colt, 'ROCKINGHAM,' ... Rider, A Yorkshire Clothier, in white and gold.

Lord H——w——d's black horse, 'BARBADOES', by Slavery; led to the Starting Chair by Peculation. Rider, a Leeds Merchant, in mourning.

Humanity's aged horse, 'ABOLITIONIST,' Rider unknown.

Five to one on the Chestnut Colt against the Black Horse, on account of the Rider.

'ABOLITIONIST' is sure to win one of the Plates, if mounted by 'Independence' but if the Jockey 'Coalition' should ride him, as is already strongly suspected, 'Plumper' will then mount the Chestnut Colt.

Nor was election rhetoric for the squeamish ('No Imbecile Infant of a factious Aristocracy. No trampling on Kings. No Popery. No Irish Papists. No Milton.'[40]) but it was also clever, funny and daring in ways we seem sadly to have lost. Mary Milton was characteristically amused by the election squibs – both for and against her husband – and tried to get hold of as many as possible:

We are very much obliged to you for squibs which we received yesterday, H. Lascelles *speech* is most excellent; Lord Dorchester was here this morning he admires Milton's very much, he told us Mr Baldwin had brought him some things on the other side, among which there was a play bill, M. is put in as the young Roscious, I should like of all things to see the squibs on the other side.[41]

No doubt Mary would have been gratified to know that she featured in a squib in her own right, although whether it was ever published is unknown. Amongst the handwritten 'Songs &c. in the Yorkshire Election of 1807' preserved at Harewood House we find 'On the appearance of the Orange Party addressed to Ld Milton':

> How ugly the Jaws, that were dropt in your cause,
> Their looks how ferocious and wild
> O keep them away from Wentworth, I pray,
> For remember your wife is *with Child*.[42]

Electioneering could clearly have its lighter side, but the anxieties held by candidates' families about the health and stamina needed to conduct such a vigorous campaign were very real. Milton's health was a great worry to his family, for the 'sickly Jacobin lad' had been close to death from fever only the year before. (His father complained he would have recovered more quickly had he not been so addicted to reading.[43]) 'I hope you all keep well', wrote a worried Mary Milton to Lady Fitzwilliam as the polling drew near. 'M says he is pretty well, I rather fear from that he is very much fatigued. I wish most heartily it was all *well* over.'[44]

Only on Sundays could the candidates gain a brief respite. 'I am amazingly fagged today', wrote Milton to his father, '& not sorry that tomorrow is to be a day of rest'.[45] Wilberforce, characteristically, stepped away from his exhausted body, and let his soul wander. 'How beautiful Broomsfield must be at this moment!' he wrote to Barbara:

> I imagine myself roaming through the shrubbery with
> you and the little ones; and indeed I have joined you
> in spirit several times to-day, and have hoped we were

applying together at the throne of grace. How merciful
and gracious God is to me! Surely the universal kindness
which I experience, is to be regarded as a singular instance
of the goodness of the Almighty ... I must say Good
night. May God bless you. Kiss the babes, and give friendly
remembrances to all family and other friends.[46]

Wilberforce had gone into the campaign as firm favourite, with
the second seat considered the focus of a battle between Milton
and Lascelles. Yet his campaign was amateur compared to those
of his rivals. Securing carriages to get the voters to York was
one major problem:

> Every day the roads, in every direction, and to and from
> every remote corner of the county, have been covered with
> vehicles loaded with Voters – and Barouches, Curricules,
> Gigs, Flying Waggons, Military Cars with eight horses to
> them, crowded sometimes with forty Voters, have been
> scouring the Country, leaving not the smallest chance for
> the *quiet* traveller to pursue his humble journey, or find a
> chair at an inn to sit down upon.

The *Leeds Intelligencer* reckoned that about eight horses a day
were to be seen dead from exhaustion on the public roads.[47]

Left standing by the activities of Harewood and Wentworth
agents, who had secured almost all the commercial transportation to be had, Wilberforce's supporters came by river, on
farmers' wagons, on donkeys, and plodding into York on their
own two feet. 'My having been left behind on the poll', wrote
Wilberforce to Barbara mid-way through the campaign:

> seemed to rouse the zeal of my friends, (I should rather say,
> of my fervent adherents,) they exerted themselves, and have

The price of the county

mended my condition. You would be gratified to see the affection which is borne me by many to whom I am scarcely or not at all known. Even those who do not vote for me seem to give me their esteem.[48]

Yet such was the strength of the Harewood and particularly of the Fitzwilliam electoral machine (the latter employed close on a hundred agents) that the outcome was soon an open contest. Within the first two days of polling, Wilberforce was in last place. Just three months after the Slave Trade Act was passed, the hero of abolition was in danger of losing his seat:

> Money was expended in a frightful profusion during a fifteen days' poll ... On the first day Mr Lascelles polled the greater number of votes: on the second day Lord Milton headed the poll: but on the fifth day Mr Lascelles passed his opponent, and kept the lead till the thirteenth day, at the close of which the numbers stood Milton 10,313, Lascelles 10,255. Now the efforts were prodigious and the excitement maddening.[49]

Slavery, Saints and sinners

To win, the Fitzwilliam camp needed to drive a wedge between Lascelles and Wilberforce. 'We cannot imagine', wrote an obliging Baines in the *Leeds Mercury*, 'how the *profane* Mr Lascelles and the *pious* Mr Wilberforce can possibly coalesce ... One of them is a *Saint*, the other a *Sinner*.' The *York Herald*'s poem on the subject was rather more graphic:

> 'Tickle me,' says pious BILLY,
> 'Tickle me, good LASCELLES, do.'

'If you but tickle pious Billy,
'He, in return, will tickle you.'[50]

In fact the two former colleagues and 'Pitt's friends', despite the slave issue, were otherwise natural political allies. A key national issue in the 1807 election was Catholic emancipation (over which the King's had dismissed the ministry) and both Lascelles and Wilberforce then opposed it. While the evidence suggests that Wilberforce himself honoured his declaration of neutrality, his machine lacked the organisation and discipline to keep his agents strictly in line, so providing plenty of ammunition for Milton's accusations of a coalition with Lascelles, and as the form guide would have it, this could bring out the clothiers against him.

Yet for all the rancour of the Catholic question, it was the bitter half-century struggle that was then beginning over the factory system in Yorkshire that lay at the heart of the 1807 county election. It was caught up in wider anxieties then current in Britain about hierarchy, anxieties that went far beyond the issue of industrial change. The brilliance of the Fitzwilliam campaign strategy was to yoke three great engines of social transformation together: to link the wool debate both to the emotive issue of slavery and to popular feelings about rank and leadership. Henry Lascelles's manners towards British working men, his family interests in slavery and his views on the wool industry all opened up a rich vein of inspiration for his opponents:

Beware of SLAVE DRIVERS!
They've dealt long in — BLOOD!!!
If they get into *Place*,
They — do — Nothing that's good.

The price of the county

So, Gentlemen CLOTHIERS,
Stand up for your Rights!
When they've bled all the Blacks,
They'll *bleed all the Whites*!!![51]

Emphasising the slavery issue, and linking it to the wool
debates, was the perfect mechanism for the Whigs to break
a possible Lascelles-Wilberforce coalition. Antislavery sentiment, after all, was a sign of all the most fashionable virtues.
In an ideological contest over who could lay claim to protecting liberty, about who had the right to lead the British nation,
Henry Lascelles was easily tarred with the brush of tyranny.
'Let us reject with becoming disdain', urged a handbill supposedly penned by 'A Clothier', one 'who, if it were in his power, I
have no doubt would treat us as ill, or worse, than his own West
India Slaves'. 'Brother Clothiers', it continued:

> if you do not exert yourselves on this occasion, your
> Freedom is gone for ever: your political consequence will
> be for ever extinguished; you will become the mere Slaves
> of the Merchants, who will dispose of you in future to
> whom they please; yea to your Greatest Enemy, to the Man
> whose very countenance speaks nothing but sullen, haughty
> and contemptuous arrogance; who seems to think one half
> of his fellow creatures scarcely good enough to look upon,
> and may even have it in contemplation, after he has ruined
> your trade, to supply his father's West India Plantations
> with Slaves, (now that the African Market is shut,) from the
> Huddersfield and Leeds Cloth-Halls.[52]

Mock playbills were posted for 'a new Tragedy, called *The West
Indian: or, Slavery Revived*'. It noted that 'The Manager being
disappointed of the Assistance of the YORKSHIRE CLOTHIERS,

Arcadia

their Places will be supplied by a Company of NEGRO DRIV-ERS, whom the Manager has lastly engaged at a great Expence':

WANTED: A Hundred Negro Drivers to be employed in
the Island of Barbadoes. Apply at Har—w——d House. No
Yorkshire Clothier need apply, as they have been found too
refractory to be insulted and trampled upon by The Son of
the Proprietor.
☞ Should the Slave Trade be revived in the next Session
of Parliament, with a View to which the Proprietor is
labouring to procure for his Son the Representation of the
County of York, the Number of Negro Drivers wanted will
not be limited, but may extend to Two Thousand at least.[53]

Slavery was evoked in moral terms, described by 'An Abolition-ist' in an attack on Lascelles as 'a curse to the British Isles'.[54] Milton's speech against slavery in the House of Commons, in which he had asked that 'the *foul stain* be washed from the character of the nation!', was quoted at length.[55] Freeing slaves made Britons feel, as historian Linda Colley argues, that they were the 'patrons and possessors of liberty'.[56] Henry Lascelles protested that he had supported the vote on abolition, but it availed him nothing. While the Lascelles *did* derive their for-tune from slavery, and would continue to lobby for planter interests, the 1806 and 1807 elections also demonstrate how the rhetoric of abolition could be a blunt instrument, used to dis-credit political opponents much as accusations of being soft on terrorism have operated in our own recent memory.

If antislavery and clothier resentment proved a power-ful combination, there was no connection made in the cam-paign between the slavery of industrialisation and the remedy of social revolution. Wentworth House, of course, was hardly likely to advocate social upheaval. Much to Edward Baines's delight, Milton would eventually come over publicly to the cause of parliamentary reform, dragging a more sceptical Fitzwilliam in his wake. But in 1807 this lay more than a decade in the future. Fitzwilliam's eighteenth-century Whiggish notion of British liberty was profoundly hierarchical, envisaging a society in which individual freedom was sacrosanct but founded securely amidst reciprocal rights and obligations. *His* liberty had no truck with the radical elements of the British political landscape, sanctioned or otherwise. For Fitzwilliam, an earl since the tender age of eight, this was bred in the bone. An enlightened aristocracy was duty-bound to lead, protecting the nation from autocratic monarchs on the one hand and popular demagogues on the other.[57] The Lascelles, for all they stood on the other side of politics, would largely have agreed. They sought to join the aristocracy, not overturn it. Wilberforce, too, was committed to moral, but never to social revolution. The 1807 debate that linked slavery to industrialisation, then, was not about attacking hierarchy as such, but about who had the appropriate credentials to lead. The power of anti-slavery sentiment meant that wealth derived from the West Indian slave colonies eroded not only a man's morality, but also his ability to represent the national voice and even his right to be British.

In an exchange of squibs entitled variously 'A few plain questions answered' and 'A few plain questions answered as they ought to be', the supporters of Milton and Lascelles indulged in unashamed social brinkmanship:

> To what does the Name of Lascelles owe its Consequence? – Ask Bleeding Africa …
> Whence is Lord Milton descended? – From a Family whose Patriotism & Virtues all the World knows.

Whence is Lascelles descended? – From a Family Nobody knows.

The counter-list included a fulsome assertion of the Lascelles family's Yorkshire pedigree in contrast to the Fitzwilliams. In asserting their political loyalty to the Crown, and their heritage in the county, it was clearly also important to counter the idea of them being 'social nobodies' and to disassociate themselves from the taint of the West Indies:

> Whence is Lord Milton descended?
> From Lord Strafford, the enemy of civil and religious
> liberty, and the traitor to the Commons of England.
> Whence is Lascelles descended?
> From one of the most ancient families in the County; their
> Names appear in the Records of Yorkshire in A.D. 1260;
> they represented Northallerton, when the Borough was
> first erected; and fought for their King and Country under
> the Plantagenets, many hundred years before the family of
> Fitzwilliam had a foot of land in the County.
> *Freeholders! Lascelles for Ever!*
> Support him against the unnatural union of Aristocratic
> pride and Jacobin principles.[58]

Milton's supporters claimed they had 'more weight in the County of York, than the Son of a Barbadoes Planter'. They urged that the 'Tyrant may fly to his African parts', and they attacked 'the West Indian domination, which has just been disappointed in its attempt of overstriding the county'. In a similar vein, 'An Abolitionist' claimed:

> whoever makes the continued Abolition of the Slave Trade,
> a motive for deciding his preference at the ensuing election,

The price of the county

cannot hesitate for a moment whether to prefer *The son of a West-Indian Lord*, not distinguished for his disinterestedness, and whose interest is deeply involved in the continuation of slavery, *or, the Son of an English Lord,* humane, loyal and generous, and of the true old Rockingham and Saville stock.[59]

Yorkshiremen were self-consciously proud of their autonomous political heritage. Lascelles claimed that the 'Representation of my native County in Parliament has for long been the first Object of my Ambition'.[60] The West Indies, by contrast, figured in the British imagination as a place of moral turpitude where fortune-hunting Europeans were in danger of turning into something dangerous, something not quite white. Henry Lascelles might have been born and raised in Yorkshire, his family might locate their historical roots there, but his wealth, social status, and political influence could be traced to a source that, by the early nineteenth century, strong elements of public opinion regarded as polluted.

'The efforts were prodigious and the excitement maddening'

In the midst of these bitter debates, fighting accusations of hypocrisy, deceit and a 'monstrous coalition' with 'West Indian' planters, the strain was too much for Wilberforce. On the twelfth day of the poll he collapsed, overcome by illness and exhaustion. (Indeed half his committee were laid low by the microbes swarming through the electioneering hordes.) Rumours flew around that their candidate was dead, but though it had been a close-run thing, it was soon clear that Wilberforce was both physically and electorally secure.[61]

The battle was now for the second seat. Henry Lascelles's emotions in these last days are lost to us, but Milton's regular despatches to his father, preserved in the Fitzwilliam family papers, chart the agonisingly close contest:

> None of Wilberforce's or Lascelles's voters are yet come, we have a great number here it is impossible to keep back the clothiers, there are multitudes come. (19 May)
>
> I was very unwilling to send an express this evening with such bad news ... We have had a terrible day; Lascelles has got above me in the whole poll ... we must make great exertion, the coalition [between Wilberforce and Lascelles] is now beyond a doubt, they have all split votes which I fear may crush us. (25 May)
>
> Wilberforce was very hard pressed by us today after the close of the Poll on the subject of the coalition, he was quite out of temper & did not know what to say, & the people were quite against him, he has lost much of his popularity; he is now accused by them of hypocrisy & duplicity in his conduct during the election, it is delightful to see that people begin to find him out. (28 May)
>
> I am now so resigned to be beaten, that I don't care much about it; we have fought a glorious battle, & that is sufficient, particularly when I think that we have ruined Wilberforce's popularity ... I shall be very glad to be at rest. (31 May)

The Lascelles supporters in the *Leeds Intelligencer* were rejoicing the following day, 1 June. They predicted the imminent defeat of 'the lesson-taught Boy with red hair'; that 'unfledged chicken of aristocracy'. 'Mr Lascelles at the York races, has tipt the young jockey of Wentworth House, the go by.' Yet on that

The price of the county

very same day, Milton himself saw light dawning:

> I begin now to hope that there may be some chance of
> success, but we have still a great deal of way to make, so
> every exertion must be made. (1 June)
> We think the election is now pretty certain, there is great
> appearance of weakness on the other side ... I own that
> three days ago I had quite given the thing up. We must still
> make great exertions. (2 June)

The clothiers were still determinedly pouring in: 'they must
have come from under ground', wrote Milton on 3 June, 'it is
impossible there should be so many upon the surface of the
country'. And finally:

> I think that after this day [3 June] there can be no doubt of
> the issue of the election; we have several people come in
> since the close of this day's poll, & I fancy they have some
> arrivals, but they cannot be equal to ours, 170 voters left
> Leeds in the course of today for me none of whom have
> polled; it seems very much as if the clothing country had
> not been completely roused till they found Lascelles was
> likely to be returned: I believe it will be a bitter piece of
> news for the *Protestant* administration.
> Wilberforce has not yet made his appearance, he & all his
> committee have been very ill. Lascelles's friends are said to
> have got the *Blue devils*, I fear it will be a fatal disorder.[62]

Milton's pun on his opponent's signature colour proved an
accurate prediction. At 3 o'clock on 5 June the poll closed and
soon after the High Sheriff declared the result from the hustings. Wilberforce stood at the head of the poll with 11 808
votes, a far smaller majority than had been predicted. Milton

had beaten Lascelles by a scant 187 votes.

The Fitzwilliams were elated. Mary Milton, quite incoherent with joy and relief, wrote to a friend two days later:

Our Victory is now complete the numbers at the Close of
the Poll were
15th Day
Wilberforce – 11,808
Milton – 11,177
Lascelles – 10,990
Majority for Milton over Lascelles 187.
We are quite mad with joy, and are covered with Orange
ribbons, Milton for Ever &c.
I am sorry it is a bad day, as we intend to go into Hyde Park
on purpose to show ourselves, with the Servants & Horses
bedecked with furious Orange Cocades. I can't write for
pure joy.
Milton says he will be here on Tuesday or Wednesday.
Oh! I am mad.[63]

Milton was chaired through York accompanied, claimed the *York Herald*, by 5000 people decked out in orange badges and ribbons. Ladies lined the windows of the streets through which the procession passed, waving orange handkerchiefs. York was a sea of orange banners, with bands of music and shouts of 'Milton forever!' rending the air. As the procession came opposite the George Inn, headquarters of the Lascelles campaign, a tile or brick was shied, narrowly missing the newly elected MP, and a 'vast number of ruffians' tried to dislodge Milton from his perch. A pitched battle ensued, but Milton kept his seat. The triumphal chair survived the assault, though its decorations were completely stripped, and was duly lodged in the Cloth

The price of the county

Hall of Leeds, 'where it is to be preserved as a memento of the glorious 5th of June'. Bonfires, processions, bell-ringing, sheep roasts and the chairing of Milton by proxy took place across the cloth districts of the West Riding. The celebrations and festivities continued for the best part of a week. Mrs Osbaldeston was toasted as 'The Female Patriot of Yorkshire' and drawn in triumph through the streets of Malton, the Fitzwilliams' pocket borough. Milton's supporters now delighted in casting the youth of their champion back in their opponents' teeth. In 'Lascelles and the Baby, or, The Glorious Fifth of June 1807' they sang:

> They *call'd him* a pitiful Baby,
> A white-looking, red-headed Baby!
> Then offer'd thcm Battle,
> And *manfully* fought, though – *a Baby!*[64]

Wilberforce was too ill to partake in the celebrations, but by 8 June he had recovered sufficiently to write to Hannah More:

> I almost feel criminal for having sent you no tidings during
> our long and laborious contest. For the last four days I kept
> my room; having at last only fallen ill under a complaint
> which had pulled down many strong men around me many
> days before … it is unspeakable cause for thankfulness to
> come out of the battle ruined neither in health, character,
> or fortune.[65]

Wilberforce's supporters made much of the fact that, by public subscription, they had preserved the 'independence' of the county in the face of aristocratic privilege. 'Perhaps it may be thought', Wilberforce announced to his more sober-minded freeholders after the election:

that we too much neglected pride, and pomp, and circumstance; the procession, and the music, and the streamers, and all the other purchased decorations which catch the vulgar eye … we catered from the impulse of our taste, no less than from that of our judgement, when we declined all competition in parade and profusion? Our triumph was of a different sort. We may perhaps have too much indulged our love of simplicity; but to our eyes and feelings, the entrance of a set of common freeholders on their own, and those often not the best horses, or riding in their carts and waggons, often equipped in the style of rustic plainness, was far more gratifying, than the best arranged and most pompous cavalcade.[66]

Lady Bessborough put in more plainly:

what I really think an honour to the Man, and a proper homage to Virtue and religion, is Wilberforce, without a sixpence, being at the head of the poll from mere weight of Character in such an Election as this, when money is suppos'd to do all.[67]

Perhaps it took a countess to consider a man of Wilberforce's means impoverished, but certainly for an independent MP to stand against the might of both the Lascelles and Fitzwilliams took an extraordinary level of broad-based support.

Wilberforce's simplicity made a virtue of necessity. But it was also politically astute. The popular literature of the late eighteenth century saw an explosion of interest in social climbing which focused resentment on the social and political ambitions of industrial manufacturers, West Indian planters, and 'nabobs' whose fortune came from India. If anyone could tap into this sentiment, it was Wilberforce. He was of the fashionable elite, but his religious conversion had set him forever apart from it. Surrounded by powerful men, he was aware of the dangers of place-seeking: 'I often detected myself in thinking, "why should not I get a title and soon?"' To keep himself from being tempted by social ambition, he carried warning notes in his pocket. In the pages of his diary, Wilberforce once described how he deliberately put a stone in his own shoe before going into fashionable company, so that the discomfort it caused might serve as a reminder of his good intentions.[68] Ambivalence about wealth's ability to purchase social status and political power could focus especial hostility on the sudden acquisition of fortunes derived from the opportunities of empire. Comedies such as *The West Indian* (Richard Cumberland, 1771), parodied in anti-Lascelles election squibs, found a ready audience in London theatres. The popularity of these images evidently struck a chord in a society anxious about the manner in which elite ranks were expanding through new sources of wealth.[69]

The Lascelles thwarted?

Lord Harewood was said to have 'staggered' under the blow of defeat. 'I was with him at Ingmanthorpe', remembered Richard Hale, 'and *saw* the pang and pitied him and went with him in his carriage to London afterwards and a miserable journey I had of it'.[70]

An alliance of clothiers, Whig aristocrats and the non-conformist urban middle class had pushed Milton over the line against the Pittite gentry and an oligarchy of Anglican merchants and would-be manufacturers who dominated the Leeds corporation. It was well recognised at the time that the cloth-

Arcadia

iers' numbers had been decisive, and had cost Lascelles the election.[71] Of the votes cast for Milton, 81 per cent were plumpers (single votes). Indeed, plumpers made up just over half of all the votes cast in the entire election. This was highly unusual. Plumpers were a sure sign of a highly partisan electorate. The clothiers voted in a body and were on the watch for any who might step out of line. Their own regalia was a leather apron, sign of their craft, 'and if one of their body appeared on the other side, they would shake it in his face, "What thee vote against t'apron!"'[72]

It is no coincidence that it was in the late eighteenth century that the term 'vulgar' took on the meaning it has today. This shift, with vulgarity coming to mean a lapse in taste and manners, is reflected in the word play of Baines's claim that 'Though Mr Lascelles has not the *populace* on his side, the filthy productions of his friends prove that he has decidedly the support of the *vulgar*'.[73] The question of status – not only wealth but its source and the use to which it was put – was intimately connected to debates over the right to act within the political realm. There were bipartisan concerns about what was termed 'Old Corruption' and widespread perceptions of elite parasitism.[74] One of the reasons Pitt was able to survive in 1784 was precisely because he was seen as being tough on graft. Attacks on government prodigality had a specifically local heritage in the form of the reformist Yorkshire Association, which had endorsed Wilberforce after his spectacular speech against the Whig oligarchy in that year. The Association coupled concerns about the need to restrict government expenditure with moderate calls for political reform, and refused to be tied to one political interest. It was yet another example of Yorkshire's reputation for political independence and experimentation.[75]

The price of the county

With the vast amounts being spent on the campaign of 1807, it was easy to draw a link between buying and selling black slaves and trading British voters:

> Shall it ever be said that our County *is sold,*
> Or that Yorkshire is *purchas'd* with *African Gold?*[76]

If buying souls was commensurate with buying political influence, Henry Lascelles was vulnerable to accusations that he was eroding British liberties. 'Lord H—re——d's Address to the Clothiers of Yorkshire', encapsulates these themes:

> What reason has a LORD to fear
> The Yorkshire Renegadoes;
> With forty thousand pounds a year
> *All* coming from Barbadoes!!
> Harry abus'd the Clothier Slaves,
> 'Tis true and it is pity;
> He call'd them 'Disaffected Knaves'
> *Upon their own Committee.*
> But let the *rascals* hoot and curse
> From July to December,
> Ye dogs, *I've money in my purse,*
> And Harry SHALL be MEMBER!![77]

Baines's *Leeds Mercury* attacked the Lascelles family pocket boroughs of Northallerton and Westbury (which Henry's elder brother, Edward 'Beau' Lascelles represented) and predicted – correctly – that if the family lost the county election in 1807, two parliamentary seats for the family would still be secured by splitting Northallerton and Westbury between the two brothers. Henry would indeed represent Westbury (now a suburb of north Bristol) between 1807 and 1812. The freeholders of 'proud

Yorkshire' were thus held up in contrast to the purchased voters of pocket boroughs. A vicious letter ostensibly directed to Lascelles by 'An Elector' attacked:

> that purse which is to give an importance to the family
> of Harewood, to which neither their talents, their public
> spirit, or their rank in society entitles them, and which is to
> level the County of York with your *independent* Boroughs of
> Northallerton and Westbury ... Retire, Sir, retire into some
> obscure borough, where you may be at liberty to say to your
> constituents, 'I have *bought* you, and I have a right to use you
> as my slaves!' Such language may be tolerated in some of
> your father's boroughs, but rely upon it, these indignities
> can never be endured by the high-minded freeholders of the
> County of York.[78]

Lascelles's supporters did not shrink from making similar arguments against Milton, but the Lascelles were more vulnerable than the Fitzwilliams to charges that they were using Yorkshire freeholders to meet their own ambitions for higher rank. Status lay at the heart of this contest, from the humblest enfranchised clothier to the candidate who had allegedly treated him with contempt. 'It is supposed', claimed the *Leeds Mercury* after describing Lascelles's insulting behaviour to the clothiers, 'that in the event of the Hon. Henry Lascelles obtaining his Election for Yorkshire, Lord Harewood has a promise from the Treasury Bench, that he shall be made an EARL'. In a poem entitled 'The Price of the County', the paper lampooned the Lascelles family's political and social ambitions since 1796, the year in which Henry Lascelles first represented Yorkshire and his father was created Baron Harewood. A few of the poem's eleven verses make the point clearly enough. Lord Harewood, a man accus-

The price of the county

tomed to buying and selling African slaves, would now buy the voters of Yorkshire for the King's interest. In the supposed negotiations described by the poem with two prime ministers (William Pitt and the Duke of Portland) a barony, and then an earldom, would be his reward:

> Said old L_c_s to P_tt, on a sunshiny day,
> 'Ev'ry man has his price, I have heard the folks say:
> 'And since *men* are purchased and sold for a bounty,
> 'Pray tell me, friend P_tt, what's the price of a county?'
> Quoth P_tt, 'Sure a Gentleman's never the worse
> 'For lacking of wit, if he owns a long purse:
> 'So to cut matters short, we'll engage at a word,
> 'You carry the county, I'll make *you* a Lord.' ...
> No longer in senate, and almost benighted,
> The dreams of past consequence make him short-sighted;
> And H_w_d, once more, at the Treasury porch,
> Asks the price of the county, for Hal and the Church.
> Says P__l__d, 'I'm not a political churl,
> 'Make sure of proud Yorkshire, I'll make thee an Earl;'
> The Pope at they elbow, throws dust in their eyes,
> And Liberty, Britain's inheritance, dies![79]

Ironically, Lord Harewood in fact later complained that the Duke of Portland had delayed promoting his request to be granted a peerage.[80]

Yet it is remarkable that the Lascelles took the decision to fight an election to poll in 1807 when they were labouring under the same disadvantages that had caused Henry to withdraw just months earlier. The 1807 election was fought in the context of a political power struggle between George III and his ministers (with particular reference to Catholic emancipa-

Arcadia

tion, as this poem suggests). Constitutional government was central to the way the British thought of themselves as 'unusually and distinctively free' by this period, ideas which had fed the popularity of antislavery sentiment.[81] Debates about the monarch's relations with his government prompted by the ministry's dismissal gave further strength to connections made in the campaign between slave abolition and notions of British identity. It was hardly a propitious moment for the Lascelles to mount what became the most expensive election campaign yet fought in British history.

<hr>

Nevertheless, it is likely that the Lascelles family considered the extraordinary expense of 1807 worthwhile, since it would have been to their advantage to show their loyalty to the monarch by securing a Yorkshire seat in his interest. Even their defeat, given its place in a struggle which had so captured the imagination of the nation, might well have served the same purpose.[82] Lord Harewood made repeated petitions for an earldom over several years, making reference in 1809 to 'My long and invariable attachment to the King – And the Exertions I have at different Times made in support of His Government'.[83] In the next Yorkshire county election, that of 1812, Henry Lascelles was much more circumspect about standing for the county.[84] It was only when they were sure that the vast expense of a second open contest could be avoided that the family announced their intention to put a member forward. There was probably not the same pressure on Henry as there had been in 1807. A month before parliament was dissolved for the 1812 election, the *Leeds Mercury* had printed the long-awaited announcement:

The price of the country

His Royal Highness the Prince Regent has also been pleased in the name and on the behalf of his Majesty, to grant the dignities of Viscount and Earl of the United Kingdom of Great Britain and Ireland, to the Right Hon. Edward Baron Harewood, and the heirs male of his body lawfully begotten, by the names, stiles and titles of Viscount Lascelles, and Earl of Harewood, in the County of York.[85]

PART TWO

Ruin and disgrace

My son, keep thy father's commandment, and forsake not
the law of thy mother: Bind them continually upon thine
heart, and tie them about thy neck. …
For the commandment is a lamp; and the law is light; and
reproofs of instruction are the way of life: To keep thee from
the evil woman, from the flattery of the tongue of a strange
woman.

Proverbs 6:20–24

Hanover Square, London, 1826

A century after three Lascelles brothers set sail for Barbados, their descendants had finally secured that necessary triumvirate of an aristocratic dynasty: wealth, a peerage, and heirs to carry the line forward. After extensive lobbying, Edward Lascelles had been created 1st Earl of Harewood, setting the official seal on one of the largest fortunes in the kingdom. Their name was already such commonly recognised shorthand for luxury and status that Jane Austen could use it to mock social pretension in her novels. In *Mansfield Park*, written at the very moment of the Lascelles's ascent into the ranks of the aristocracy, the shallow and self-absorbed Maria Bertram decides on 'giving her hand without her heart', and marries the dullard Mr Rushworth. For all he is 'a very stupid fellow', his income and fine estate would launch Maria into fashionable society. Austen has Mary Crawford, wise in the ways of the corrupt world, write of the newly married Mrs Rushworth:

> Then she will be in beauty for she will open one of the best houses in Wimpole Street. I was in it two years ago when it was Lady Lascelles's, and prefer it to almost any I know in London, and certainly she will then feel – to use a vulgar phrase – that she has got her pennyworth for her penny.[1]

Wimpole Street had indeed been the home of Edward Lascelles. But when he inherited the Harewood fortune from his cousin in 1795, his horizons broadened. He bought a three-storey Adam mansion from the Duke of Roxburghe, favourably situated on the north side of Hanover Square.

It was at this address that a series of sinister letters were directed to his son Henry Lascelles, by then 2nd Earl of Hare-

Ruin and disgrace

wood, in 1826.[2] They claimed knowledge of the shame that had come to the 'family of Harewood' some eight years previously, events that the family had done their best to keep quiet, and they hinted that the writer had information that could restore the 'tranquillity of your house'.[3]

Until these troubles had come upon them, the difficulties of succession that had plagued the Lascelles family through the eighteenth century had seemed at an end. In 1812, the year of their earldom, the lineage appeared secure. No longer would a failure to produce sons make it necessary for nephews to inherit, or for various branches of the family to merge or re-merge. To be sure, the immediate heir, Edward 'Beau' Lascelles, remained more interested in collecting porcelain than in find-ing a suitable bride. But Henry Lascelles (of 1807 election fame) had married Henrietta Sebright, the daughter of a baronet, in 1794. Their first son arrived two years later, and their second a year after that.

Henry's match had inspired some tart gossip from the pen of Queen Charlotte:

> The younger Lascelles, Alias Cupid, is to marry Miss
> Sebright. The Gay Lothario is to Wed the Sedate & retired
> Wife; how they will suit, time will shew; for Beauty
> there is none, nor Fortune on the Female side. I do not
> mean by that, that much of either is necessary for real
> Happiness; but as on the one side there has always been so
> much pretension to Beauty, I wish there was more Money
> on the other side. She has been well Educated; as I hear,
> is possessed of many Talents, & has behaved with great
> attention to Her Mother; I hope she will be happy.[4]

Happy or not, the couple were conscientious. Henrietta soon

Ruin and disgrace

produced the first of her twelve offspring, of whom eight were to prove the all-important sons. Perhaps Henry and Henrietta suspected the 'Beau' of misliking matrimony. In any event, their first son, heir-presumptive to the title, was christened after both uncle and grandfather. It was to prove one of the few prudent choices in the younger Edward's life.

If 'Beau' Lascelles was indeed reluctant to wed, it was one of several traits he shared with the Prince Regent. Both were noted connoisseurs, passionate collectors of Sèvres porcelain, and so much resembled one another that it became a well-worn joke amongst their contemporaries. The Prince was not amused. 'Young Mr Lascelles of Harewood House', wrote Farington in 1796:

> is reckoned very like the Prince of Wales. The Prince is
> not pleased at it. He calls Lascelles *the Pretender*. Making a
> remark on a portrait painted of him by Hoppner He desired
> an alteration, at present, said He, '*It is more like the Pretender*'.
> At Brighton the Prince has been struck on the shoulder
> familiarly with a 'Ha Lascelles, how is it?' – To which He has
> returned a marked look of disapprobation.

Beau Lascelles was also well-known in artistic circles, both as a patron and as one who had 'practiced a little' himself, as Farington put it.[5] He invited Thomas Girtin, JMW Turner and John Varley to Harewood, the three artists leaving a matchless record of the house and surrounds before the formidable wife of the 3rd Earl unleashed her renovation forces to bring Harewood into the Victorian era.

Even when Beau Lascelles died without issue in 1814, the Harewood succession seemed secured in the shape of Henry's five surviving sons. It certainly looked less perilous than had

Ruin and disgrace

their rivals the Fitzwilliams a generation earlier, when only Milton, the slightly built 'boy with red hair', stood between the Wentworth inheritance and the children of a runaway match with a footman. Milton's own eldest son died before he was blessed with an heir. Three years later, however, the next son married and, shortly after, the first of no fewer than eight boys was born. Perhaps the Fitzwilliams were haunted by fears for the continuation of their name. In any event they took no chances. All eight were christened William.

In 1818, six years after his grandfather became 1st Earl of Harewood, young Edward Lascelles, then aged twenty-two, occupied an enviable position. Until such time as he inherited, he was kept occupied in a manner traditional to his family's newly attained rank, as officer in a cavalry regiment.[6] Edward had the year before been made a lieutenant in the Yorkshire Hussars, the regiment then on high alert as fears of an uprising swept the West Riding.[7] Unlike the host of demobilised and impoverished men and officers on half-pay, to whom the end of the war with France was a mixed blessing, Edward was financially secure. Unfortunately his judgement was not equal to his situation. At the apex of British society, and certainly one of its most eligible bachelors, it was only a matter of months before, as reported in that Sydney courtroom, 'the son of the Earl of Harewood ... disappeared from England'.

Ruin and disgrace

3

HAREWOOD AT BAY

'Ah, but I'm not a gentleman,' said the Marquis. 'I have it on
the best of authority that I am only a nobleman.'

Georgette Heyer, *Devil's Cub*, 1932

In the summer and autumn of 1818, Edward Lascelles was enjoying a dalliance with a woman named Ann Elizabeth Rosser. 'My
Dearest Edward', she wrote to him on 18 August:

> please try and come for I have been anticipating the
> pleasure ever since you sent word in your letter that you
> thought it would be most probable that you would be there,
> please to send me word whether you are coming and what
> you think of us being together … I can assure you that
> I have been perfectly steady to you and *depend* upon me
> remaining so … a thousand kisses with my best love.

Her letters chart clandestine meetings, and requests for money
and for news of 'the particulars what they said to you at home'.[1]
The lovers met in secret, for Ann Elizabeth was apparently

Ruin and disgrace

the daughter of Hereford publicans. For a man of Edward's rank to have an affair with a woman such as Ann Elizabeth was both common and, largely, condoned. But by no contemporary standard was she an acceptable *public* mate for the heir to an earldom, nor indeed (so some claimed) for any respectable man. A double standard allowed for sexual licence amongst young men, so long as they adopted a reasonable degree of discretion. The stereotype of eighteenth-century elite masculinity – drinking, gambling and wenching – is not without foundation. Sons were expected to sow their wild oats; potency and heterosexuality, after all, were important attributes if a family lineage were to be preserved.[2] Men like Wilberforce were preaching loud enough for moral criticisms of masculine sexual license to be gaining ground within the aristocracy. But youthful sexual experimentation was still widely condoned. Whatever social transformation were taking place as the eighteenth century gave way to the nineteenth, the 'sexual *rite de passage* of young men on the threshold of manhood', so long as it was followed by responsible household headship, remained one of the most enduring models of proper manly behaviour.[3]

For young Edward Lascelles, then, it was a case of so far, so conventional. But things rapidly became very messy. On 12 November 1818, the Earl of Harewood received an anonymous letter from Bristol. It claimed that 'a plan was in agitation to strike a severe blow at the honor of the house of Harewood, by the marriage of the Honorable Edward Lascelles to a person of low situation with whom He had kept up an illicit connexion for some time'. The writer gave an address in Bristol where this 'person' might be found, warning that 'She lodged at the house of a respectable old widow, with whom great caution must be used, as She was bribed highly to secrecy'. The marriage, it was

Harewood at bay

claimed, 'was intended to be solemnized within a few days from the date of this letter' and if it were to be prevented, then 'no time was to be lost'.[4] By the next day, the family's agent, Mr Sherrard, was in Bristol, looking frantically for Edward.

Sacrificed on the altar of family honour

It was too late. On the night he arrived, Sherrard discovered from the register of St James' church, that 'Edward Lascelles of the Parish of Westbury upon Trim & diocese of Bristol Esqr Batchelor' had married 'Ann Elizabeth Rosser of this Parish Spinster' on 3 November. Both parties declared that they were above twenty-one years of age and that no impediment existed as to their marriage. Ann and William Lodge were listed as witnesses. (William Lodge was obviously on hand if witnesses were scarce on the ground, for his name appears again in another marriage two days later.) Unlike the two other brides whose 'marks' appear on the same page of the parish register, Ann Elizabeth had neatly signed her name.[5] The proof of the marriage was there in black and white for Sherrard to report to Harewood House, but the happy couple were nowhere to be found.

Some two weeks later, Sherrard was still looking. He believed them to be in Bristol or Birmingham, he wrote to Henry Lascelles:

> I have been incessant in my inquiries in as private a manner
> as possible, and which I am a little facilitated in, from the
> circumstances of two other clandestine marriages having
> taken place in this city about the same time ... your
> Lordship must however be sensible that things of this
> nature cannot long remain obscured.[6]

Ruin and disgrace

In the meantime he was doing his best to see if the marriage could be declared invalid. The licence bore no date, and Ann had not lived in the parish for the requisite twenty-eight days before it was granted. In 1753, legislation commonly known as Lord Hardwicke's Marriage Act was passed to deal with the significant problem of clandestine and irregular marriage in England. Any marriage not performed by a regular clergyman in a church or chapel and preceded by banns or a special licence was deemed illegal. Both parties needed to be older than twenty-one, or to obtain the consent of their parent or guardian. As both Ann Elizabeth and Edward were of age this provision wasn't of much help to the Lascelles. It was also technically required that a couple marry in their local parish church, again to prevent clandestine unions. A loophole, however, known as 'the Lord Holland clause', existed, which laid down that a false statement of place of residence on a licence did not nullify a marriage. Lying about a place of residence, or renting rooms for a month in a parish in order to marry without unwarranted attention, were both common practices.[7]

As well as investigating the legalities, Sherrard was assiduous in finding out as much as he could about the bride. The news was not good. Gossip credited Ann Elizabeth with being not only mistress to Edward, but to his younger brother (predictably, another Henry) as well:

> the woman is supposed upon a former occasion, to
> have permitted the familiarities usual to Women of her
> description, to have taken place between herself and another
> son of your Lordship in the Army, though the fact is not
> vouched therefore very delicate mentions should be made
> of it.[8]

To the Lascelles, the news of the marriage came as a bitter blow. It took Henry several attempts to draft a response to his son's actions. One version is especially chilling. With no salutation, dated Harewood House 26 November 1818, it opens as follows:

> As you have thought proper to disgrace yourself and distress
> your Family by marrying a common prostitute I think it
> right to make the following communication to you.
> You and your Heirs will be totally cut off from the
> succession to any part of this property. The only means you
> will have of subsistence now, or hereafter, therefore depends
> upon me.[9]

As Edward's father laid out in devastating clarity, he was henceforth to be allowed a mere £300 a year: 'I do not feel myself bound to do more than afford you the necessary means of support whilst you are living in habits of vice and under circumstances of ruin and disgrace to your character'. As well as being cut out of the succession, Edward's debts would not be covered, and his creditors would be warned of this fact. 'Convinced', declared Henry:

> that every effort has been, and will continue to be made by
> the abandoned person to whom you have united yourself
> and her friends, to destroy in you every vestige of the moral
> and religious principles in which you have been brought up,
> I have reason to apprehend that if money can be obtained
> the means however discreditable or dishonest would not
> be an impediment, I therefore apprize you that I may deem
> it expedient to advertize a caution in the public papers,
> against making you any loans, as you are cut off from the
> power of ever repaying them.

Ruin and disgrace

Evidently keen to remove his son from Ann Elizabeth's influence as quickly as possible, Henry indicated that he was willing to see Edward at Harewood 'provided you seek that Interview quickly, but beware of protracting it, lest the door be shut against you for ever'. The letter was signed merely 'Lascelles'.

Once the couple were discovered ('I find the connexions he had got amongst are exceedingly bad', wrote Sherrard[10]), Edward was hastily dispatched via the Birmingham Mail to Yorkshire. On 11 December, a day after he arrived at Harewood, Edward wrote to his wife, informing her that there would be a separation and that he would never see her again. A family connection, John Russell, was appointed to act as intermediary. The bridegroom, it seems, was easily persuaded of the necessity to give up his bride. Of all the gifts the heir of Harewood had received in life, the one most lacking was strength of character. While they saw the truth too late to prevent his disastrous marriage, those closest to him came to realise that he would be led by whatever stronger personality was to hand. Edward's younger brother, William, put it best: 'Weakness and excessive weakness is the only fault he has, but it is so deeply engrafted in the very existence of his mind, that I fear no time or exertions of his own can work any change'.[11]

In all his actions and correspondence, Edward comes across as an amiable, if not especially intelligent man; one disastrously prone to errors of judgement, but generally contented to live his life in happy obscurity. The accident of being first-born son to one of the most prominent fortunes in the country made this impossible. Had the sexual politics of the day been reversed, things might have been quite otherwise. The eldest daughter of the family, Edward's sister Harriet, was of a very different calibre. Born in 1802, she inherited the undoubted intelligence

Harewood at bay

possessed by both her parents. Henry's wife, Henrietta Saunders Sebright, came from a family much given to entertaining the leading intellectuals of the day. Harriet was known to her circle not only as a talented artist (as was her mother) but also, less conventionally, as a scientist. Her experiments were guided by two of the leading lights of British chemistry, Humphry Davy and William Hyde Wollaston. The latter addressed her as 'the renowned chemist of Harewood' and made her a gift of a hydrometer to measure specific gravity. In 1825 Harriet had married the Earl of Sheffield and though she continued to sketch, there is no evidence that she continued with her scientific labours.[12] The tyranny of primogeniture worked as much to thrust responsibility onto the shoulders of the unwilling as it did to deny it to the more capable.

Three days after Edward wrote to his wife informing her of their separation, the articles were drawn up. They laid down that 'neither party [was] to have any intercourse of any kind or nature whatever, either by letter or otherwise, without the consent of Lord Lascelles'. Ann Elizabeth was to hand over all letters between herself and Edward. She was to have an allowance of £300 per annum, paid quarterly. What Ann Elizabeth's feelings were we cannot know. Her only documented response is a formulaic letter to the Lascelles solicitor dated 4 January 1819: 'it shall be my study never intentionally to give his Lordship or any part of the family any unnecessary trouble'.[13]

Shortly after the arrangements were made, Henry received another anonymous letter, this time from Hereford, cautioning against making any provision for his son's wife:

> if you do – you will put it in her power to do an injury
> to your Lordships family you at present little think of as I

Ruin and disgrace

know her whole thought is at present of putting a spurious
child to be hereafter Earl of Harewood for Heaven sake
then my Lord if the Honour of your family was ever dear
to you do not let such as woman remain in it one moment
for there is not a gentleman in Hereford that as not had
concerns of an improper nature with her she is a most
unprincipled wretch but how can she be expected when
her father is a common barge man and her mother keeps
a house of ill fame and for the last ten years she as been
a common prostitute sometimes in Hereford at others
in London nay even since she as been a member of your
Lordship family she as had no less than four gentlemen with
her when she only remaind two nights in Hereford to see
her friend.

If, continued the mysteriously well-informed writer, the Lascelles family were to pay her, the money would be used to
employ attorneys to 'act against you'; whereas if she discovered
that it was impossible to obtain 'an yearly allowance she will
then of course go to her old occupation of street walking which
will of course enable your Lordship to have a divorcement'.[14]

The prospect of an heir to the house of Harewood springing from such unsavoury origins had clearly already occurred
to the Lascelles, who acted accordingly. The first step was to
discover whether Edward was already a father-to-be. Ann Elizabeth Rosser had testified on 29 December that she was 'to the
best of my knowledge and belief … not at present pregnant'.
A doctor who had treated her in June 1818 wrote to give his
medical opinion that she was unlikely to be able to conceive,
given her former lifestyle. The second step was to ensure that
no child of hers could reasonably be declared legitimate. Plans

Harewood at bay

were already well in train to spirit Edward out of the country. At the end of January, Edward wrote to his father from Harewood House giving him authority 'during my residence abroad' to proceed against Ann Elizabeth and 'to act on my behalf, to obtain a separation, or divorce, provided the conduct of my wife should authorise such proceedings'. He signed these directions 'your affectionate Son, Edward Lascelles'.[15]

It was 1819. Four years earlier, some two decades of global warfare between Britain and France had finally come to an end with Napoleon's defeat on the field of Waterloo. The victory, of course, had profound global consequences. But at a more mundane level, it re-opened the continent to disgraced members of elite British families. Their black sheep could once more be packed off in the traditional manner.

Not by any to be taken in hand unadvisedly, lightly or wantonly

Modern sensibilities might be tempted to condemn Henry Lascelles for ruthlessly parting young lovers. But to their peers (in both senses of that word) the family's actions were more likely regarded as a necessary response to a disastrous event. Much ink has been spent by historians debating the rise of the 'companionate' marriage and ideals of sensibility in the eighteenth century, the tension between romantic and arranged matches, and the implications of all of these for equality between men and women.[16] In terms of marriage choice, the most convincing eschew any artificial opposition between, as Amanda Vickery puts it, 'cold-blooded arrangement' and 'idyllic freedom'. Novels of sensibility might promote the fantasy of giving up the world for love, but those who acted upon this advice were

Ruin and disgrace

the 'deluded exception'. Indeed, if the advice of literature was sought there was the trenchant mantra offered in Colman and Garrick's 1766 play *The Clandestine Marriage*: 'Love in a cottage? ... Give me indifference and a coach and six.'[17]

Any marriage amongst the propertied class had direct consequences for far more people than the actual couple involved. Social and political authority amongst the aristocracy was quite literally grounded in land. The integrity of the estate was protected through the system of primogeniture. It was in the interests of an aristocratic family's power to transmit the title, the land, and the wealth required to maintain both of these, intact to the eldest son. In their anxiety about maintaining a direct lineage, then, they differed fundamentally from the mercantile middling sorts, where liquid capital could more easily be split between children. Claims of lineage, however, needed to be reconciled with the need to provide for other members of the family. A system of property inheritance known as the 'strict settlement' was designed to balance the financial needs of the individual (particularly younger children and widows) with the demands of keeping the lion's share of the family property in trust for the enduring interests of the family. Such settlements were generally made upon either the marriage or the majority of the eldest son.

Negotiated marriage settlements amongst the landed elite were protracted affairs, and the resultant documents 'read like treaties between sovereign states'.[18] Endogamy was the norm for the peerage, and wealth was no automatic passport. Partners from lower down the scale were generally permissible if they haled from the professions – the clergy, law or medicine – but not from 'trade'. As we know, even the political alliance between the Lascelles and the Leeds merchant community did

Harewood at bay

not stop the portly Mary Lascelles from having to engineer an elopement with the mayor's son Richard York in 1801.

Marriages where a partner was unable to make an equal financial contribution and lacked social respectability were even less common. Virtually all such marriages were made by elite men who, unlike Edward Lascelles, were not dependant upon their fathers for financial support. Disinheritances like Edward's were not frequent, but they could and did occur when a father disapproved of his heir's marriage choice. Historian Randolph Trumbach gives us the example of the 1720 disinheritance of Richard, Lord Willoughby, when he married a seamstress. While his father could not prevent him inheriting the title, the money and land were settled on a younger brother. Given an annuity of £300 a year (the same sum as Edward) Willoughby soon found himself in such dire financial straits that his clothes and peerage robes were seized by creditors.[19] While scandalous marriages amongst the elite did exist, the recklessness of Edward's actions is hard to exaggerate.

None of this meant that questions of emotion were cast to the winds, or that parents commonly acted as tyrants in their children's matrimonial choices. By the early nineteenth century, increasingly rigid boundaries were being drawn around elite sociability. Clubs such as Almacks (familiar to modern readers of Regency romances) were presided over by powerful patronesses who, at least in theory, applied strict criteria for entry and behaviour. Such establishments began to replace less exclusive sites of recreation such as the pleasure gardens at Vauxhall, where the elite might mix with the *demi-monde*. Masquerade balls, which hid personal and status identity, were falling out of favour by the time of Edward's marriage.[20]

Education in proper moral values, combined with an exclu-

Ruin and disgrace

sive marriage mart, meant that unsuitable choices amongst the elite were usually avoided. Prudential marriages arranged between two people of equitable property meant that the bride and groom came from similar social backgrounds, had friends and interests in common, and had enough money to prevent financial stress on their relationship. Put this way, the system seems not without sense. At the very least, it is more attractive to modern values than the cold stereotype suggested by 'arranged marriage'. A delicate balance needed to be struck between strategic, financial and emotional considerations. Elizabeth Bennett probably spoke for many when she articulated this conundrum in *Pride and Prejudice*, a novel published just five years before Edward's marriage: 'what is the difference in matrimonial affairs, between the mercenary and the prudent motive? Where does discretion end, and avarice begin?'

For mutual society, help and comfort

The tragedy for Edward was the loss of his family. And for that family, the tragedy lay in one heedless choice that placed the dynastic work of more than a hundred years at naught. It was not that they expected their heir to marry against all inclination. Sensibility could be combined with sense. They had only to look across the 1807 political divide for a poignant example of what might have been. If neither the Lascelles nor the Fitzwilliams escaped scandalous runaway matches, be they with footmen, publicans' daughters or Leeds manufacturers, their sanctioned matches were equally strategic. Yet in the extensive family correspondence that survives from Henry's 1807 electoral rival, we can witness Milton at the heart of an extremely close and affectionate family.[21] Personal desires and affec-

Harewood at bay

tive bonds were woven with apparent seamlessness into the responsibilities of lineage.[22] Two days after Milton's birth, the new baby's aunt wrote that Lady Fitzwilliam's breastfeeding was going well. By refusing to use a wet-nurse, the Fitzwilliams declared themselves part of a growing number of aristocrats in this period who chose to emphasise domestic values. 'I never saw so happy a creature as Ld. Fitz', continued Lady Duncannon (he *had* waited more than sixteen years, after all). 'He really is almost out of his senses with joy, & can see, think & talk of nothing but his child.'[23]

When Milton became engaged to Mary in December 1805, he was not yet twenty. She was a year younger, his cousin and a childhood friend, the fourth daughter of Thomas, 1st Baron Dundas. Georgiana, 5th Duchess of Devonshire and sister to Milton's aunt, wrote to her mother that the undoubtedly eligible heir was 'both clever and amiable but so odd in person and so unlike other people it was a great chance against him ever finding any woman who liked him for himself'. However, he was so steady, she continued, that 'there is no fear of his finding out in a few years that he likes many better than her'. It was, clucked the gossip, 'a very young marriage'.[24] When Mary Dundas married Milton in that temple of fashionable alliance, St George's in Hanover Square, it was five years since Richard York and Mary Lascelles had snuck into the same building to celebrate their more clandestine nuptials.

Milton and Mary's marriage was a political union, linking two families in the same Whig faction, as much as it was a dynastic and personal one. But while the connection may have been politically fortuitous, the surviving letters of Milton's young family also paint a vivid picture of domestic felicity. Mary's anxiety and joy for her husband in the midst of his gru-

Ruin and disgrace

elling 1807 campaign are characteristic. The Fitzwilliams had an endearing habit of mixing high politics and domestic minutiae in their correspondence. At the height of national alarm about revolution, Fitzwilliam (as Lord Lieutenant of the West Riding) wrote to Milton with news of a 'premature rising', But this news rubbed shoulders with Charlotte & George (Milton's children) getting through their vaccinations, Mary Milton choosing wallpaper, and Lady Fitzwilliam searching for a 'garden engine' for the grounds.[25]

We get an engaging snapshot of their family life from letters written during Milton's prolonged absence in Ireland eleven years into their marriage. Mary missed her husband acutely ('all day, I fancied I heard yr foot, such is the force of imagination'), worried constantly about his health (she recommended steak and port wine for strengthening) and wrote to him almost daily from Wentworth of the small trials and triumphs of their children's lives. Mary was known as a woman of great humour and charm, and this comes shining through her domestic vignettes:

> How my letter will proceed is very doubtful, for Tom tit [William Thomas Spencer, not quite two] is amusing himself pulling all the parcels about that lay in the window, he is now spitting on the floor & rubbing it with his hand, in short to recount all his mischief would require the quickest short hand writer, for he has played at least a dozen of his monkey tricks since I began to write.

The visit of that formidable electioneering campaigner, Mrs Osbaldeston, caused a collective family groan: 'Mrs Osbaldeston only made a morng visit of at least an *hour & three quarters*, unluckily Lord Fitzwilliam was out; all the Children passed in

Harewood at bay

review, & she expressed her approbation of all, but particularly the boys, Tom shewed of[f] amazingly'.

'Pray write to the Children by turns', she wrote to Milton, 'for they [are] very anxious every morning to know if there is a letter for them'. The Miltons' brood were eager correspondents in their own rights, and their carefully kept letters have a powerful immediacy. Charlotte, aged ten, wrote labouriously in her own childish hand (her mother sent excuses that it was written 'in a great hurry').[26] The younger children used their mother as secretary, and were immensely proud of their efforts at composition. Mary, the second daughter, was seven:

> My dear dear Papa
> I hope you are very well, and that you will be here soon,
> I want to tell you that Jet is grown quite fat, when will you
> come back to me; I want you very much.
> I am a very bad driver because I let go the reins, because
> I was very frightened going down the slope.
> Your Affectionate
> Daughter
> Mary Wentworth-Fitzwilliam.[27]

William Charles ('That Rogue William'), the heir, was five, and much addicted to climbing the hornbeam until he was eight or nine feet up. 'Grannyma told him of a man who was killed by a *bough breaking*, upon which he replyed "ah! but he was much heavier than I am"'.[28] His mother confessed herself 'vastly amused' by taking down his jumbled observations verbatim. He 'desired me to stop once for he had not more *stuff* in his head & after considering a minute or two he proceeded, *I* think it is a capital letter, it is every *word* his own':

Ruin and disgrace

My dear Papa

I am very happy, and very well, and we have seen a great
many Waggon loads of Grandpapa's hay; & I have got new
wheels to my waggon, with spokes in, & twelve nails in
them, & that my large waggon load, has got almost set
on fire, that us three big ones could not drag, for it was
so heavy; & I have been reading my lesson, & learning
geography.

And they have mown the grass twice.

They have been thinning those little bits of clumps where
Granpapa's waggon loads of hay & stuff goes through.

Yr Affectionate Boy

William Charles Wentworth-Fitzwilliam.[29]

For the procreation of children

Domestic joy, then, could marry well with dynastic responsibility. But the burden on a woman's body was high. By 1830 Mary
had been married for twenty-four years. She had borne thirteen children and buried two. She was six months into her four-
teenth pregnancy when the Fitzwilliams attended divine service
on 31 October at Wentworth Church.[30] The chaplain took as
his text James 4:14 – 'Whereas ye know not what shall be on
the morrow; for what is your life? it is even a vapour which
appeareth for a little time and then vanisheth away'. Mary, it
was observed, was visibly moved, in tears as she helped her aged
father-in-law from the church. A day later she was dying.

Milton had been due to leave for London that Monday
morning, but, with the carriage waiting for him by the door,
he changed his mind at the last minute. His wife was feeling
increasingly unwell. Mr Branson, the family surgeon, was called,

Harewood at bay

but Mary went into premature labour. All through the rest of that day, Branson struggled against the inevitable. Towards evening things looked more hopeful, but by nine o'clock it was clear the battle would be lost. With Milton by her side, in desperate haste the children were 'torn from their beds and assembled in their night dresses to witness the agonies of death in a parent whose life had been devoted to the duties of a Christian wife and mother'. It was, tragically, a common enough end for women of the time, no matter what their status, but it was no less of a blow for that. Milton was devastated:

> Lord Milton's state of mind may be more conceived than expressed. It is well known that the noble lord and his lady lived in a state of the warmest affection. Having a large family, they were united in giving them a solid education, carefully watching over them both in their studies and recreations. Except when the Duties of public life occupied his lordship, he courted privacy, for the purposes of domestic duties and enjoyments; and so sudden has been the change, that his lordship is quite frantic, and almost sceptical as to the reality of the awful event.[31]

Wilberforce was deeply shocked when he heard the news some days later. He immediately began a letter to his one-time rival Milton, offering what comfort he could muster:

> I really never felt so deeply any Event that did not relate to my own family. I knew, as we all know, the uncertainty of life; but We none of us live sufficiently in the habitual consciousness of the uncertain tenure by which we hold our dearest Earthly Enjoyments, & such Events as these astonish as well as afflict us. Such is really the Effect produced on

Ruin and disgrace

myself by the sudden Blow of which the sad tidings have just now reach me.

In the event, Wilberforce delayed sending this, fearing to 'intrude on you while in the first paroxysm of your sorrow'. Nevertheless, he felt compelled to write, in memory of:

> the Kindness with which you treated me at Wentworth, I should *very* unwillingly forego the earnest Impulse I feel, to express to you the Sincerity of my Sympathy – Tho' of different Ranks, We have a common nature & it is soothing to the mind in seasons of deep affliction to know that those whom we esteem & love feel for us & with us in such trying hours.[32]

Milton was so distraught that he announced his retirement from public life, though he was later persuaded to return to politics. It was said that the responsibilities of his 'numerous family' lay heavily upon him. As Mary lay dying, she commended their children to 'his personal care; and the Noble Lord is too good a father to neglect so solemn an injunction'.[33] Though he survived Mary by almost thirty years, Milton never remarried.

The gossips begin to cluck

Back in 1818, gossip about Edward's misalliance, couched in the innuendo of the day, was soon current amongst the *bon ton*. Charles Percy wrote to Ralph Sneyd that Edward 'has espoused a sister of Lady Berwicks, a younger one, with whom his brother intrigued, which was the origin of the acquaintance. I am sorry for poor Lord Harewood.'[34] From another of Yorkshire's great houses, Castle Howard, Lady Cawdor wrote to Mary Stewart Mackenzie:

Harewood at bay

the Harewood family in this Country are all in great despair at the Marriage of Mr Lascelles, (Ld Lascelles' eldest son) with a girl of very infamous character, old Lord Harewood it is said is very miserable, & moving to separate them, but Mr L. is of age, the marriage is a good one, & I don't see what can be done. He says he married her to *reform* her, Lord Berwick married her sister.[35]

Lord Kinnaird, politician and art collector, wrote to the MP Thomas Creevey, that 'Lord Lascelles' son has married Harriet Wilson's sister'. After listing a number of other similarly unsuitable matches, Lord Kinnaird noted, perhaps in a train of thought prompted by such signs of general dissipation, 'Lord Byron's poem [*Don Juan*], which I brought to England, is returned to Venice. Murray the Bookseller is afraid of printing it.'[36]

Ann Elizabeth Rosser was born in Hereford in 1793 (making her three years older than Edward), the daughter of William and Elizabeth Rosser. Her father was a barge owner, who also, according to investigations ordered by the Lascelles, kept a public house.[37] Ann Elizabeth's parents were later described to Henry Lascelles as being 'of the lowest order', but this view needs some qualification. Firstly, many of the slights on their character and behaviour come from anonymous informants. Secondly, if neither the Rossers nor their relatives were of unimpeachable virtue, this did not put them on the lowest rung of provincial society (though the telescopic view from Harewood House might have suggested otherwise). Not only was Ann Elizabeth literate, but in 1824 her younger sister Eliza married William Cooke, a local timber merchant who probably met the Rossers through the barge business, in which he also had an interest. William Cooke was a man of 'superior education' and 'some respectability' in Hereford's commercial com-

Ruin and disgrace

munity. Or so, at least, was the view reported in the local press in 1838. Unfortunately for Cooke, it was articulated by a judge, then passing sentence of transportation for life on charges of forging bills worth £1500.[38]

In the gossipy letters quoted, Ann Elizabeth's sisterhood to the courtesans Harriet Wilson and Lady Berwick was intended as figurative rather than literal. Harriet Wilson was the most famous courtesan of the age. Her notoriety was redoubled when she began blackmailing her admirers by offering them the opportunity to pay her rather than appear in the forthcoming instalment of her memoirs. The Duke of Wellington was famously reported to have responded 'Publish and be damned'. She took her revenge by portraying him in print in a less than flattering light as 'the rat-catcher'. Harriet Wilson's younger sister, Sophia, also a courtesan, married one of her protectors, Lord Berwick, in 1812.

If Edward married Ann Elizabeth to 'reform her', in Lady Cawdor's ironic phrase, he broke faith with his caste in doing so. The more practical younger brother, Henry, while he might have amused himself with the dalliance, acted with less recklessness by marrying Lady Louisa Thynne, daughter of the 2nd Marquis of Bath, in 1823. Unlike Edward's alliance, Henry's 'Marriage in High Life' was duly reported in the social columns with an account of the 'grand déjeuner' given for the couple at the Lascelles house in Hanover Square. Shortly after, the press reported, 'the happy pair left town in an elegant new chariot with four horses and out-riders for Oakley Park, the seat of the Marquis of Tavistock, in Bedfordshire, where they will pass the honey moon'.[39] Whether Louisa ever heard of the scandal of her husband's earlier involvement with the woman married to Edward is unknown. We can only speculate that this formida-

Harewood at bay

ble woman – for it was she who remodelled Harewood House along Victorian lines to accommodate her own brood of thirteen children – would have brushed the rumours aside with the same ruthlessness with which she treated the designs of Carr, Brown, Chippendale and Adam.

Despite all the inequalities of the Lascelles's world, they could not act against Ann Elizabeth with impunity. As a wife she had certain rights, and as her husband Edward had certain obligations. Divorce in this period was available to elite men by means of a (vastly expensive) private Act of Parliament. But even then, it was not there simply for the asking. Without plausible evidence of a wife's adultery, testified by two or more witnesses, Edward had no grounds for divorce. Judicial separation (which did not allow either party to remarry) was possible in the ecclesiastical courts, but it also could only be made on the grounds of adultery, life-threatening cruelty, or a combination of both. For Edward to free himself from Ann Elizabeth, to remarry and to produce legitimate children for the lineage to be continued, his only escape route was proof of a prior husband still living, her adultery, or her death. A close watch was correspondingly kept on Ann Elizabeth, in order to see whether there were any grounds for either annulment or divorce. The vicar of Harewood church, Richard Hale, had a somewhat vexed relationship with his cousin, Henry Lascelles, whom he considered arrogant and overbearing in comparison with Henry's popular father. Nevertheless, Hale was doing what he could. His connections were investigating rumours that Ann Elizabeth might already have a husband still living, but these came to nothing. Sherrard was continuing his enquiries ('I have heard many reports of the Woman's Conduct which is bad in the extreme – previously to her leaving her lodgings to go to

Ruin and disgrace

Hereford, she was I understand in a state of almost perpetual drunkenness.') Ann Elizabeth sent monthly letters to the Lascelles family agents from Hereford, where she had grown up and where she now returned, to inform them of where she was living, so that her quarterly allowance might be paid.[40]

Henry Lascelles now employed a Mr Flexney in a capacity we would describe as private investigator. Surviving letters from Flexney to Henry making reports on Ann Elizabeth span the period 1819 to 1822. Flexney (who took the highly suitable pseudonym Hunt) despatched an informant called Townend to Hereford to make discreet enquiries. Townend made regular reports to Flexney on Ann Elizabeth's behaviour and conduct. Although she drank liquor, she was otherwise depressingly (at least for the Lascelles's purposes) well behaved, dressing more modestly than before, going to church and visiting her sister. She was living in Norfolk Terrace, Hereford: 'at the entrance to the town from Glocs', reported Flexney to Henry, 'it consists of a row of small houses, pleasantly situated, & suitable for persons of small income'. Her parents, he continued:

> kept a public house, & when she was very young she was found in bed with a young man … They keep a good look out for her, as the Father is afraid of the money (of which it seems he gets a great part) if she goes wrong, & they think there is a watch upon her in the town … He [Townend] says he believes she conducts herself properly. Nobody notices her as her character is well known, besides which her parents are of the lowest order.[41]

When Edward was separated from Ann Elizabeth and sent to Europe, he was not the first Lascelles to suffer this fate. While Edwin Lascelles, builder of Harewood House, married suitably (first the daughter, and then the widow, of baronets), Daniel, the second son of Old Lascelles, did not. In September 1740 he secretly married Elizabeth Southwick in London. His furious father immediately cut Daniel out of the family business. A year later the couple separated and Daniel sought a reconciliation with his father. He was summarily sent off on a tour of Italy and France, afterwards leaving for the East Indies and only returning to Britain in 1750. Elizabeth Southwick, divorced and abandoned by her husband, sank into poverty and was repeatedly consigned to debtors' prison.[42] Like Ann Elizabeth Rosser, she was collateral damage in the dynastic ambitions of her husband's family.

Removed from the eyes of Britain's polite world, Edward was also now touring Europe, in the company of the same John Russell who had acted as intermediary in the negotiations with Ann Elizabeth over the settlement. Edward was clearly remorseful. He wrote to his father from Paris in April 1819 that 'I have thought a great deal upon the melancholy event, under which I am come abroad, and every day impress still more strongly upon my mind the madness of such an act'. But Henry was concerned that Edward was gambling and behaving badly, and wrote warning him to stay within budget. Edward's younger brother, William, reported to his father a month later, from Dresden, that 'I have of course talked to [Edward] a good deal upon his affair, he appears to view the whole of that subject in a proper light, and I am quite sure you need be under no apprehension of his giving you any further trouble on that point'.[43]

Russell certainly had his work cut out for him with Edward's 'complete weakness for women'.[44] 'The prejudices of English travellers in favour of their own country are now proverbial', wrote Russell in the book which he later published about his travels. Evidently he had good reason to prefer being at home. *A Tour in Germany, and some of the Southern Provinces of the Austrian Empire, in the years 1820, 1821, 1822* contains not a word as to who was funding his time in Europe, or of his purpose there. It was published anonymously in 1824: 'These volumes are ushered into the world with a modesty not common in our days', wrote the *Quarterly Review*. 'Will our readers believe that they are … actually without name, dedication, preface, introduction, vignette, or margin'.[45] The copy at Harewood House is inscribed to Henry Lascelles 'with the Author's most respectful compliments'.[46] A second edition of 1828 contained the author's name. Possibly Russell felt the dust had settled sufficiently now that ten years had passed since Edward's marriage.

The *Tour* was generally well reviewed as 'a sensible clever work' by a 'reasonable Traveller' unaddicted to flights of poetic fancy.[47] Indeed, a rather jaundiced air pervades the entire account ('The German kitchen is essentially a plain, solid, greasy kitchen'). Russell spent some time attacking the loose morals of their hosts, from the 'Protestant countries of Germany' ('Morality cannot but suffer from the impolitic and indecent facility with which the marriage tie is dissolved') to the dancing halls of Vienna ('There cannot be a more dissolute city, one where female virtue is less prized, and therefore, less frequent').[48] Perhaps unsurprisingly, Russell wrote to Henry Lascelles that Edward preferred Vienna to any other

Harewood at bay

European capital.[49] No doubt in compliment to his politically active patron, Russell ascribed the contrast between the 'high-minded and well-informed peerage of Britain' and the 'servile and corrupted aristocracy of Vienna' to the former's involvement in British public life.[50]

Russell's familiarity with the seedier side of European life, which finds such a prominent place in his narrative, was coloured by his somewhat ineffectual brief to keep his aristocratic charge out of trouble. His account to Henry Lascelles written from Berlin in June 1821 describes events that Russell later considered to mark a change for the better:

> During the six weeks we have been here Lord Lascelles
> conduct has been extremely inequal. Sometimes he has
> behaved with perfect propriety, and sometimes returned in
> a great degree to his former extravagances … on the 11th
> and 12th of May he staid out all night.[51]

When Edward failed to return, Russell went searching for him, and found he had moved in with a local woman. 'Lord Lascelles himself was perfectly docile; the woman was loud, furious and vulgar to a degree that was utterly revolting. I succeeded in bringing Lord Lascelles home.'[52] Edward routinely got into amatory (mis)adventures at every stop, whereupon he was hastily extracted by Russell, and the two men moved on.

Knowing how open he was to influence by others, it was the object of Edward's friends to give him some kind of steady example combined with a motivation to behave well. In August 1821, Russell wrote to Henry Lascelles of a suggestion that Edward might join the staff of the British embassy in Vienna:

> It is not necessary I should say any thing of the advantages
> which would result to Lord Lascelles from the proposed

Ruin and disgrace

arrangement. As to any *occupation* it might give him, that is a matter of very little moment. All connected with diplomacy have in general very little to do. The important object is that he should fill a station which will impress upon him daily the necessity of supporting the character of a gentleman, and which while it never allows him to lose sight of all that he must forfeit by relapsing into his former errors, furnishes to him at the same time both means and motives for avoiding them.

The suggestion was taken up, the long-suffering Vienna embassy staff doing their best:

> to find or make work for him, and every forenoon he has three or four hours employment. He then goes a walking, frequently rides to the Prater alone or with Mr Gordon; dines at the Embassy, and is always at home early in the evening.[53]

This was the career-diplomat Robert Gordon, fifth son of George Gordon, Lord Haddo, and secretary of embassy (the rank next to ambassador) in Vienna for the past seven years. Gordon was only five years older than Edward, had also attended Christ Church (though not at the same time), and the two men appear to have struck up a friendship. For all Gordon's apparent willingness to keep an eye on Edward, he was known to express frustration with those who saw diplomacy as an agreeable hobby for an amateur elite. Twenty years later, when Gordon was ambassador in Vienna, he would complain bitterly to his brother (then foreign secretary) of the quality of his staff. Gordon wanted men who could 'collect the opinions and command the good will of the people'. None of those sent out to him 'could boast a quality of this nature. To drink a glass

Harewood at bay

of wine, to smoke a cigar and to damn the natives – such are the characteristics of most British attachés'.[54]

For all Gordon's steadying influence, Edward was inventive, and determined, enough to find time in his respectable schedule to pursue his personal interests. By this time he had a regular mistress, a twice-widowed Bavarian baroness named Phillipine Testa. 'The singular thing is', continued Russell:

> that his visits to the woman whom I have mentioned to
> your Lordship are paid early in the morning. In the depth
> of winter, and in the roughest weather, he gets up and
> breakfasts between six and seven o'clock; immediately
> goes out, and by ten o'clock is at his desk in the Embassy.
> The interval is spent, I know, with Madame Testa, and in
> general I believe the only portion of his time he spends
> with her. This singularity originates in his wish to avoid
> exciting notice, to be able to spend the day and the evening
> in a more becoming way, without entirely sacrificing his
> amour. Altogether he shews a desire to avoid every thing
> which might make him an object of notoriety. He does not
> feel the immorality of the connection; neither does he feel
> the ridicule ... but he feels the necessity, and probably the
> propriety of conducting an indecent connection in a decent
> manner.[55]

At least this caution was an improvement on Edward's previous 'total abandonment'. In a lengthy discussion of Edward's state of mind and behaviour shortly before Russell left Europe, he wrote to Henry that his son had improved in behaviour, and had recently showed a 'strength of resolution' towards female temptation that 'I certainly did not expect from him'. Nevertheless, he cautioned:

Ruin and disgrace

I would only deceive your Lordship did I allow you to believe that this reformation is a complete one or that if left to himself it would certainly be a lasting one. In a very short time I must leave Lord Lascelles; and from all I know of his conduct, and have observed of his character I could not have advised you to leave him upon the continent free from every sort of inspection. His deviations have been wide, and he has still many steps to retrace before regaining the former confidence.

In Russell's opinion, the greatest hope for reformation, or 'continuance in well-doing', as he put it, lay in Robert Gordon, who 'has over him a greater moral influence than I can pretend to possess'. In keeping Edward occupied in a 'demi-official character' with 'regular employment', and in surrounding him with a proper social circle, much might be achieved. Edward's liking for Vienna ('dissolute as it is') was a force for good, as it inspired him to behave sufficiently well there that he might avoid having to decamp. It was, concluded Russell, to Edward's credit 'that he has voluntarily placed himself under the influence of these circumstances and restraints. It is his own choice. He has always said to me that he wished to be in a situation which would keep him back from doing "foolish things".'[56]

Defending the lineage

Russell returned to England in 1822, and his 'sensible' travelogue appeared two years later. Edward continued on the continent and all the evidence suggests that his family considered it impossible for him to return to England while he had a wife still living. The reasons for this, and for Henry's constant con-

Harewood at bay

cern for how Edward was behaving in Europe were no doubt partly moral. Letters bear witness to family anxiety about both personal conduct and social reputation.

But there were also practical legal implications to Edward's hasty removal from Britain. The arrangements that were made between Edward and Ann Elizabeth constituted a deed of private separation. Such deeds were popular with the middling and elite ranks of society in the eighteenth and nineteenth centuries, but they were a real headache for lawyers because of the confusion that reigned over their implications and provisions. Historian Lawrence Stone calls them 'a form of quasi-legal collusive self-divorce', a 'popular institution which flourished in the margins of the law, but was totally reliant upon the legal skills of conveyancers in drafting the deeds in such a way as to survive the hostility to them of many distinguished judges'.

Around the very time of Edward's marriage, a conservative attack was being mounted against the legal validity of just such deeds. They were vulnerable to challenge, and thus relied on both parties coming to a mutual agreement not to take legal action against their provisions. As the anonymous warnings about litigation offered to the Lascelles family suggest, they were not in this fortunate position. Many of the common provisions of judicial separations, for example promising not to molest a spouse over the freedom to live with whomsoever he or she wished (a tacit agreement to allow adultery), were technically illegal. Such clauses could even be put into articles of separation to lull a wife into a false sense of security, trap her in adultery, and thus allow a husband to obtain a divorce. This had happened just two years prior to Edward's marriage, when the family of the Honorable John Augustus Sullivan extricated him from a reckless marriage by precisely these means.[57] As we have seen, Ann Elizabeth (or her family) were careful to avoid any grounds for claims of adultery. An allowance of £300 a year might have seemed a small sum to Edward Lascelles, but the price of her abstinence clearly represented a goodly amount to the Rossers.

For the Lascelles, the real danger in a private separation lay in the attitude of the law to the legitimacy of any children conceived and born after the physical separation of the spouses. The assumption of the law was that a child conceived after separation was legitimate unless proven otherwise. The onus was on the husband to prove that he could not have had access to the wife. Given the repeatedly expressed concerns about lineage and inheritance in the letters about Edward's marriage, it seems certain that this was one factor in removing him from the country. Ann Elizabeth could not put a 'spurious child to be hereafter Earl of Harewood', as the anonymous warnings had put it, if Edward were kept abroad.

So Edward remained in Vienna until 1829, when he moved with his mistress, the Baroness Phillipine Testa, to Munich, apparently because she had inherited property from an aunt in Bavaria. Gossip in Vienna put another interpretation on things. Lord Harewood received yet another anonymous letter, this time from Vienna, claiming to be from a friend of Edward's, reporting that Edward had left that city 'on account of so many reports spread by [the] English relative to his unfortunate marriage'. The tale had grown in the telling since 1818, for the whispers were now of a conspiracy hatched between a Lascelles servant, Ann Elizabeth and Edward's brother in order that the second son 'might take his place in succeeding to the fortune'.[58]

The close watch kept by Lascelles agents on Ann Elizabeth was in vain. No grounds were ever found for divorce. But on 21 August 1831, Lord Harewood received news from Hereford that

Harewood at bay

his eldest son's wife was gravely ill. Two days later came further news that Ann Elizabeth Lascelles had died. She was thirty-eight years old.

If the Lascelles had prevented Ann Elizabeth from having any children by Edward, her family was clearly happy to enshrine their connection with the house of Harewood in the names of the next generation. Amongst the children born to Eliza Cooke, Ann Elizabeth's sister and wife of William Cooke, were Ann Elizabeth Lascelles (born 1833) and William Montague Lascelles (born 1836) and the name 'Lascelles' would continue to crop up in the ranks of their descendants. Eliza and the children managed to join William after he was transported to Australia. By strange coincidence, Eliza died not far from the Hunter Valley, where a certain convict rebellion would inspire a man calling himself 'Lord Lascelles' to embark upon a tour of investigation into convict conditions. Even decades later, the Cooke family made sure their illustrious connections were not forgotten. With a careful selection (and omission) of facts, in 1873 the Hunter Valley's *Maitland Mercury* reported the death of 'Eliza Rosser, the beloved wife of Mr. William Cooke, formerly a merchant of the city of Hereford, and sister of the late Lady Ann Elizabeth, wife of the late Lord Viscount Lascelles, aged 73 years'.[59]

'I am not fitted to being at the head of a family in England'

'There is now no impediment to your return to this country', wrote Lord Harewood to his son a few days after Ann Elizabeth's death, and asked to know his intentions. 'My former communications expressed the regrets of all your Family at the necessary separation, that existed, and we all look forward

Ruin and disgrace

with pleasure to the prospect of seeing you again.'[60] This letter was signed 'Your affectionate Father', but Edward was destined to disappoint Henry yet again. He expressed his happiness 'at being free from that person to whom I was unfortunately so long joined', but also his immediate determination to marry the Baroness Testa. He was then suffering from 'Rhumatic Gout' and his physician did not advise travel, but he was willing to visit in the Spring:

> I feel that I never could reside in England after what has
> happened. I could come for a few weeks next Spring when
> you were in London, and I conceive that some months
> passing over after the death of that person may be of
> advantage to me before my arrival in England. My dear
> Father I am now free; you can render me very happy for
> the rest of my life, if you will grant the request I am now
> about to make, and that is your consent to my marrying a
> Bavarian Lady of good rank and family, here.[61]

The baroness was no Ann Elizabeth, but she was hardly a happy alliance for the house of Harewood. She had been widowed twice (her second husband died in 1814), she was Catholic, she was older than Edward – and she was German. Above all, perhaps, she was well known to have lived publicly with Edward for many years as his mistress. 'She is a few years older than myself', wrote Edward, anticipating disapproval:

> but will never have any children. I feel the deepest and
> sincerest affection for her, and it is impossible for the best
> wife to have shewn a more sincere or more affectionate
> conduct than this lady has done towards me from the first
> moment of our acquaintance up to the present time; we
> have lived so happily together. You will perhaps say that you

Harewood at bay

hesitate, since you are not acquainted with the Baroness, but I will take upon myself to say that in no way would she do a prejudice to your family; on the contrary I feel assured you would much admire her excellent disposition. At my age [35] my dear Father, and after ten years of acquaintance with the character of an individual, and convinced by every action of her sincere and affectionate attachment for me I trust you will give me the credit for my judgement to be correct.

Edward's characteristic naïveté is rather touching, but he was also careful to say that:

Notwithstanding the sudden late event, I remain perfectly of the same feeling relative to the arrangements made at the time of my late unfortunate marriage; that is to say that Henry should be considered as your successor; I should never meddle with any affairs of the family or have other sentiments than those for the welfare of you and the rest, and should thankfully receive what you may think good to allow me in the shape of allowance. I entreat you for the fulfilment of my wishes for my marriage with the Baroness; I never could give my hand to any other person.

Edward suggested he could visit once a year, or every two years, but would make his home in Munich, where he had many friends and where the baroness 'goes into society' – though she was not received at court.[62] Edward pleaded repeatedly throughout the letter for his father's consent, possibly (disregarding the affection he clearly did hold for Henry) because he regarded it as necessary to a financial settlement:

Do not my dear Father conceive, that this case and the last

Ruin and disgrace

have the slightest comparison one with the other. If my
proposal should not be quite what you wish, still let me take
the responsibility upon myself and marry the Baroness ...
I am not fitted for being at the head of a family in England.
I prefer the Continent and a humble station in life with
sufficient to live upon and united to a person who loves
me to the bottom of her heart. I state this fact in order to
quiet any alarms either you or the family may have as to any
pretensions I might set up by the sudden change to meddle
with the affair.

By this marriage, claimed Edward:

I shall bury in a great degree the former disgraceful
transaction in oblivion, and can form my domestic state
upon solid and honorable grounds. The Baroness is very
economical, and conducts her financial affairs with the
greatest regularity. My heart is irrevocably given to her, you
will easily be able to understand what it is to concentrate
all one's affections in an individual; you have enjoyed for
so many years a state of perfect domestic happiness with
my Mother, and may you enjoy for many years to come this
state together. Believe me my dear Father, all my happiness,
my very existence, is concentrated in the Baroness; She is
of a family that would do me honour, and of a birth that I
could present her any where. Were it otherwise I should feel
ashamed of asking you.[63]

Lord Harewood's reply to his son's impassioned letter was succinct:

I am quite sensible of the strong manner in which you
have expressed yourself, upon this subject. I shall not enter

Harewood at bay

minutely into some parts of my objections, but will merely
state, as to them, that the arguments you urge in support of
the step in question, do not produce the same result upon
my mind that they appear to have produced upon yours. I
have however an insuperable objection to your marrying
a Foreigner. I cannot give my consent to such Marriage.
I certainly had conceived an expectation, that if released
from your first unfortunate engagement, you might have
felt disposed to return to England with a view to establish
yourself, & to marry a suitable person in your own country.
Such a course, accompanied by such an event, would have
received every assistance from me.

While he denied his consent to this or any other 'Foreign
Alliance', he expressed a conviction that Edward was already
'resolved' upon the marriage. In the circumstances:

it would be unprofitable & even useless to urge the matter
beyond the declaration of my objections to the Marriage in
question. If therefore it should take place, you are aware of
the amount of your allowance, which will be continued, but
I must positively to decline to make any other or additional
provision of any kind in consequence, or in contemplation
of it.

Your affectionate Father.[64]

Lord Harewood evidently knew his son only too well. If any
man could be persuaded to give up his own interests in favour
of his mistress's, that man was Edward Lascelles. Phillipine
might even have hoped for a reconciliation with her husband's
family. Less than a week after writing from Munich to request
permission to marry the baroness, Edward wrote again to say

Ruin and disgrace

that the marriage had taken place. The opportune presence of an English clergyman in Munich had facilitated his wish.

Edward may have chosen personal happiness over family obligation, but he was fully alive to the claims of lineage. In all his correspondence about the marriage, he repeatedly mentioned both his satisfaction with his younger brother's inheriting the estate, and the baroness's inability to have children to disrupt the succession. 'In adverting to family arrangement', wrote Edward in another letter:

> I would beg humbly to state, that I have never felt the
> slightest irritation on account of the alterations made
> some years ago ... I have wished to regard myself from that
> moment as a younger son, and have always thought that
> Henry was infinitely better adapted to succeed you than
> myself in many respects; he takes an interest in all that
> constitutes the habits and customs of a person residing in
> England. I much prefer the Continent ... It would indeed
> be highly unjust in me, on account of the unforeseen death
> of that individual to feel uncharitably disposed towards my
> brother Henry who has been for many years regarded as
> your successor, and particularly as he has several children.

He reiterated again his desire to relinquish any claims on the estate, and that his wife 'will certainly not have any children'. The letter closed with a brief note from 'Philipinne Lascelles' to Lord Harewood, in which she expressed the 'honour I feel in being now related to so illustrious a family as yours, and at the same time my great happiness at being the wife of your son'.[65]

Lord Harewood was unsurprised. His delayed response to Edward's second letter stated merely that he had already said all he meant to say 'upon the subject of your recent marriage':

I did not think it necessary, or even discrete, to enter upon the topic, when first the information reached me. From circumstances of which I was not ignorant I was led to expect that such a result might probably be the consequence of the intimacy you have described. My former letter will have explained to you the views I could have wished to have seen accomplished, after the death of your former wife; they are however at an end. It is useless now to say more upon the subject of your recent marriage. I therefore purposefully abstain from extending my correspondence concerning a matter, which if I do not approve, I will not, by that means, aggravate.[66]

Though Edward had been sent into exile, the public was not silenced. Lord Harewood, so his daughter-in-law complained, repeatedly got 'annoying' letters about his son's first marriage.[67] In September 1826, one Edward James wrote to the earl from Plowden Hall, Ludlow, in Shropshire, enquiring 'where the young gentleman now resides who made an unfortunate marriage some years ago likewise where the female *now* lives it is not curiosity but a desire to serve the family of Harewood which produces this letter and perhaps may many more'. A month later the assiduous James wrote again:

My Lord

I again address you because I understood that the tranquillity of your house had been greatly disturbed by a Mr Lascelles marrying a person quite unworthy of him and if my information is correct the family *may be* restored to its former tranquility. I have no interest. I do not personally know you I take this trouble because I think it my *duty* to

Ruin and disgrace

do so and necessary information can be had by applying to

Your lordships
Obedient Humble Servant
Edward James.[68]

By this time Lord Harewood had put discrete enquires in train as to his correspondent, whose murky testimonial was duly transmitted back, courtesy of a network of respectable local gentry. Edward James, his informants found, had been a servant in the employ of Mr Beddoes of Longville and succeeded in entrancing the daughter of the house. He enlisted in the army but '*Miss Beddoes* bought him off and he ran away with her and married her of course very much against the approbation of her Parents'. James was now living at Plowden Hall where:

> he takes boarders or lodgers into his house some of whom
> are military men and not very respectable; he is not
> considered to be living in a respectable way though I believe
> his wife has a very good Property from her Father who was
> considered a rich man.[69]

It may be that Edward James had heard the story of that scandalous first marriage and subsequent separation in military circles. Whatever the source of the rumours, two things are clear. First, knowledge of Edward's unfortunate alliance was not restricted either to his immediate circle, or even to the confines of the polite world. Second, those in the know included some who would seek to profit from it. Edward had indeed 'disappeared from England', as would be claimed in an antipodean courtroom. But his destination was not Van Diemen's Land.

Who then was it who stood before a Sydney judge in 1835 claiming the viscount's identity?

Harewood at bay

4

★✿✿★

THE LOST HEIR

'when a man's an h'impostor, you want to know *why* he's
an h'impostor,' said Constable Hurst didactically.
'Naturally,' I said.

Agatha Christie, *The Murder at the Vicarage*, 1930

In September 1824, as John Russell was pulling Edward Lascelles out of the fleshpots of Europe, another prodigal young
man arrived at the door of the Reverend Dr William Singer in
southern Scotland. He was 'in a state of great destitution' and
described himself as John Colquhoun, 'the eldest lawful son of
Sir James Colquhoun of Luss'. He told a sad story of misspent
youth: 'been misled by bad company', cashiered by his regiment and cast off by his father. Singer was wary, but willing
to help. He wrote to Sir James about the circumstances, and
under Singer's suggestion the young man did likewise, 'solicit-
ing forgiveness' from his father.

Singer also took the precaution of insisting that his visitor sign a 'voluntary declaration' as to his identity and circumstances.[1] In it John Colquhoun swore that his father had

Ruin and disgrace

purchased him a commission in the 10th regiment of Hussars, which had 'cost ... a great deal of money', but that he had been cashiered for being absent without leave. He then drew on his father for £1300, but had:

> squandered the proceeds among gamblers; and that his father has been so highly offended with him as to dismiss him with orders not to see him again; and that he has been for sometime in distress and of late even in want of the necessaries of life.

He declared, with the same reckless regard for the truth that he would later display in that Sydney courtroom, 'that he is accordingly sorry for the misconduct which has occasioned so much offence to his father Sir Jas Colquhoun, and also to his other friends and relatives'. Aware that someone must vouch for him, he mentioned that he had lately met with some gentlemen who knew him, amongst them 'Daniel Fisher Esq Solicitor Forth Street Edinburgh'. He wished to be reconciled with his father, but was afraid that his parent would refuse to see him. He would shortly come of age and would then enter into some property, but at present he was 'so destitute he cannot determine what to do'. If 'his father be not reconciled to him, he sees nothing before him except to go, if accepted, into some Regiment wanting Recruits, where he could enter as a volunteer until fa[r]ther means can be taken to insure at least a decent maintenance'. He hoped some 'neutral person' might intercede with his father and persuade him that 'he would be happy in future to conduct himself so as to gain the approbation of his relatives'.[2]

The lost heir

William Singer was silent upon any thoughts he might have had about how such profligate behaviour should have sprung from the loins of so respectable a family. The Colquhouns were famed throughout the area both for their piety and for their disapproval of the loose morals of the fashionable classes. Sir James Colquhoun had become an elder in the Scots church in 1816, much to the delight of his evangelical wife, Janet (née Sinclair, 1781–1846). It was she who would prove the family's most prominent member.

At the time Lady Colquhoun was known for her activities in local religious and charitable institutions, having established a school of industry for girls where she taught Sunday School. While the family lived in neo-classical splendour at Rossdhu, on the banks of Loch Lomond, Lady Colquhoun deplored the fashionable round of life in which her class had placed her, and was especially pained by the prejudice against evangelical religion she found in her social circle. 'This week have the prospect of being four days following *in the world*', she confided to her diary in 1816, 'have prayed for support. I feel the influence of worldly company less hurtful than I once did, and can lift up my heart to God in the midst of it much more frequently.' When her health declined in 1820, she was unable to continue her more active philanthropic ventures, and turned to religious writing. It is probably around this time that she penned a series of poignant letters to her children, to be opened in the event of her death. To her eldest son, she wrote, 'If you live you will have much of this world's good things to dispose of; value them, I beseech you, only as giving you more of the power to do good. Oh! let all you are and all you have be devoted to God.'[3]

Ruin and disgrace

In the event, her immediate fears were groundless. Lady Colquhoun lived another twenty-six years, found considerable fame as a religious author, and those 'death-bed' epistles were published for the edification of Victorian morality. In 1823, a year before her 'profligate' eldest supposedly turned up on Singer's doorstep, she published a pamphlet entitled *The Higher Classes*. Wrapped in the comforting blanket of anonymity, she launched a stinging attack on the gentry for finding immorality in the lower orders without looking clearly at their own sins. She deplored the theatre and other 'fashionable amusements of the age', found Lord Nelson, the nation's hero, 'a brave but misguided sinner' (his love affair with a married woman was notorious), and she recommended Wilberforce's *Practical Christianity* as 'a work that can hardly be too highly esteemed'.[4] It was only after the death of her husband in 1836 that Lady Colquhoun admitted publicly to the authorship of her numerous religious works. Around the time her son was allegedly carousing with drinkers and gamblers, Lady Colquhoun was also writing *Despair and Hope* (1822), *Thoughts on the Religious Profession* (1823) and *Impressions of the Heart* (1825). The diary she began keeping in 1805, large sections of which were also later published for religious inspiration, was full of pious hopes for her children's dedication to Christ. 'Oh, my God! protect my children! Make them Thine, early Thine, for ever Thine! I ask nothing for them but in subservience to this. My whole drift in their education has been towards this end; but, Lord, thou only canst give the increase.'[5] Hearing the sad stories told by the Colquhoun heir, the Reverend Dr Singer could only have despaired that these hopes had so plainly failed to flower.

We have no knowledge of why Singer's visitor plucked his identity from amongst the Colquhoun family. Perhaps the

The lost heir

moral high ground this evangelical gentry family occupied in 1824 lent an added drama to his supposed fall from grace. (Ironically, the real John Colquhoun — second, rather than eldest son of Sir James — was a forerunner to those 'Saints' of our own time: he would end his life a passionate environmentalist.) The Colquhouns, then, may have had a worthiness that appealed to the impostor. More likely, they were simply the elite of the area, a family whose members it was politic for others to treat well. 'If he had known he was an impostor and not Sir James's son', Singer later testified, 'he would not only not have given him a shilling, but adopted means to put a stop to his impostures'. There was evidently sufficient plausibility in the young man's story, though, for Singer to hedge his bets, and to feel it his 'Christian duty to assist him if he was Sir James' son'.[6] A less charitable interpretation might suggest he thought it inadvisable to offend a local baronet with considerable social and religious patronage. As it was, the prodigal was sent off that day with a letter of one pound's credit, on the strength of which he made for the nearby spa town of Moffat. Here he spent five enjoyable days at the Spur Inn, leaving without notice and without giving his name to the innkeepers, who were left to obtain payment from Dr Singer himself. Singer duly covered the bill of sixteen shillings, without expecting he would ever be recompensed.

Playing the prodigal son

On 24 October, a somewhat dishevelled figure, 'apparently travelling on foot' and carrying no luggage, arrived at the Dumfries and Galloway Hotel in Assembly Street, Dumfries. To the innkeeper Ambrose Clarke and his wife Amelia, evidently a

Ruin and disgrace

sympathetic couple, he repeated his sad and cautionary tale. He was 'short of money' on account of an estrangement between himself and his father. He could redeem his bill, he assured the Clarkes, as soon as he came of age, for then he would 'succeed to a property through his Grandmother', inheriting the estate of Coyleckie plus £12 000. His father had thus far prevented him from entering into his inheritance, but it would be his by right some five weeks hence (his birthday now having moved from October to December). He admitted he 'had behaved ill & was wild & dissipated and had much offended his father', and had been cashiered from a lieutenancy in the 10th Hussars for being absent without leave. Having been only seven months an officer, he carefully explained, he had fallen between the publication of two army lists, which accounted for his name not appearing there.

Dumfries was a bustling town. Scotland's Liverpool, said some; not only the metropolis of the country's south but also its gateway to the Atlantic. Situated on the left bank of the river Nith, by the 1820s it was already a place of pilgrimage for those who came to pay their respects at the grave of Robert Burns. The poet had died there on 21 July 1796, suffering the effects of rheumatic fever and abscessed teeth, aged only thirty-seven but bound within a body worn out by hard living. Crippling farm labour as a youth had not been helped by a lifetime testing out all those celebrated drinking songs. Prescribed sea bathing in the icy Scottish seas, such rigours had only hastened his demise. It didn't take long for the town to attract Burns tourists. Samuel Taylor Coleridge and William and Dorothy Wordsworth came in 1803. For the faithful, or the curious, there was Burns's mausoleum (1815), his final abode (clad in the red-coloured Permian sandstone distinctive to the town), and his epigrams and

The lost heir

verses scratched into the window panes of the Kings Arms and the Globe Inn. He left his mark at the Globe in other ways also. The landlady's niece bore one of the numerous Burns progeny scattered across the region.

Ambrose and Amelia Clarke trusted the stranger living with them 'solely on the faith of the truth of his statement' and did not expect payment until such time as he came of age and, as they had planned, took Ambrose with him to Edinburgh to arrange for his inheritance. Their guest was of an open disposition, eager to tell his troubles to the assembled company. He was much given to reading aloud letters sent to him concerning the estrangement between himself and his father. He:

> often showed these letters & appeared to be fond of doing
> so even to persons who had no interest in the matter &
> particularly mentioned who were the writers of them &
> showed the addresses on the back, but never gave a letter
> into any persons hand.

It was the letters that 'Colquhoun' wrote to and received from 'respectable people' that, Amelia Clarke testified, particularly persuaded her and her husband that their guest was who he said he was. Nevertheless, 'her husband intended not to part with him till he went to Edinburgh and got his money'.

For all his supposed past dissipation, Colquhoun 'lived very moderately' at the inn. The Clarkes were concerned for his comfort and, as the bitter cold of a Scottish November swept into Dumfries, Ambrose urged him to order 'some decent clothes' as 'his own were getting shabby'. He recommended a local tailor, Benjamin Oney ('Clothes made in the newest fashion. Liveries on the most reasonable terms.') to have a warm cloak, vest and surcoat made, and lent Colquhoun money to

Ruin and disgrace

buy boots and gloves. As rumours 'as to his character' began to swirl around their guest, all of which they related to him, 'he solemnly assured them that he never had deceived them never would and this led them still more to believe in his story to the last'.[7]

In ways that would be familiar to New South Wales settlers James Roberts and Francis Prendergast – the swindlers 'Colquhoun' and 'Lascelles' being of course one and the same – the Clarkes' credulity would later figure as the butt of a courtroom's scorn. But this was amusement after the fact, and we should be just as wary of indulging in it. The fact is that people *were* convinced by the impostor – and repeatedly – and they were not in some way innately more credulous than ourselves. Their credulity was simply moulded differently. None of the people to whom the impostor played his roles had actually met either Colquhoun or Edward Lascelles. And in any case, in a time before photography, before identity cards, television or bright lighting, facial recognition was not necessarily the key means by which the identity of strangers was established. Dress, demeanour and other symbols of authority or status established such identity far more plausibly.[8] And the impostor made consummate use of his props – be they a gold chain, a mysterious tin box, the writing and receiving of letters, or even the conspicuous consumption of poultry. He was equally canny about what roles he chose to play, and the lost heir was a personal favourite.

As novelist Richard Flanagan puts it in *Gould's Book of Fish*, 'swindling requires not delivering lies but confirming preconceptions'. To persuade, one must be credible. By their very nature, confidence men have to inspire precisely that. If not, their careers would be brief indeed. The man who turned up

The lost heir

at the Reverend Singer's door, or at the Clarkes' inn, had to have a plausible story. And his story was plausible because it drew directly on common familiarity with the way status and property worked in British society in the first decades of the nineteenth century. As the real Edward Lascelles found out to his cost, the most reliable way for an aristocratic or gentry family to establish and perpetuate its consequence was to keep the majority of the landed estates, the title, and the money to support them, in the hands of one member: the eldest son. Land remained the most visible and effective way of exhibiting wealth and status. When Old Lascelles converted part of his West Indian fortune into a Yorkshire estate crowned with a palatial home, he was playing by this rule. Land was the setting for the family seat, for entertainment, sport and for the patronage that linked that family into reciprocal bonds of social and political obligations above and below. It gave influence in ways that other forms of property did not. Even in an era when the peerage was being dramatically expanded, and when the reward of honours for political support was accepted practice, those called to the peerage were those (however their initial fortunes had been made) who had established landed estates. They were country gentlemen before they were peers. Mere income might derive from a variety of sources, but land meant social prestige, and would do so for far longer than the upwardly mobile industrial middle class desired. Those vast tracts of land required primogeniture to avoid being eroded into smaller and smaller portions.

This meant that the demands of the lineage had to be considered above those of the individual. Land was not a personal possession, it was held in trust for generations to come. In practical terms it created a distinct class of heirs-in-waiting,

Ruin and disgrace

men who had to occupy themselves in some appropriate way before they could take their appointed place in control of the family estate. The army was one frequent recourse. It provided social acceptability in terms of elite masculinity, congenial company and civic virtue. The connections between military – as opposed to civil – governing prowess and aristocratic obligations would wane over the course of the nineteenth century, but they remained strong.

Strict settlement, then, was designed to preserve the estate for the lineage rather than the individual, and unless a family was extraordinarily wealthy, it could cast a temporary poverty over the heir. This of course was relative. When Elizabeth Bennet listened to complaints on this score from an earl's son, her response was characteristically astute: 'What have you ever known of self-denial and dependence?' But a combination of being raised in expectation of substantial means, while having little personally disposable income until the death of one's father, often set the stage for youthful indiscretion. The prodigal son of a high-status father was a common trope in fiction (and a suitable role for an impostor) precisely because he was a familiar figure in life. The prodigal son who had come to grief in the army was an even more convincing role to play. The end of the Napoleonic Wars had not only demobilised a mass of men from the ranks. It had also dispensed with the services of many gentlemanly officers, now subsisting somewhat perilously on half pay and seeking what means of preferment they might.

The poverty felt by the heir to a landed estate was temporary, and here was a contradiction tailor-made for a swindler's purpose. Inheritance would come eventually, and in the meantime there were a host of influential relatives and friends who

The lost heir

could give temporary support, even if a youth were estranged from the man who currently held the lineage's purse strings. It was with letters to these 'respectable people', as witnesses put it, that a web of deceit was spun over five weeks at the Clarkes' inn. This was a key tactic in sustaining 'Colquhoun's' identity. But it would also prove to be his undoing.

On 4 December 1824, the procurator fiscal's office in Dumfries received an unexpected letter from Edinburgh warning of a 'swindler' at the Dumfries and Galloway Hotel 'who passes himself for the eldest son of Sir James Colquhoun of Luss'. Patrick Miller, Justice of the Peace, urged the local sheriff to take action. The impostor should 'be taken up & examined & if he is what there is no doubt of his being deal with him as severely as the Law will permit'. Miller was acquainted with Sir James ('I mentioned the circumstances to one of his brothers today who told me that this fellow is nothing but a low swindling ruffian') and the matter had come to his attention by means of the letters streaming out of Clarke's hotel. 'Be particular in finding out his real name', ended Miller in a postscript, 'that he may be exposed by the Edinburgh papers while you have him in jail'.

Acting on this advice, the authorities called at the Dumfries and Galloway Hotel, but the landlord told the sheriff that:

> he was satisfied from the various letters he had shewn
> him that Colquhoun was not an impostor & that he
> had no doubt he would get payment of his account –
> that Colquhoun had heard of the suspicions that were
> entertained against him but had shewn no dread or any
> inclination to leave the place in consequence and that he
> was perfectly willing then to shew the letters before alluded

Ruin and disgrace

to, to the Sheriff or any other person who might choose to examine them.

The names of several 'most respectable people' who had written to Colquhoun were sent on to Miller, Clarke explaining that 'He has also letters on business from Daniel Fisher W.S. [Writer to the Signet; a solicitor] who he says is his father's Factor and agent and to whom he refers for any information that may be required respecting him'. The procurator fiscal's office did not doubt, they assured Miller, that the letters had been obtained as he suggested, but no charge could be brought since 'Clark will not complain but seems certain of getting payment and there is no other person appears to have an interest'.

Miller was not going to let the matter rest, and as a local magistrate he was sufficiently well connected to do something about it. He began by systematically tracking down all the supposed John Colquhoun's correspondents in Edinburgh who had been named by Clarke. All testified as to the swindler's false identity. Miller then took up the matter with the Lord Advocate himself and the earlier story of the connection with Singer was flushed out. So too was our single piece of evidence (albeit hearsay) as to the impostor's real identity:

> Mr Daniel Fisher knows him from the circumstance of his
> being agent to Sir J Colquhoun to be a swindler & the son
> of a collier & alehouse keeper in Sir James's neighbourhood
> at a place called Knightswood colliery. If he has not
> committed in [Dumfries] any act of swindling he has in the
> country to a certainty for by representing himself to Dr
> Singer to be the son of Sir J C the doctor thereon gave him
> a note to Workman the Innkeeper in Moffat to furnish his
> wants as far as untill he could hear from Sir James who by

The lost heir

return of Post informed the doctor that he was an arrant impostor.

The Lord Advocate's office was advised that:

> The step you ought therefore to adopt as to this individual is to take him up for examination if he has not fled (which I make little doubt of his having done by this time) & first ask him if he is the eldest son of Sir J Colquhoun & if he answers yes ask his first name & if he says John propose rebaptising him as Sir James eldest son's name is James — then ask if he knows Mr Daniel Fisher *his father's agent* & if he says yes tell him you will produce that gentleman to prove that he is not Sir James's eldest son but that he is John Dow son of John Dow collier & publican in Stirlingshire & keep hold of him till you hear from Dr Singer whom he has imposed upon then you can easily make out a case independent of Clarke of 'Falsehood Fraud & Imposition' in the Sheriffdom of Dumfries which you are unquestionably called up by such respectable evidence as that of Dr Singer to report to the Lord Advocate as soon as you make it out.[9]

Sprung up out of the ground

During the swindler's subsequent career in Australia his name was spelt mostly as 'Dow', but it also appears variously as 'Dowe' and 'Doe'. To our ears the name seems patently false, an almost laughable title for a serial impostor. It would have sounded somewhat differently to those listening to courtroom arguments in the 1820s and 1830s. John Doe (plaintiff) and Richard Roe (defendant) had been used as generic names in legal actions of ejectment since the eighteenth century. But

Ruin and disgrace

to use the name 'John Doe' to denote 'an ordinary or typical citizen' would only come into common usage (and particularly in the United States) in the twentieth century.[10] We should also take note that the first mention of the name John Dow comes from Miller, who had every reason to assign the impostor a concrete rather than a figurative identity. It was only later that 'John Dow' became usefully vague to the man himself as a name to hide behind, a mask said to conceal the convict shame of 'Edward Lascelles'.

Was the impostor's name John Dow? The man masquerading as Colquhoun repudiated that name when put on trial (given what we know of his methods, this seems rather to prove it than the reverse) but the authorities looked no further. Their interest lay in proving fraud, not in investigating the impostor's real identity. Given the tissue of lies with which he surrounded himself, it seems unlikely that we will ever know Dow's origins. Miller's investigations threw up enough incidental detail (and potential witnesses, albeit they were never challenged) to suggest that the coalminer's son story may have been accurate.

If so, then Dow really hailed from a background that was peculiarly apt. For he had sprung up out of the ground, from a lineage widely regarded as murky, blackened in body as much as in reputation. All coalminers worked in terrifyingly harsh conditions. Before the close of the eighteenth century, Scottish miners also laboured under the stigma of serfdom. The 'inspector' of convict conditions in 1830s New South Wales was in all likelihood the son of a bonded labourer.

Unlike the gargantuan system of Atlantic slavery, the little-known history of Scottish coalminer 'enslavement' had emerged more by accident than design. It was a system of slavery more in fact than in name, though this was cold comfort for those

The lost heir

who suffered under it. As one critic put it in 1778, 'nothing seems to be wanting in the said acts to constitute real slavery, but the name! and that want hath been abundantly supplied by the decisions of their courts of law'.[11] This was not a survival of earlier agrarian serfdom, but arose in the seventeenth century out of the need to secure a labour force in the coalfields. An Act of 1606 prevented colliers and salt-workers (the two industries often operated in tandem in Scotland) from being employed without permission of their master. It was intended more to eliminate labour poaching by rival employers than to establish a system of servitude. But for the next two centuries it would result in a very real bondage. Subsequent Acts in the seventeenth century tightened controls, and while no piece of legislation explicitly enslaved miners, the interpretation of the law by masters made this an empty letter. Vagrants could be forced by law into the coal mines; miners could not leave the estate without a pass (which they were unlikely to get); and they could be removed and redeployed to other mines of their masters at will. With their families, miners could be disposed of by sale or lease, along with the mine itself. When an estate was sold, described one critic in 1808:

> the colliers and their families formed part of the inventory
> or livestock, and were valued as such; in short, they
> were bought and sold as slaves. This system secured,
> indeed, a race of colliers, but it was disgraceful to a free
> Government, and therefore every man must rejoice at their
> emancipation.[12]

Coalmine owners usually laid automatic claim to the labour of children born of colliers. This practice was often underscored through a baptismal payment to the family known as 'arles' or

Ruin and disgrace

'larigeld'. As the eighteenth century wore on, debates over the condition of Scottish coal-workers became shot through with the same language of liberty that would be bandied about so much in the Yorkshire elections a generation later: 'Shall a free-born Briton, the favourite of heaven and envy of the world, lose for ever his much-loved and invaluable liberty, by entering to work in a Scotch colliery?'[13]

An Act of 1775 technically ended such servitude, but it was so toothless as to be virtually without meaning. Subsequent legislation of 1799 was more effective, but the death knell of bonded labour in the Scottish mines was really rung by the industrial revolution. And it was reforming coalmine owners, not workers, who led the charge. Bonded labour was inefficient, and its association with slavery added significantly to the stigma already carried by what was difficult and dangerous work. Nor was it especially cheap. Miners were paid relatively good wages compared to other manual labourers, though even this was not enough to tempt many recruits. The miners themselves (unsurprisingly, considering the conditions in which they lived) were not replenishing their population quickly enough to meet the labour needs of increased coal demand. Strikes and labour unrest in the Scottish mines punctuated the 1790s, with associations built between workers in different mines. There was anxious talk of an energy crisis in both Edinburgh and Whitehall. It was, finally, the desperate Irish families who flooded the west of Scotland after the wars with Napoleon ended in 1815 who would solve the labour problems of the industry.[14]

If he were a collier turned tavern-keeper, John Dow senior would have gone down the mine at age eight or so. Education for collier children was patchy, and depended very much on the attitude of the local laird (most aristocracy and gentry

The lost heir

were involved in the coal industry where conditions permitted). John Dow junior's literacy certainly shows the marks of someone who received more than the basics, but was largely self-taught in the art of polite discourse. Yet whatever paternalistic advantages might be had, all colliers laboured under a social stigma. 'This class of men', wrote an engineer in 1808:

> from their peculiar habits, form a distinct society, living
> in houses together at a distance from towns, intermingling
> very little with the other classes of the community, and
> generally marrying among themselves, particularly where
> women are employed to carry coals, as no one but a collier's
> daughter would choose to be a collier's wife in such a case. [15]

They were a race apart. As the lines of *The Collier's Bonnie Lass* (a poem sometimes wrongly attributed to Burns) would have it:

> The collier had a dochter, and O she's wonder bonie;
> A laird he was that socht her, rich in lands and money;
> She wadna hae a laird, she wadna be a leddy,
> But she wad hae a collier lad, the colour o' her deddie. [16]

In 1824, then, the stigma of Scottish coalminers was not a distant memory. Was it this tainted heritage that first prompted the swindler on his progress of reinventions? If so, it would not be long before his journey took a turn back towards servitude.

'Crimes of a heinous nature, and severely punishable'

On 10 December the Sheriff's office informed Miller that they had 'caused Colquhoun alias Dow to be apprehended'. [17] The

Ruin and disgrace

wheels of justice began slowly to grind. The prisoner made a declaration asserting that he was 'John James Colquhoun, eldest son of Sir James Colquhoun of Luss Baronet', aged 21. He declined to say what his mother's name was, he denied that he was John Dow, and although he answered some questions, he was generally unco-operative. He did, however, admit to receiving a letter of credit from Singer which paid for his bill in Moffat. He declined to say how much he owed the Clarkes, but declared that he 'intended going to Edinburgh on Monday and taking Mr Clarke with him, and settling accounts with him there, as he expects money there, but declines saying from what quarter he is to get it'. Evidence was taken at length that day, and through the month of December, to ascertain whether there was a case to be made. The innkeepers of Dumfries and Moffat testified, as did Benjamin Oney the tailor (who evidently had his suspicions and had already retrieved the clothes he had made on the pretence that they were needed to copy a pattern).

Ambrose Clarke seemed particularly distressed by the betrayal. He testified that he had confronted:

Colquhoun in Jail and asked him how he could think of imposing on [him] as he had done. That on this occasion Colquhoun confessed he was not the son of Sir James Colquhoun and said at the same time it was no matter who he was but his name was not Dow and he also mentioned that if he had got to Edinburgh with [Clarke] he would have received his money in the Royal Hotel.

Miller and Clarke submitted letters from the impostor to the court as evidence. The declaration that had been signed at Singer's parish in Kirkpatrick Juxta in September was produced. Slowly the case was assembled and in due course 'John Dow,

The lost heir

Junior, alias John Colquhoun alias John James Colquhoun, present prisoner in the Tolbooth of Dumfries' was indicted in the requisitely imposing tones of the law:

> That albeit by the Laws of this and every other well
> governed realm, Falsehood, Fraud, and Wilful Imposition,
> particularly when practised in order to obtain by false
> pretences the money or goods of others … are Crimes of
> a heinous nature and severely punishable: yet true it is and
> of verity, That you the said John Dow, Junior, alias John
> Colquhoun alias John James Coquhoun are guilty of the said
> Crimes.[18]

As the Scottish winter wore on, the prisoner awaited the spring court session in the jail of Dumfries. Here he built up a certain degree of local notoriety. In the start of an article headlined 'JAIL REFORM', which detailed efforts to get prisoners to read, the *Dumfries & Galloway Courier* reported that 'We are happy to state that our old friend Colquhoun, the pretended heir apparent of Sir James Colquhoun, of Luss, still plies his vocation in the Jail, to the no small advantages of divers of its inmates'. He was teaching his fellow prisoners to read. 'Altogether', concluded the *Courier*, 'the reputed swindler is a strange compound'.[19]

The Dumfries Circuit Court of Justiciary opened on 25 April 1825 under the authority of Lords Hermand and McKenzie. The trial was duly heard, sandwiched between several cases of assault, the locals seemingly much given to discharging fowling pieces into their neighbours. As Dow waited to hear his fate, the audience in court was entertained by the case of the unfortunate Robert Wallace, clandestinely courting the sister of his friend John Smith on a 'cluddy' night in January. Perhaps

Ruin and disgrace

the poetry of Burns ('Scots, wha hae wi' Wallace bled') had inspired him to emulate his more heroic namesake. If so, things rapidly took a turn for the ludicrous. Mistaken for a potato thief by his sweetheart's brother, Wallace was challenged by Smith (whose gun duly 'gaed off'), peppered with small shot in the buttocks, and laid up in bed for six weeks. Cross-examined by the court as to why he was courting Mary in the dead of night with plaid wrapped furtively about his head, Wallace insisted that it was 'customary in business o' that kin', Sir'.[20] Despite the hindrance of a profoundly deaf witness, who persisted in answering questions 'with a vociferous Eh!', the case was eventually resolved. The protective John Smith, with his 'previous orderly and inoffensive conduct' taken into account, 'as well as the goodness of heart he displayed in offering to support Wallace during the time he was confined', was sentenced to imprisonment in the Dumfries jail for one calendar month – during which time Mary was presumably wooed at more reasonable hours.

Dow would receive less indulgence from the court. Accused 'of falsely and fraudulently assuming the name of John or John James Colquhoun ... and under that false and assumed name ... imposing upon and cheating various persons', his crimes specifically entailed three offences: the letter of credit provided by Dr Singer; the bill he had run up at Ambrose Clarke's together with the money lent to him by Clarke; and the clothes he had obtained on credit from Benjamin Oney. The prisoner pleaded not guilty. The Reverend Dr Singer, Mrs Workman of the Spur Inn, and the Clarkes all testified against him in court. Mrs Clarke explained that she and her husband credited his story for 'he said he was acquainted with Messrs Jeffrey, Cockburn, and other gentlemen in Edinburgh (Every person

The lost heir

in court was tickled with this last answer, and Lord Hermand laughed heartily at it).' It would not the last time the impostor's victims faced ridicule in court.

The final witness was Sir James Colquhoun himself. Standing before the supposed prodigal, he testified that in the autumn of the previous year he had received a letter from Dr Singer as to the young man who 'called himself his son'. Sir James informed Singer by letter that the reverend had been imposed upon by 'a most nefarious impostor' who, Sir James had been informed, 'had been practicing the same tricks in the north of Scotland, particularly at Inverness' some two or three months previously. Sir James confirmed to the court that Daniel Fisher was his Edinburgh agent and that 'he never saw the [defendant] before to his knowledge, and he is not his son'. He also confirmed that his son 'is not, and never was, in the 10th Hussars'. Fisher, who was then in London, was never called upon to give evidence as to his claim that the impostor was John Dow, although he was listed as a witness prior to the trial. Dow's real identity was irrelevant. It was sufficient for the court's needs to prove that the prisoner was *not* John (or James) Colquhoun. The declarations that Dow had made when he was first apprehended were entered into the record, but he did not give further evidence.[21]

The prisoner's counsel tied himself in knots attempting to prove that no swindling had taken place, that Dr Singer had helped the prisoner from Christian charity, that the Clarkes were shortly to be paid, and that they were in expectation of payment before the prisoner was taken up by the sheriff's office. Lord Hermand made short shrift of these claims, remarking to the jury that the charges were not of swindling but of 'falsehood, fraud and wilful imposition', and that it was quite clear that the prisoner had falsely claimed to be the son of Sir James

Ruin and disgrace

Colquhoun, who, moreover, had testified against the prisoner's claim to this identity. Furthermore, 'was it not a little extraordinary that when asked about his mother's name, he would neither give it, nor answer a single question?' The jury returned a verdict of guilty on the first and second charges, evidently dismissing the third since Oney remained in possession of those clothes which had been made. Both judges were agreed, in Lord McKenzie's words, that the prisoner's crimes were 'of the most impudent and base kind' and that he 'was a person whose longer remaining in the country would be attended with great danger to the community'. Giving sentence of seven years transportation, Lord Hermand pronounced that 'the man at the bar was indicted under the name of John Dow; he did not know whether he had any title to that name or not; but he had none to the other honourable name assumed by him'.

With unknowing and profound irony he informed the prisoner:

> it was only because he represented himself as the son
> of Sir John Colquhoun, he was enabled to carry on his
> depredations; he ought now to reflect that he was going to
> a country where a more strict watch would be kept over his
> conduct, and that, by repentance and improvement of his
> time, he might still recover his character, and return to this
> country a better man than he left it.

He ought, observed Lord Hermand, 'thank the Court for sending him out of the Country. He was a young man; and by the blessing of God might yet return a reformed character.'[22]

The lost heir

'Torn from all that was dear to me on earth'

Lord Hermand might have had confidence in the 'strict watch' of the penal system, yet when a man like Dow is swallowed up by the maw of transportation, he vanishes at the very moment he is most definitely pinned down in paper and ink. Thanks to the meticulous record-keeping that sustained the antipodean gulag, we can track his progress through the system with relative ease. But any kind of detail, any hint of the rich amalgam of truth and fantasy we get when Dow tells his own story, almost completely disappears. He becomes a cipher; a few sparse notations made by the army of clerks completing the necessary paperwork.

Some seven months separated his conviction in Dumfries from his departure for Van Diemen's Land. Dow was incarcerated in one of London's hulks, worn-out ships converted into floating prisons to serve as holding areas for those sentenced to transportation. Jorgen Jorgensen, transported on the same ship that later bore Dow to Van Diemen's Land, left a vivid account of his time there:

> Humanity would almost shudder at the sight of the sufferings which one must endure on board one of those receptacles of criminals. The moment a convict passes over the gangway his person is searched for money, or other articles of value; he is taken below, is entirely stripped, is obliged to undergo an ablution, his hair often cut off, and the prison-dress put on him; a pair of irons are then placed on his legs, when the following morning he is sent to hard labour in the dockyard.[23]

Listed under the versatile portmanteau 'adventurer' in the

Ruin and disgrace

Australian Dictionary of Biography, Jorgen Jorgensen was a Dane, born in Copenhagen in 1780. Press-ganged into the British navy, by his own account he sailed with Mathew Flinders (famed for circumnavigating the antipodean continent) and was present at the founding of the British settlement of Van Diemen's Land in 1803. In 1809, in the midst of an Anglo-Danish war, Jorgensen masterminded a military coup in Iceland, declared the island independent from Denmark and installed himself as head of the government. He lasted a scant eight weeks before the arrival of English warships transformed him from uncrowned king to prisoner of war. He then spent two years on the continent spying for England, before a life of drinking, gambling and bad debts collapsed with an arrest for petty theft in 1820. For the next five years he was in and out of Newgate prison, famed for doctoring to his fellow inmates, and eventually having a sentence of death commuted to transportation for life. Jorgensen would go on to an equally varied career in the antipodes as explorer, negotiator with the Tasmanian Aborigines and general pen for hire.

Processing in the hulks was merely the beginning, wrote another who underwent the same ordeal, of a 'metamorphosis' which transformed the victim into something new and alien. Weighing some 14 pounds (6.3 kilograms), the leg irons were heavy enough to discourage escape by swimming.[24] With few exceptions (Jorgensen was relieved to be one of them) convicts worked by day at stone-breaking and similar tasks in the government dockyards and were locked in overcrowded quarters in the rotting, leaking ships by night. Jorgensen complained that no-one who had not suffered the hulks really knew what went on there. Inspections by conscientious government officials were all very well; things were put 'in admirable order'

The lost heir

for their visits. The reality was a 'school of abominable pollution' that rendered all 'ten-times more the children of darkness than they were before'. 'On board the hulks, anyone who should complain to the superiors of any of those heart-appalling scenes which he could not help seeing, would be destroyed by the other prisoners, and incur the resentment of the officers.'[25] All we know of Dow's time amidst these horrors is the curt note that his conduct was 'orderly'.[26]

From the hulks, Dow was transferred to the *Woodman*, a 419-ton chartered merchantman, captained by Irishman Daniel Leary. They set sail from Sheerness, at the mouth of the Thames, on 6 December 1825. Prisoners were supplied with 'new clothing of the coarsest description' and each 'had a pair of double-irons placed on his legs'. In the haste to catch the tide, the *Woodman*'s departure was a scramble, and circumstances on board were chaotic. As she was a charter rather than a regular convict transport, the *Woodman* needed to be refitted for the voyage, and carpenters were still trying to finish building the convicts' berths at the last minute. Regulations stipulated two rows of sleeping berths, one above the other, extending on each side of the 'between decks'. Each berth measured 6 feet (180 centimetres) square and held four convicts – they were allowed to choose their own mess mates – giving each one a scarce 18 inches of space in which to sleep.[27]

Friends and family were hastily allowed on board the *Woodman* to take their final farewells and 'swearing, cursing, wrangling, lamentations, and tears, deafened all within hearing, and it appeared as if ten thousand demons had been let loose'. The strong, complained Jorgensen, stole anything they could snatch from the weak, and a thriving trade in purloined articles ensued between the thieves, 'looked up to with a great deal

Ruin and disgrace

of respect by their less hardened fellow convicts', and the sailors and soldiers on board.[28] When the ship was sufficiently far out of port to prevent temptation, the leg irons were struck off and the convicts were allowed on deck for exercise. The *Woodman* would round the Cape of Good Hope on its way to Van Diemen's Land, a voyage of 144 days. It was a time in which Dow would do his utmost to slip free of the exacting bondage of the convict record, and recast himself as author of his own story. If it was Dow alias Colquhoun who went on board the *Woodman* in 1825, it was 'Lascelles, a son of Lord Harewood' who disembarked in Hobart some five months later.[29]

On board the *Woodman* were a guard from the 39th Regiment, military reinforcements for the Van Diemen's Land garrison, a number of their wives and children, a handful of free passengers, and 150 male convicts, including Dow and Jorgensen.[30] Like Dow, Jorgensen was the tireless author of his own drama, though in the Dane's case less as an impostor than as a man addicted to embroidering what by any set of standards amounted to an extraordinary life. Determined to publicise his own uniqueness, Jorgensen was a habitual scribbler, for which habit we are duly grateful, as it leaves us with an account of the voyage of the *Woodman*. It was, compared to many a convict transport, a relatively uneventful sailing. Neither punishment nor disease caused any noteworthy degree of suffering, but the immediacy of the pain for the captive souls on board was no less exquisite for that. Jorgensen can speak for those who watched the coast of England blur into the horizon: 'I now found myself torn from all that was dear to me on earth … I stood in silent agony, taking a last and lingering view of those shores.' In his case the bitterness was only more acute for being suffered under sail: 'I saw myself an exile and a captive

The lost heir

on that element on which I had once been a commander'.

It wasn't long before the *Woodman* ran into bad weather, and after the haste of setting out the stern was found to be so loose that water was soon lapping around the unhappy sojourners. The convicts, then still in irons and heartily sea-sick, found the situation, said Jorgensen in a moment of withering understatement, 'very disagreeable'. Several were convinced the whole lot of them were bound for the depths.[31]

The Dane spoke well of the captain, chief mate and surgeon-superintendent on board. The last of these was required by government regulation to oversee the health of the convicts, and Jorgensen, who 'had dabbled a little in medicine' during his time at Newgate, worked under him. It was common practice for some prisoners to be selected to perform certain tasks and wield some petty authority on board in return for better rations and living conditions. As the *Woodman* entered the tropical waters off the coast of Africa, an infectious 'brain fever' carried off four convicts, laid many more in the ship's hospital and finally saw the surgeon, a man 'of a meek and kind-hearted disposition', himself sicken, unnoticed to the others. One morning, 'he suddenly dropped down dead from his chair, to the grief of all on board'. Jorgensen was left in sole charge of the sick. No more died, though the 'melancholy ... manner of disposing of dead bodies at sea' put him into a profound depression.[32] The *Woodman* arrived at the Cape of Good Hope on 4 March, and Surgeon Cornelius Kelly was secured as a replacement.

Though both Kelly and Captain Leary were Irishmen, they were 'totally opposed in political principles' and each was reluctant to uphold the other in proposed punishments when regulations were breached. This divided authority (another common

Ruin and disgrace

problem on convict transports) may have contributed to the surprisingly benign atmosphere that seems to have prevailed on board during Dow's voyage. The convicts proved themselves an orderly consignment after their irons were struck off. 'As the prisoner[s] conducted themselves extremely well, and as they were permitted every day on deck, it soon produced a sort of goodwill on board, and the soldiers and marines were very obliging'. To keep the convicts fit and well, the surgeon needed, in the words of Peter Miller Cunningham (who made four voyages in this capacity) to promote 'cleanliness, comfort and hilarity among them'. Boredom was a dangerous influence on the convicts' mood. Gambling was endemic (Cunningham was not much bothered by it) and the Bibles, Testaments and Prayer Books distributed to convicts could be pulled apart to make playing cards.[33] Dancing on deck was encouraged every afternoon for exercise, and singing at all times. Impromptu plays were sometimes enacted. One surgeon passing across the 'stage' as the performance was about to begin asked the name of the play. 'Oh, sir, the "*Forty Thieves*" was the response of the facetious rogue next him'; no loss for actors then, came the riposte.[34]

It was in such relatively tolerant circumstances that Dow found ready outlet for his own dramatic talents. Philip Lander Fell, a cabin passenger on board the *Woodman*, later remembered that Dow stated his name to be Lascelles, and that he was 'anxious to propagate a belief that [he] were Lord Lascelles, the eldest son of the Earl of Harewood, but no one on board believed it'. Fell described how 'Lord Lascelles' went so far in refusing to answer to the name of John Dow that he was put in hand-

The lost heir

cuffs 'for his obstinacy, and narrowly escaped corporal punishment'.[35] In time, the prisoner would learn that a convict
pseudonym was a canny mask to wear; it was more effective to
use the identity 'John Dow' than to deny it outright.

Ruin and disgrace

'I am not fitted for being at the head of a family in England.' Edward Lascelles, painted not long before he relinquished any claim to the family title and fortune.

'Edward Lascelles', F von Lutzendorff, 1826: The Earl and Countess of Harewood and Trustees of the Harewood House Trust

The tyranny of primogeniture worked as much to thrust responsibility onto the shoulders of the unwilling as it did to deny it to the more capable. Edward's four sisters. Harriet, 'the renowned chemist of Harewood', holds the portfolio.

'The Four Daughters of the 2nd Earl of Harewood', John Jackson, c 1820: The Earl and Countess of Harewood and Trustees of the Harewood House Trust

Edward's father, Henry Lascelles, later 2nd Earl of Harewood. The plaque records
that this portrait was presented to his wife 'by a numerous body of the freeholders
of the county of York, in testimony of their deep sense of his public services during
the time of his representing that county in parliament'.

*'Henry Lascelles', Sir Thomas Lawrence, c 1823: The Earl and Countess of Harewood
and Trustees of the Harewood House Trust*

Harewood House, painted a year after Edward's birth. Capability Brown's lake,
which covered the site of the demolished Gawthorpe Hall, irritated Edwin Lascelles
with its persistent leaking.

'Harewood House from the South West', JMW Turner, 1797: The Earl and Countess of
Harewood and Trustees of the Harewood House Trust

William Wilberforce Esq. M.P.

Nature imprints upon whate'er we see,
That has a heart & life in it — Be free.   Cowper.

London. Pub.d April 28. 1792. by I Read. Coventry Co.t Coventry S.t

'As I listened, he grew and grew until the shrimp became a whale.'
William Wilberforce around the time he began his parliamentary campaign against
the slave trade. Note the quotation from Cowper: 'Nature imprints upon whate'er
we see, / That has a heart & life in it ~ Be free.'

'William Wilberforce', after J Davies, 1792: National Portait Gallery, London

Henry Dundas joins Pitt in riotous conviviality at his house in Wimbledon.
William Pitt's lanky frame and love of the bottle made him a gift to the country's
satirical artists.

'God Save the King — in a bumper, or An Evening Scene Three Times a Week at Wimbleton',
James Gillray, 1795: National Portrait Gallery, London

'Both clever and amiable, but so odd in person and so unlike other people it was a great chance against him ever finding any woman who liked him for himself.' Lord Milton soon after the 1807 election.

'Charles William Wentworth-Fitzwilliam, 5th Earl Fitzwilliam', William Ward, after JR Smith, 1808: National Portrait Gallery, London

'Delightfully easy and pleasant.' Mary Milton
in the year of her marriage, aged nineteen.

'Mary, Viscountess Milton', detail, Sir Thomas Lawrence, 1806

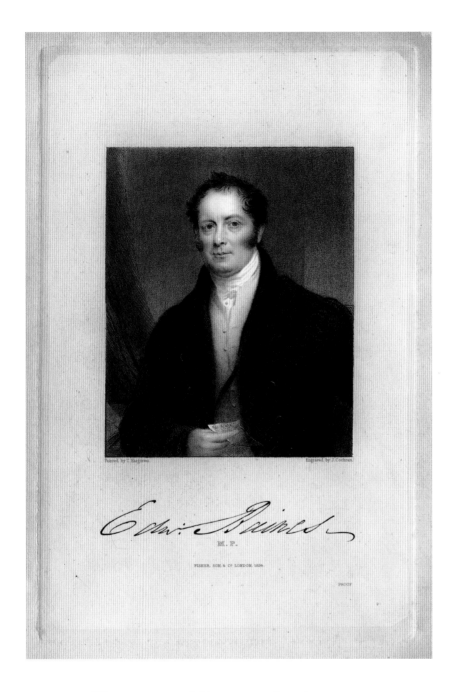

'There was a remarkable correspondence between
the spirit of Mr Baines and the spirit of the age.'

*'Edward Baines', John Cochran, probably after Thomas Hargreaves,
1834: National Portrait Gallery, London*

'Orange Jumper is as well known in Yorkshire as the King of England ...
He was the most conspicuous Partisan at Lord Milton's Election – They call Him
Orange Jumper from Lord M's color, (F Hawkesworth to J Gillray, 16 Feb 1809:
BL ADD MS 27337).'

'Orange Jumper', James Gillray, 1809: National Portrait Gallery, London

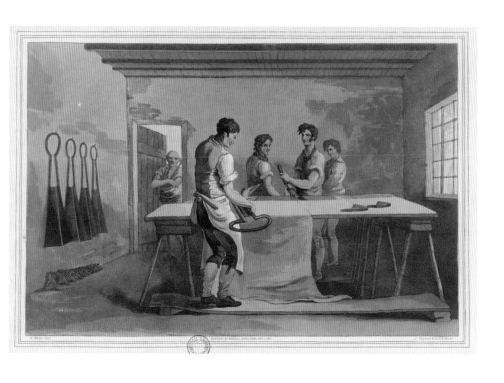

Cloth dressers preparing cloth by hand. This skilled labour, described as 'the nicest [meaning most precise] and most difficult part of their employment', was made redundant by the introduction of gig mills, shearing frames and factory production.

George Walker, The Costume of Yorkshire, *p 23: Mitchell Library, State Library of NSW*

'It is almost as difficult to trace each stage of this man's chequered career, as
it is to follow Harlequin through the various changes of a Christmas pantomime.'
James Mudie, the 'tyrant' of Castle Forbes.

Portrait of a man thought to be James Mudie, artist unknown, c 1810–1820:
Mitchell Library, State Library of NSW

Making Arcadia in the Antipodes. The three sons of artist John Glover were granted
substantial property in Van Diemen's Land during the 1820s exodus that saw many
would-be gentry leave post-war Britain for the colonies. Glover joined them in 1831.

*John Glover, 'Padderdale Farm', c 1840, oil on canvas, 76.6 x 115.2 cm, purchased 1974, Art
Gallery of New South Wales (photo Christopher Snee)*

A GOVERNMENT JAIL GANG.
Sydney N.S Wales.

The first act of the Castle Forbes mutineers was to liberate two of their mates who had been sentenced to labour in a chain gang for twelve months. Note the prisoners' trousers, with buttons down the sides, that could be removed without unshackling the wearer.

'A Government Jail Gang, Sydney N.S. Wales', Augustus Earl, 1830: Mitchell Library, State Library of NSW

ST JAMES CHURCH, SUPREME COURT HOUS

A view of St James' Church, where Edmund Smith Hall battled Archdeacon Thomas Hobbes Scott for control of his family pew. The Supreme Court, the dilapidation of which belied the dramas enacted within, sits immediately behind the church.

'St James Church, Supreme Court House', Robert Russell, 1836: Mitchell Library, State Library of NSW

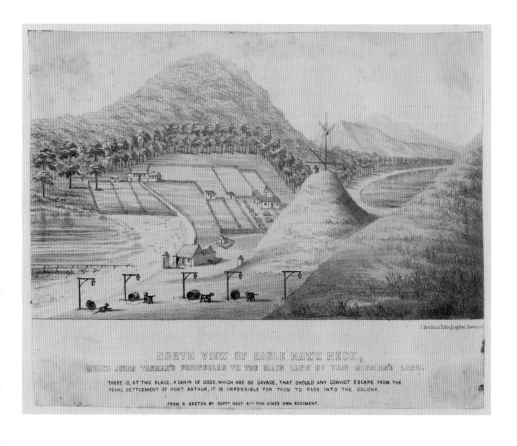

'Whether Port Arthur is, as called by some, an "Earthly Hell" or not, it has at all events its Cerberus.' The view from the Tasman Peninsula to the mainland across Eagle Hawk Neck, showing the notorious line of guard dogs.

'North view of Eagle Hawk Neck', C Hutchins, c 1845: Mitchell Library,
State Library of NSW

PART THREE

Antipodes

A very large proportion of the population consists
of branches lopped for their rottenness from the tree of
British freedom.

James Mudie, *The Felony of New South Wales*, 1840

The Hunter Valley, New South Wales, 1834

As convicts Anthony Hitchcock and John Poole made their way towards Castle Forbes, a military escort stood on guard. Poole distributed religious tracts to the spectators come out to watch the two men's melancholy progress. Hitchcock appeared stunned into silence. The men were on their way to a Hunter Valley settler's estate notorious throughout the entire colony as the scene of a recent convict uprising. The 'Castle Forbes Revolt' of November 1833, for so it is known to history, hardly merits the scope or drama suggested by that name. Yet this in no way softened the offence in the eyes of the authorities, or eased the penalty that the rebels would pay. As Hitchcock and Poole jolted by horse cart beside the Hunter River, they were seated upon their own coffins.[1]

Castle Forbes was the domain of one whose murky past was matched only by his social ambition. Known in the colony as 'Major' Mudie, it was 'almost as difficult to trace each stage of this man's chequered career', wrote a Sydney barrister, 'as it is to follow Harlequin through the various changes of a Christmas pantomime'.[2] A scoundrel, a Scot, a man determined to reinvent himself whatever the cost to others: to those following the progress of John Dow, James Mudie seems almost uncannily familiar.

Dismissed from the army and bankrupted in a shady business deal, Mudie was given free passage out to New South Wales by a compassionate patron. In the Hunter Valley he reinvented himself as a pillar of the colonial gentry, a local magistrate who styled himself 'Major' (a rank he had never attained) and lorded it over his assigned convict servants. He boasted that his homestead, run by his overseer and son-in-law John Larnach and guarded by savage Newfoundland dogs, provided an impregnable fortress against convict attack. Mudie soon became as infamous for the harsh treatment of his own convict servants as he was for his excessive sentencing from the Maitland bench.

On 5 November 1833, six of the convicts assigned to work at Castle Forbes had been unable to bear their lives under Mudie and Larnach any longer. Seizing weapons, and liberating their mates who remained under guard, they had made for the homestead in search of revenge. Larnach was away, down by the river, supervising (from the safe distance of the bank) some fourteen men in the dirty, exhausting and smelly work of washing sheep. Exported to industrial mills, Yorkshire's amongst them, Australia's 'golden fleece' promised to make fortunes for men like Mudie, so long as they could survive the rigours of a frontier penal colony. But Emily Larnach remained at the house, so the rebels rounded up her and the house servants, threatening to 'blow her brains out'. They wished her father was home, they told her, so they could settle him too.[3] The prisoners were bundled into the wood store and locked in. The rebels were off to the river to deal with her husband, was their parting shot. They would cut off Larnach's head, and 'stick it on the chimney piece'.

It was around midday when John Larnach heard a loud voice calling 'Come out of the water every bloody one of you, or we'll blow your bloody brains out'. Three of the convicts were armed, and approached, the others spread out to prevent the hated overseer's escape. They appeared keen to avoid wounding the others, urging the sheep washers to stand clear as they might be hit. Larnach hastily jumped into the water, took cover behind two of the unfortunate men, and called for them to stand fast with him.

He was waist deep when Hitchcock fired the first shot. There was a babble of confused shouts from the rebels:

Why don't you get out of the way, I would have shot him by now; Fire again – I'll take care you shall never punish another man; shoot the bugger; you will never take another man to Court; I'll blow your head off – you are a bloody old rogue; You villain, you tyrant, I'll make you remember flogging, I will, you tyrant.

Several more shots were fired, but the dual-charge flintlock weaponry of the period was notoriously unreliable, and the rebels were anxious not to hurt the innocent. In the general chaos, Larnach waded to the far bank, his boots and clothes so sodden with water that he stumbled and fell as he reached the edge. This probably saved his life.

The attackers assumed he was hit: 'Fire again, let us finish him', called out Poole and Hitchcock. 'He is almost finished', as a third shot rang out, 'fire again'. 'Don't', said another, 'but take care of your ammunition'. Larnach, in fact, escaped without a mark on him, and ran to the house of a neighbour. The convicts made for the bush, but not before they had turned the tables on another of the Hunter Valley's masters: stripping him, tying him to a post, flogging him with a cat-o-nine tails, and taunting him with 'how he liked it? and whether he would ever get another man flogged?'[4]

When the dust had settled, a government investigation found that Larnach's and Mudie's treatment of their convict servants had not been marked by any unusual 'harshness or oppression'. Mudie, it seems, was no worse than his neighbours.[5] This only underlines the banality of the misery he and Larnach had inflicted. 'I have seen the overseer take maggots off the meat', said one convict. The flour was poor, 'mixed with grass seed and smut', 'as black as a gentleman's hat', the clothing provided was often inadequate.[6] Life on the farm was a constant war of attrition between pilfering convicts and vengeful masters. It differed from countless others only in the co-ordinated violence of the rebels' response – and the political use to which it could be put.

The events at Castle Forbes were of that almost mundane brutality so familiar to many who suffered the convict system. Yet, in the words of historian Manning Clark, they 'led inexorably from a story of outrage on the frontiers of human civilization into a debate on the future of New South Wales'.[7] For all the sneers made by James Mudie about rotten branches, the tree of British liberty was sprouting fresh and green in the antipodes. With Britain locked in debates over the limits of freedom, two factions in colonial politics were squaring up in a propaganda contest of their own. Who could lay claim to 'the rights of freeborn Englishmen' in a penal colony? Castle Forbes would prove a gift for lobbyists of all stripes, and they were not alone. Equally self-interested was a convict called John Dow. Finding inspiration in the rebellion for his last and greatest role, Dow would be swept up in the struggle to direct the course of colonial destiny.

5

♪♫♪

A WILD AND DISTANT SHORE

Security of property! Behold, in a few words, the definition
of English liberty. And to this selfish principle every nobler
one is sacrificed.

Mary Wollstonecraft, *Vindication of the Rights of Men*, 1790

As the *Woodman* sailed up the Derwent River on a fair April
wind in 1826, Jorgen Jorgensen was moved by the changes in
the decades since his last visit. Where once there had been wilderness, now there were farms and cottages lining the shore,
with the town of Hobart approaching in the distance. Upon
the ship's arrival, the *Hobart Town Gazette* found a few individuals worth mentioning by name: Jorgensen was 'well known to
most of the prisoners in the Colony'. There was also a 'person
who comes out under the name of Dow *alias* Colquhoun, [who]
at the usual examination previous to debarkation stated that his
name was Lascelles, a son of Lord Harewood, and a cornet in
the 10th Hussars'. The antipodean masquerade had begun.

The morning after the *Woodman* anchored, the convicts
were landed in their prison clothes, and marched over to the

prisoners' barracks. There they were inspected by His Excellency, Colonel George Arthur, Lieutenant Governor of Van Diemen's Land, then in the second year of his office.[1] In the dutifully recorded register of convicts, the physical description of 'Dow, John, the younger, alias Colquhoun, alias John James Colquhoun' puts him as five foot five inches tall, with light brown receding hair, hazel eyes, and a large pockmark near to the left wrist joint. His 'trade' was given as 'Cornett 10th Hussars'. In all his roles, Dow stuck loyally to the 10th, the first hussar regiment in the British army. (Edward, as we know, was actually in the Yorkshire Hussars.) The prisoner gave his age as twenty-two and his 'native place' as 'Harewood'. Jorgensen's literacy and good conduct meant he was assigned work in the Naval Office, though he was the first to admit he was never much good at it. Dow's first assignment is unclear. In the *Woodman*'s disembarkation record the entry under 'how appropriated', meaning where he was assigned, is illegibly scratched out, with no replacement noted.[2]

'If thou be'st born to strange sights'

In less than a week, Dow would have some of the darker and more savage aspects of his new world thrust into his face. On the day the *Woodman* docked, sentence of death was pronounced upon twelve men convicted of bushranging. The group included Matthew Brady, whose daring exploits against the social pretensions of the Van Diemonian gentry had gained him much popular support. As Brady awaited sentencing, supporters garlanded his cell with flowers. Not so that of the most despised criminal in the colony, held in the same building. Thomas 'Monster' Jeffries, child murderer and cannibal, had torn a baby

A wild and distant shore

from its mother's arms and dashed out its brains against the trunk of a tree. Later, as would other convict escapees lost in the harsh Tasmanian wilderness, he had shot and partially eaten a compatriot before being recaptured. In the sensational trial, Mrs Tibbs confronted the 'insatiate murderers of her babe' and collapsed in shock before the horrified spectators.[3]

Matthew Brady and thirteen other convicts had made a daring escape by boat from the penal settlement of Sarah Island in Macquarie Harbour in June 1824. The authorities quickly gave chase. Pursuers and pursued sailed around the rugged western coast of the island, the former passing their quarry unawares. Nine days after the escape, the guards sailed up the Derwent and raised the alarm in Hobart Town. Next day the fugitives landed secretly on a deserted stretch of coastline and secured a cache of arms by force. While part of the gang was soon recaptured, Brady and the rest remained at large for almost two years, thumbing their noses at authority and, in contrast to Jeffries, gaining a reputation for chivalry towards women along the way. When the authorities posted a proclamation against the outlaws, gossip had it that Brady responded with his own notice on the door of a local inn: 'Mountain Home, 20 April 1826. It has caused Matthew Brady much concern that a person known as Colonel George Arthur is at large. Twenty gallons of rum is offered for him.'[4]

Governor Arthur ordered that all convicts in Hobart be present at Brady's execution on 5 May 1826. Some two to three thousand free citizens also came out, some to sympathise with Brady, others to see justice done on 'Monster' Jefferies (whom Brady had threatened to kill in prison). An unprecedented orgy of hangings would follow: 103 in Hobart between 1826 and 1827 alone, the bodies left to rot in the colony's gibbets as warnings to the populace. Arthur was determined to stamp out insurrection, and to bring forth a new colonial order.

Van Diemen's Land was fifteen years the junior of the parent colony to the north. When Dow arrived in 1826, the colony had achieved administrative independence from New South Wales only the year before. The British established a foothold on the southern side of the island in 1803, primarily as a result of concern for French interest in the region. This would become the town of Hobart. Famine menaced the first decade, and the settlement only survived because its inhabitants managed to live off the land. The government had perforce to relax a certain degree of control over its convicts, or the colony would have starved. Accompanied by their dogs, many of those supposedly under sentence spread out into the interior and made a living from hunting kangaroos. While the numbers of Europeans were small and impact on the land was light, relations with Indigenous people could remain relatively cordial. Centralised control was tenuous at best. The only effective response to stock theft was to hand over some control to convict stockkeepers, who then had an incentive to keep flocks safe. What emerged in the decade before Dow arrived in the colony was a cultural melting pot. It was the world of the eighteenth-century plebeian gone bush: clothed in animal skins, using Aboriginal land management and hunting techniques, and acknowledging as little obedience to government authority as it was possible to get away with.[5]

It was from this independent counter-culture of the frontier that a generation of bushrangers drew their support. Michael Howe, who styled himself 'Lieutenant Governor of the Woods', had posed the most serious challenge to official authority in the earlier years. Things got so bad that Lieutenant Gover-

A wild and distant shore

nor Davey lived under a state of virtual siege in Hobart Town. His own farm, Carrington Park, was repeatedly raided (Howe took a dictionary on one visit, saying he would return it on his next). Davey declared martial law, banned the traffic in kangaroo skins and clothing which was sustaining the bush convicts, and issued instructions that all dogs capable of hunting kangaroos be destroyed. The establishment should surely have known better than to think they could part a Briton from his dogs. Since watch dogs were exempted, the solution was simple: the island's rag-tag canines were hastily chained up and listed as such for the authorities.

Howe's bushrangers chose to mark Christmas Day 1816 at Carrington Park, calling on all present (Davey was sheltering in Hobart) 'to join them in a Yuletide drink or else suffer being shot for Christmas'. Howe's pretensions were more than mere cheek. Bushrangers were so much in league with individual settlers and officers as to pose a near-effective alternative to the governor's rule. Howe and his gang were eventually tracked down, in part through the efforts of his Aboriginal partner, known to the authorities as 'Black Mary'. The couple were supposed to have fallen out when Howe shot at Mary to avoid her being captured alive. In 1818 Howe was killed during an ambush, his head struck off and brought back in triumph to Hobart.[6]

The root of the bushranger problem lay in control over the pastoral interior of the island. Before the early 1820s nearly all Europeans, even convicts in Hobart, had ready access to unallocated land. But Arthur had the situation well in hand. It was to the free settlers that he looked to establish discipline and morality. And they would do so from the powerful promptings of self-interest.[7] A new land policy and a crackdown on

lawlessness would recast the colony along English lines, popu-
late its interior with gentry, and relegate the earlier inhabitants (both black and white) and their culture to the status of
savages whose day had passed. The defeat of Matthew Brady,
executed within days of Dow's arrival in the colony, saw the
end of the last bushranger emergency. Arthur's hangings sent a
clear signal that the governor was determined to exert control.

Violence alone, however, was not enough to remake the
island in a new image. The administration would do so with
the aid of a rush of new emigrants who would displace the
older bush culture of the Tasmanian frontier. The government
backed these arrivals (at least at first) precisely because their
self-interest made them such powerful allies. As they fought to
put themselves at the apex of an ordered social hierarchy, these
would-be gentry, so Arthur hoped, could sweep away the pandemonium of convict lawlessness.

'Spies and Bloodites!': the hopes and terrors of reform

For all their wealth and status, these new arrivals were also
refugees of a sort. An industrial juggernaut was sweeping away
their ordered gentrified world. Britain appeared to be facing
revolution. If they were to regain Arcadia, they would have to
make it anew in the antipodes.

The story of John Dow and Edward Lascelles is a drama
enacted across two continents, and one that goes well beyond
their individual lives. To put it another way, there 'can be no
satisfactory history of Britain without empire, and no satisfactory history of empire without Britain'.[8] Convicts like those on
board the *Woodman* certainly tasted the bitter fruits of exile as

A wild and distant shore

their ship sailed from home, but in another sense they never really left. When Dow landed in Hobart, he was stepping foot on what was the farthest edge of an interconnected British world, and his fate remained bound up in events unfolding in the place he had left behind. As the game was played out, those who have already crossed these pages – Edward Baines, Lord Milton, Earl Fitzwilliam – all took significant roles. Colonial society in Van Diemen's Land and New South Wales was about to be taken apart and put back together again in a radically new form. To understand how this came to be, we must return to the Yorkshire members of our cast once more.

Edward Baines and the *Leeds Mercury* emerged from the 'paper war' of the 1807 election with a solid reputation for reform-mindedness and Whig support, a mouth-piece for the urban middle class of the industrial north. Ten years later, Earl Fitzwilliam sent a page of the *Mercury* to Lord Grenville (former prime minister and Whig power-broker) and scribbled in the margin that the events there reported had put the paper 'in the hands of persons of every rank'.[9] The name Baines was suddenly on the lips of the entire kingdom.

In 1815, just a decade before Dow sailed up the Derwent, the battle of Waterloo saw Britain finally emerge victorious from the titanic struggle against Napoleon. But peace at home proved fleeting. The nation dropped into a profound economic depression as the war ended and continental manufacturing and food production began to pick up. The 1816 harvest was a disaster, industrial demand slumped. Misery and want stalked a country also dealing with the upheavals of mass demobilisation. Some 300 000 soldiers had returned by 1817 and unemployment was skyrocketing.[10]

Amidst the general distress, the men and women who survived by domestic cloth production were fighting a desperate rearguard action. In 1806 Wilberforce, Lascelles and the wool commission had effectively sanctioned their demise. The following decade, the battle would spill out of the Houses of Parliament and into torchlight processions and blackened faces on the moors. Across the textile districts, the machines that were destroying the livelihood of generations were themselves broken in Luddite protests. 'Throughout England', wrote Edward Baines the younger in his father's biography, 'there was uneasiness and apprehension, and the alarm was the greater because the danger was unseen'. As crowds of 10 000 or more assembled before men like Henry 'Orator' Hunt (brandishing a liberty cap atop a pikestaff at Spa Fields, London) rumours of uprisings, of plots and of revolution simmered constantly below the surface.

In 1816 the government formed two secret committees to investigate alleged seditious activities. Henry Lascelles, Wilberforce and Milton were all amongst the Commons members, as was Earl Fitzwilliam in the Lords. When Edward Baines himself came to write his history of these events, he insisted that their reports were misleading, their 'object being to establish the existence of a widely spread conspiracy against the government and constitution' by linking together a series of disparate and unconnected happenings into 'a regular and formidable plot'.[11] When the Prince Regent's coach was attacked in January 1817, *habeas corpus* was once more suspended, 'treasonous' meetings were banned, and printers of seditious material arrested.

Repressive legislation pushed political activity underground. This had the added and unwelcome effect of making it near-impossible for the authorities to garner accurate information. The government under Lord Liverpool had no regular police force, in the modern sense, and the line between the informer and the *agent provocateur* was indistinct. Being paid piecemeal for information meant there was an obvious incentive for spies to 'sex up' the threats upon which they reported. Nineteenth-century spymasters were not fools, and generally allowed for such practices. Nevertheless, it was a dangerous game for Liverpool and his Home Secretary, Lord Sidmouth, to be playing. Beliefs about British liberty must have seemed pretty hollow to many political Radicals who felt the brunt of government repression in 1817. But if we are to understand this period at all, we must understand, to quote historian EP Thompson, that there were 'limits beyond which authority did not dare to go'.[12]

Spying against one's own people was widely considered to be one of these limits: a sign of despotism, a betrayal of patriotic values. It was no accident, claimed the author of the 1817 pamphlet 'Spies and Bloodites!', that there was no English word for *agent provocateur*. The 'system of domestic espionage' was:

> as odious as it is unconstitutional, a system as directly at variance with the operations of a free government, as it is consonant with tyranny and despotism, a system which is of foreign, of *French* origin, for which, as a patriotic nobleman has remarked, our language has not even a name; forcing us to borrow from our enslaved neighbours its appellation.[13]

In the 1790s, Pitt had silenced critics of his domestic secret service by arguing that invasion was imminent, and that English democrats and French revolutionaries were all but one and the same.[14] In the aftermath of war with France, though, there was less tolerance for using spies.

On 6 June 1817 a group of men were arrested at Thornhill Lees in Yorkshire's West Riding, amongst them one William

Oliver, known to be a radical 'delegate' from London. Three days later, an armed rising of some 400 boys and men occurred in Pentrich, Derbyshire. It was quickly put down, but three leaders would be hanged and fourteen transported to Australia for life. Oliver, meanwhile, had attracted some unwanted attention. John Dickenson, a linen draper and radical sympathiser, who knew of the Thornhill arrests, was surprised to see Oliver at large some days later, boarding the Leeds coach when he was supposed to be in gaol. Oliver hastily explained that he had been released since no incriminating papers had been found on him. But it was at this point that Oliver was undone by a social gaffe. Keeping a clandestine watch, Dickenson saw a servant in livery go up to Oliver. This was unexceptional so far as it went, but then the servant doffed his hat, as to a gentleman, before opening a conversation. When Dickenson realised that the servant was employed by Major-General Sir John Byng, commander of the troops in the north, the game was up. A bookseller friend of Dickenson took the story to Edward Baines, and the editor began digging.[15]

In a series of sensational articles in the *Leeds Mercury*, Baines exposed 'William Oliver' (also known by the name WJ Richards) as a government agent. He would go down in history as the notorious 'Oliver the Spy'. Historians have debated the role of this 'archetype of the Radical Judas' ever since.[16] It seems clear he did not *cause* unrest in the region, notably the Pentrich rising, though he probably influenced its timing. What shocked readers of the *Mercury*, though, was that Oliver's reports had alerted the authorities. They could have stopped the Pentrich rising before it started, but they had permitted it to go ahead. Then they had used the uprising to further their repressive political ends. Baines himself, in the history he wrote three

A wild and distant shore

years after the events, probably gets the balance of government culpability pretty much correct:

> They sent him [Oliver] out, as they afterwards asserted, for the purpose of discovering treason, not of encouraging it: yet when they heard of his active instigation, his endeavours to organize a regular conspiracy, the extensive mischief he was producing, and the alarm felt by the magistracy, they forbade his course to be checked, and thus sanctioned his nefarious acts. The original commission to the spy might proceed from an error of judgement; but his continued employment, after this intimation, betrayed a greater anxiety to find grounds for renewing the suspension of the habeas corpus act, than to prevent the necessity for that measure.

Oliver's importance lies less in his activities as a spy than in his exposure as one. The public outrage prompted by his activities was, in retrospect, one more step on the path to reform. Baines's revelations ensured a quite different outcome from the activities of Sidmouth's agent than the one the Home Secretary had planned. Working-class activists were only too well aware of the government's use of informers. It was a tactic regularly used among industrial workforces, as also amongst convicts on the other side of the globe. For countless middle-class readers around the country, though, the information in the *Leeds Mercury* was a profound shock.

Baines's account of Oliver the Spy was printed in a special edition of the *Leeds Mercury* on 14 June 1817. Two days later it produced a 'strong sensation' when read in both Houses of Parliament.[17] This was however not the first that Fitzwilliam, as Lord Lieutenant of the West Riding, had heard of the spy, although Sidmouth had kept the matter very close. Amongst Fitzwilliam's correspondence is a copy of a letter from Sidmouth to Hugh Parker, magistrate of Sheffield, marked 'private and confidential' and dated 31 May. It reluctantly confirmed that 'O is employed by me – that he is travelling under my directions at this time'. Yet Baines's exposure of Oliver as an alleged *agent provocateur* deeply shocked Fitzwilliam, as it did many others, both powerful and humble. Sending a copy of the *Leeds Mercury* to his son, Fitzwilliam wrote:

> you have no idea of the sensation this paper has made
> in the country, indeed well it may, for the case calls for
> indignation – I will not say, I do not believe, that an agent
> was sent for the purpose of stimulating poor ignorant men
> to acts of insurrection or rebellion, but in my conscience I
> believe, that without his presence & his active incitement,
> insurrection w[oul]d never have taken place.

A day later Fitzwilliam wrote again to Milton, declaring that he had come around to his son's opposition to the suspension of *habeas corpus*: 'I have now seen so much of the extent of mischief here, & also of its cause, still a more important consideration, I sh[oul]d not hesitate to oppose what is not required by existing circumstances'.[18] The exposure of Oliver, wrote Fitzwilliam to Grenville, had caused a complete change in his opinion on the repressive measures adopted by the government. It would prove a decisive break between the two Whigs, but Fitzwilliam was adamant: 'I see no cause for the continuation of greater power than the ordinary ones, because I see no chance of disturbance if the people are left to themselves: if there are no Agents to incite them to mischief'.[19]

A wild and distant shore

Fitzwilliam was joining an increasing majority. In turning the tide of elite public opinion, it was perhaps Edward Baines's finest hour. *Habeas corpus* was restored in 1818, a year that brought a brief respite of domestic peace, but it did not last. The harvest was bad once more. Industry was still languishing. As was the case in Leeds, there was increasing frustration in growing industrial centres like Birmingham and Manchester that these cities had no representatives in Parliament to call their own. In August 1819, a crowd assembled at St Peter's Fields in Manchester to call for parliamentary reform. Estimates of numbers varied but there were upwards of 60 000 people present to hear the speakers, chief amongst them 'Orator' Hunt.

On a hot summer's day, many took advantage of the spectacle for a family outing. Bands played, flags and banners waved, many were dressed in their best, as for a gala occasion. Countless women and children were present, but the magistrates, fearing a riot, sent in mounted yeomanry to arrest Hunt. It was a fatal mistake. The crowd cheered in support of Hunt, the horses panicked, the yeomanry charged. Edward Baines the younger, aged nineteen and on the hustings with Hunt that day, escaped the fatal bottleneck with his life. Others did not. In the chaos that followed, eleven people were killed: shot, cut down by sabres and trampled to death. Some six hundred more were maimed and injured. A mere twenty minutes later, the field was empty, save for the dead and dying, lying amongst the scattered hats, shoes and musical instruments abandoned in desperate flight.[20] In blackly ironic reference to the final great victory against Napoleon, the incident became known as 'Peterloo'.

As protest meetings against the Peterloo massacre began to sweep the country, Sidmouth, as Home Secretary, defended the actions of the magistrates in dispersing a seditious gathering. Then he sat tight, waiting to see whether prominent members of society would break ranks. The first to do so was an unpleasant surprise. Earl Fitzwilliam, Lord Lieutenant of the West Riding, might have been a Whig, but he was still a pillar of the establishment. He was also, it was easy for Sidmouth to assume, distracted, caught up in preparations for the major event of Yorkshire's racing calendar.[21]

In the pantheon of Fitzwilliam's house, the gods of turf had always stood high. Wentworth's stables were so large that if grooms walked to the house for a drink, they complained they were thirsty again by the time they returned.[22] Covering more than two acres, the stables had been built, so rumour had it, entirely from the winnings of Rockingham's most famous racehorse, Whistlejacket. In the house itself, the Whistlejacket Room, a Palladian wonder forty-foot square, was designed to set off the stallion's portrait. George Stubbs's masterpiece (now in London's National Gallery) was a fitting centrepiece; so lifelike, said admirers, that the canvas had nearly been destroyed when the subject tried to attack his own image.[23]

Yet for all this family obsession, Sidmouth had miscalculated. Even in the midst of a dispute with the stewards of the Jockey Club over a false start, Fitzwilliam organised a protest meeting calling for a government inquiry into Peterloo. Held on 14 October in the York Castle Yard, site of the son's famous 1807 election victory, the gathering now became the occasion for the father to enact a high-profile political martyrdom. No sooner did Sidmouth hear of the meeting than he asked for, and got, Fitzwilliam's resignation as lord lieutenant. Henry

A wild and distant shore

Lascelles, Milton's former rival, was appointed in his stead.

In the immediate aftermath of Peterloo, parliamentary reform seemed further off than ever before. In 1819 Lord Liverpool's government passed the so-called 'Six Acts' that further suppressed public assembly and 'seditious' meetings. Magistrates received extended powers of search and arrest. The authorities categorised all cheap publications as newspapers, thus imposing a fourpenny stamp duty, in the hope that this would place them beyond the means of working people. But if Peterloo was a tragedy, in the longer term it was also a gift for the reform-minded liberal Whigs under Lord Grey. These were the men to whom Milton had been increasingly drawn, but of whom his father was more wary. Grey's challenge was to steer a course through the factional waters breaking around him. Even by the standards of the day, the Whigs were still an extremely loose alliance. If they were ever to come out of opposition, they needed to stop pulling in different directions. The debate over Peterloo conveniently split off the right-wing faction of the party under Grenville. It was a cause that naturally belonged to the Radicals, but Grey's strategy was to attract support away from them in order to overturn the government without their help.[24]

Fitzwilliam played a crucial role in eclipsing the Radicals and securing the issue of Peterloo for the centre of his party. His presence at the meeting in York did much to convince more moderate sentiment that Peterloo had been an outrage. His dismissal from the lord lieutenancy for supporting this matter of principle only compounded the government's poor reputation, and made the old Whig a temporary hero. In 1795 Fitzwilliam had himself been in command of a yeomanry troop that rode down a protest gathered in Sheffield. But his views were changing. The events of two years previously, when Baines had exposed Oliver the Spy, profoundly shocked him. It was the beginning of a transformation that would bring father and son into closer political alignment. The year of Peterloo saw Milton's official and public conversion to what he had probably believed in private for far longer: the cause of parliamentary reform, the dismantling of the rotten boroughs, and the enfranchisement of the new industrial towns. With his calculated attack on the events in Manchester, 1819 also saw Fitzwilliam's somewhat 'grudging acquiescence', in the words of his biographer, to the same measures.[25]

Milton had to tread a delicate path between his father's political principles and his own growing conviction of the need to support reform. The pair had always been close, and Milton had found their difference of opinion on this issue very hard, writing that while on ordinary political matters he had no scruples in acting against Fitzwilliam, on this one his father felt so strongly that it was painful to go against him. Fitzwilliam, for his part, wrote to Grey:

> I cannot bring myself to indifference, when I contemplate how much his [Milton's] influence and efficiency may be thrown away, when he becomes a prominent supporter of parliamentary reform, for from that instant he becomes the tool and slave of every worthless adventurer. He is born aristocratic, that is his station in the country; one that enables him if he acts in that sphere, to defend the rights and liberties of the people, whom he ought to consider as under his special care and guardianship.[26]

It would be hard to find a better distillation of eighteenth-century Whig ideas about status, power and liberty. According to

A wild and distant shore

these lights, aristocratic birth endowed one with a paternalistic responsibility to protect the people from the tyranny of both autocracy above and the mob below. Milton had been born into the very heart of Grand Whiggery, an intermarried cousinhood of five extraordinarily wealthy and politically influential families – the Cavendishes, Ponsonbys, Howards, Spencers and Fitzwilliams.[27] But as early as 1796, when Milton was a child of ten, his father seems to have realised, perhaps only dimly, that these days were drawing to a close. Fitzwilliam had then written to a disciple of Edmund Burke, the Whig politician and philosopher, who had recommended the boy take a course of reading in English constitutional history: 'he is growing up in awkward times; God knows what rank in society he has to fill; but it is our duty to proceed with him, and fit him to fill that rank to which he was born.'[28]

By 1822, when he expressed his concerns about Milton's future to Grey, Fitzwilliam was increasingly becoming an anachronism, a throw-back to an earlier era of Whig politics. It was precisely this reputation that made his Peterloo conversion in 1819 of such strategic importance in attracting the moderates. It was with men like Baines, with the rising commercial and professional classes, that the future of the Whig party really lay, and Milton, for one, could see it. In the following decade, he was at the centre of a group of noblemen known as the 'Young Whigs', men who would play an important part in the evolution of the party into the Liberals of the Victorian era.[29] Those childhood lessons in constitutional history had clearly borne fruit.

In retrospect it was clear that these political realignments would be important for the parliamentary reforms of the next decade. In their fear of revolution from below, the aristocracy

Antipodes

would unbend sufficiently to incorporate the political ambitions of the rising middle classes. This self-interested embrace between the propertied would spawn the 1832 Reform Act. In the shorter term, though, Peterloo seemed one of a series of seismic shocks to the ordered arrangement of existence. Prime Minister Spencer Perceval, who had taken office in the 1807 election, was assassinated in the lobby of the House of Commons in 1812. There were the Luddite disturbances of the same year, riots against the laws restricting the sale of corn in 1815, the 'Pentrich Revolution' (supposedly fomented by Oliver) in 1817, the Peterloo massacre of 1819, and the 'Cato Street Conspiracy' to assassinate government ministers a year later. The repressive 'Six Acts' were an expression of increasing panic.

Flight of the would-be gentry

It was these events that would turn the development of New South Wales and Van Diemen's Land in a new direction. Those who had the wherewithal to help themselves out of the mess at home began to cast their glance over the seas to Britain's colonies. And their anxieties dovetailed neatly with some pressing administrative concerns: costs must be cut, and convict transportation must be made a proper deterrent in uncertain times. For those tempted to defy the law, exile to a penal colony must be reaffirmed as an object of terror, not a paradise of unfettered opportunity.

If, amidst the birth pangs of an industrial society, the poor were suffering real want, many on higher rungs of the social ladder were finding their perch increasingly precarious. These 'pseudo gentry', as some historians have called them, feared loss of caste. They were dogged by financial insecurity, made

A wild and distant shore

worse by the fact that they had been born, bred and educated to a lifestyle that required an income, preferably one grounded in land.[30] Officers released from service on half pay, younger sons stymied by primogeniture, men of limited property with numerous and hopeful offspring: these were the emigrants who left for Britain's settler colonies in the 1820s. They knew that if they stayed in England they would drop from the ranks of gentlemen. In the colonies they would not only have greater economic opportunities, they would be automatically placed in the first class of those new societies. Many marshalled what claims on patronage they had at their command and found their way into the imperial civil service across the globe. Those who contemplated a move to the Australian colonies swallowed their anxiety about living amidst the social refuse of Britain's criminal classes, and took its advantages to heart.

For reasons of its own, the government was eager to oblige them. In 1817, the year of Oliver's exposure and the Pentridge rising, the Secretary of State for the Colonies, Lord Bathurst, determined on an investigation into the transportation system. He was concerned that it did not act as a sufficient deterrent to crime, that it did not reform offenders and (to add insult to injury) that it was costing far more than it ought. John Thomas Bigge, former chief justice of Trinidad, was despatched to the antipodes to head a wide-ranging Commission of Enquiry. Bigge arrived in Sydney in 1819 and over the course of the following years his investigation poked its nose into every conceivable aspect of colonial life. Under the sympathetic administration of Governor Lachlan Macquarie, many former convicts had managed to acquire wealth and become more or less incorporated into the general population. This was the moment 'the empire struck back'.[31] (It would set a precedent brilliantly exploited by John Dow, dubbed 'a second Bigge' by the Sydney press in 1834.[32]) Three detailed volumes of evidence were published before the House of Commons in 1822 and 1823. And this was only the beginning. Bigge would spend the best part of a decade travelling the British empire, producing voluminous reports not only on New South Wales but also on Mauritius, Ceylon and the Cape of Good Hope.

The Bigge investigations confirmed a widely held fear amongst the propertied in Britain: in the midst of social upheaval, when the threat of transportation was needed more than ever before, balmy reports from the antipodes could act as an encouragement to crime. Bigge complained that Macquarie had treated former convicts ('emancipists') with too much leniency. Favourable circumstances meant they could enrich themselves and reclaim or even improve their rank in society. A raft of new legislation tightening up discipline was designed to reverse this trend. There would be fewer indulgences for those under sentence, and fewer pardons. Emancipists were to be kept from public office or social preferment. Convicts would no longer receive land grants after the expiry of their sentence; the government would encourage emigrants with capital instead.[33]

If a man had sufficient funds as well as testimonials as to his respectability, he could now proceed to New South Wales or Van Diemen's Land where, in return for employing convicts, he would receive a grant of land in proportion to his wealth. Bonded labour would be provided to make that land productive. The new master would become part of the apparatus of punishment recommended by Bigge. His authority would help instil the proper degree of terror to potential offenders in Britain. His ambitions would ensure convicts laboured through

A wild and distant shore

their years of punishment rather than working for their own benefit. Work on a master's rural property would keep convicts away from town pleasures. Since he needed to feed and clothe the convicts assigned to him, the master's capital would help defray the costs of administering the whole system. Britain's would-be gentry were hardly the worst off amongst those suffering the traumas of industrialisation. But their want supplied an imperial need. And so it was that landed wealth, that rock-solid basis of social status, was offered to them for the asking. Unto those who had, more would be given.[34]

Prominent amongst such imperial opportunists was James Mudie of Castle Forbes, to whose story we now return. Mudie arrived in 1822, one of a wave of emigrants who added a new layer to the colonial elite. Those who were already in place and busily feathering their nests included many former army officers and colonial officials. Amongst them was even one Thomas Allen Lascelles (1783–1859), who had arrived in New South Wales in 1811 with the 73rd Regiment and departed for Van Diemen's Land two years later. He was appointed private secretary to Lieutenant Governor Thomas Davey and, like many of his contemporaries, took ruthless advantage of his government connections. In later years Van Diemen's Land would be decried as the 'Sodom and Gomorrah' of the British Empire. It was a moral panic that had more to do with propaganda against transportation than it had to do with the incidence of sex between men.[35] In fact, the island's chief transgression against the state had always been embezzlement. With his hand in the till up to the elbow, Thomas Allen Lascelles made judicious misuse of government labour and provisions, and managed to escape prosecution for both. He resigned his commission in 1814 and farmed extensive grants of land received from the state. By the time John Dow was serving out his sentence in Van Diemen's Land and claiming descent from the house of Harewood, Thomas was proving himself a controversial police magistrate and justice of the peace, relieved of office after only two years on the grounds of malpractice, whereupon he briefly took on a role increasingly common in these pages, that of rabble-rousing newspaper editor. Unlike Dow, Thomas's relation to the Harewood dynasty was genuine, albeit extremely distant. However tenuous the connection, though, antipodean society was not allowed to forget it. In this place of relentless social one-upmanship, Thomas Allen's grandson was duly christened Edward Harewood Lascelles in 1847.

The new policies encouraging capitalist emigration made it increasingly difficult for poorer emigrants to make it under their own steam. Land regulations of 1825 and 1828 were explicitly designed to prevent settlers without sufficient capital from acquiring land. The period in which new immigrants were eligible for government rations was cut down from six months to two months, and then stopped altogether. Through the 1820s, what suitable land was left on the island was granted with almost reckless abandon in an attempt to promote capitalist immigration. In six years, Lieutenant Governor Arthur handed over more than a million acres. Speculators profitted and many settlers inflated the value of assets they had brought to the colony in order to secure grants. By 1832 most of the best land in the southern colony had already been given away.[36] The possibilities for those on the margins of society were receding. When government policy shifted direction once more in the 1830s, and began selling Crown land to finance assisted immigration amongst the deserving poor, the change came too late to have a real impact in Van Diemen's Land. Large landholdings

A wild and distant shore

worked by bonded labour were already characteristic of the island, and this was the pattern that stuck. It would be otherwise in New South Wales.

The vast government-sponsored land grab by would-be Tasmanian gentry coincided with the ruthless conquest and attempted destruction of the island's Indigenous population. The wool factories that Wilberforce and Lascelles had authorised were cranking up production and the country's flocks could not keep pace with an insatiable demand for wool. Between 1810 and 1850, Britain's imports of fleece increased tenfold and an growing proportion came from the antipodes. Industrial progress had destroyed Yorkshire's domestic weavers. Now these same forces would deprive another and very different community of its livelihood also. As the tragedy unfolded, in most cases these new victims would lose their lives as well. In the war against Australia's Aboriginal peoples, sheep would prove 'the shocktroops of land seizure'.[37] In Van Diemen's Land, the die was largely cast by the time of Dow's arrival. The colony had never known peace, as such, but while the number of whites competing for resources was small, some kind of accommodation with the Indigenous inhabitants could be reached. By the middle of the 1820s, most of the best Aboriginal hunting land in Van Diemen's Land had been distributed to Europeans under freehold title and was beginning to see intensive use by permanent settlers. The days of shared land use and co-operation between races, however self-interested it might have been, were no more. There was a change in the balance of power on the frontier, for the new settlers had the money, arms and manpower to back up their claims in a way the earlier itinerant bushmen could not.

In recent years, frontier conflict in Australia, particularly on the island of Tasmania, has been the subject of heated debate by historians, politicians and the public. Here I will say only that any account that does not acknowledge the violent and deliberate dispossession of Australia's Indigenous population is deeply unconvincing. One of the most recent analyses of Van Diemen's Land, by historian James Boyce, mounts the plausible argument that the murders there were mostly conducted by small-scale armed parties of men who knew the environment and ways of the Aboriginal Tasmanians intimately. This took place well before these activities were sanctioned by the proclamation of martial law in 1828 and before the formation of official military parties.[38] It was, ironically, the skilled bushmen of the previous era of colonisation who would pave the way for the gentry's conquest of the island. Those whose hands had done the actual killing would find the land wrested from them in turn.

Public works and colonial morality: 'Lascelles' turns informer

Outlaws, child murderers, cannibals, a swathe of executions, bodies swaying upon the gibbet, all in the midst of a bloody frontier war: we cannot know if Dow was cowed by the horrors that confronted him within days of his arrival in Van Diemen's Land. What is certain is that he kept his head down for most of his seven-year sentence there. Since it is only in court that he emerges with any clarity, his success in keeping out of trouble means we know very little of him during this time. His official prisoner conduct record is sparse. From those who later testified against him in court, we know he had a short stint as a clerk in the dry store of the government engineer's depart-

A wild and distant shore

ment in Launceston, the colony's main northern outpost, but he was soon after dismissed 'on account of bad penmanship, and bad orthography'. He seems to have remained assigned to the colony's Public Works department, as he was subsequently employed as gatekeeper at the lumber yard in Launceston. It was known in the town that he claimed to be Viscount Lascelles, and he persuaded one resident to carry letters to London under that name.[39] His sole offence as transportee (confined for four weeks in the penitentiary in February 1831) was for allowing one Eliza Davis to come into the yard without permission.[40]

In 1828, however, three letters arrived for Governor Arthur, signed 'Lascelles' in a bold hand. These place Dow at the Middle Arm lime quarry, though his official record makes no mention of him being there. The quarry was situated north of Launceston, about twenty kilometres from George Town at the mouth of Port Dalrymple on the Tamar River, the northern-most edge of the island. Dow's letters to Arthur give us some hint of his life on the public works. The writer would, he explained, have written before, but 'I could not upon the account of not having paper being in this deserted place of misery'. It *was* an isolated spot. Convicts were stationed around the various inlets of Port Dalrymple as timber sawyers and lime gatherers. Lime was quarried and carried back to George Town to be burnt at the brick kilns there. Despite Governor Macquarie previously declaring that George Town should be the headquarters of the north coast settlement, development there had languished, and the town had only some five or six hundred inhabitants, 'destitute of even the necessities of life' when district headquarters were moved south to Launceston in 1825.[41]

Provided with a few sheets by a 'friend', Dow felt it his 'duty' to address the governor on two issues. The first was a conspiracy he had unearthed amongst his fellow convicts to steal government tools and throw them in the river. This was a plot allegedly hatched by the assistant overseer, George Morgan, the object being to take revenge upon the chief overseer, Kerrigan, whose place Morgan would then take. Dow enclosed the testimony of three other convicts, men, he assured the governor without a hint of irony, of 'good moral characters'. He complained that Morgan had escaped punishment, even when the men had gone to Kerrigan and alerted him. Though signing the letter 'Lascelles', the writer made sure that his 'duty' would be recognised by helpfully explaining 'I am convicted by the name of John Dow'.[42]

The second problem occupying Dow was an issue of morality. He made haste to write, knowing the governor's character for 'putting a stop if possible to every wicked and obnoxious practice – which the following is the most infamous'. Evidently Dow, that pillar of respectability, was concerned about the relations between boatmen and convict women being transferred down the Tamar River from Launceston to the Female Factory at George Town. The 'factory' (so-called as its female internees were set to work making clothes and shoes, though the inmates' obedient respectability was a hoped-for by-product), had been in operation since the first years of the 1820s. In 1824 there were complaints that it was a small and inconvenient building with no place for the women to sleep. The boatmen obviously had a few suggestions to make.

Nor, complained Dow, was the sex the worst of it. The women's language was:

> such as my capacity cannot describe nor give your
> Excellency the distinct idea of – rather could I before

A wild and distant shore

conceive that such discourse could proceed from the Human mind and I am confident that its physically impossible that such an invective speech of undecorum could be more expressed by either sex.

When Dow challenged the captain, 'he only laught at my insinuation and gloryd in it as a bravado'. This 'horrid intercourse', claimed Dow, 'has been carrying on a considerable length of time without being cognized'. He assured the governor that he had 'no pecuniary interest, nor tincture motive' in thus addressing him, 'but an ardent desire if possible to put an end to such wicked and pernicious practices'. He ended with a pious hope of turning the minds of prisoners to the path of 'duty towards *God*' that 'a reformation may be observed in their moral characters'. Two years after Dow's complaints, an investigation into the George Town female factory felt that the institution was not performing its purpose of filling women with a dread of being punished there. The local press complained that the boats conveying the women down river were more in the nature of a pleasure cruise of licentiousness, stopping along the way at all the huts and cabins of the convict sawyers.[43]

If Dow's penmanship and orthography was indeed faulty (as these letters painfully underline), he had not lost his ability to match his tale to his audience. Arthur, a fervent evangelical, was a man much concerned with Christian morality. The governor saw the moral improvement and discipline of the convicts to be the main point of the government of the colony. His administration, indeed, was conducted with a 'sense of public duty so lofty that ordinary mortals could scarcely encompass it'.[44] It made him many enemies, not least amongst local officials like Thomas Allen Lascelles who had spent years happily

Antipodes

helping themselves to government resources.

What Dow hoped to achieve for himself (as we must assume was his real object) in writing to Arthur is unclear. The letters did prompt investigations, and Dow wrote once more on 23 March thanking the governor for looking into the matter, underlining the purity of his own motives, and again giving instances of his 'duty' towards the authorities. Having recovered a stash of stolen nails 'I immediately give thame [sic] to Bennett the overseer for so doing I became obvious to my fellow prisoners and solicited Bennett to allow me to sleep in the Jail as I was in danger of my life'.[45] There is no evidence that Dow ever bettered his own circumstances by this correspondence. The letters were duly lodged amongst the interminable correspondence of the penal regime. They were similarly filed away in the recesses of their author's fertile imagination. Years later, Dow would pull out this correspondence between his excellency and his lordship to serve a quite different purpose.

Once his seven-year sentence expired in 1832, Dow was free to take his destiny in hand once more. He made his way first to Hobart, where the majority of the colony's population lived. There he was a regular attendant at the town's principal church, St David's, and was later remembered as a 'little prim gentleman, of rather an eccentric, poetic appearance', some thirty years old but balding despite it. He approached the *Hobart Town Courier* with several poems he hoped to get published, chiefly in praise of local dignitaries, but the paper declined. With his tongue firmly in his cheek, the editor later explained that 'we did not conceive that the taste of our readers (they belonging principally to the middling classes) would be able to reach or relish the very *recherché* aristocratic flavour of his Lordship's literary olio'.[46]

A wild and distant shore

The under-appreciated poet of the lumber yard and the lime quarry did not remain in Van Diemen's Land for long after his sentence expired. Perhaps he was too well known in that colony for his aristocratic identity to really take wing. On board the aptly named schooner *Defiance*, Dow departed Hobart for Sydney in 1833. Setting some distance between the island of his penal servitude and his Lascelles persona, Dow could make himself over once more. There was the flavour of new possibilities in the air. A new era, as much as a new colony, would offer wider opportunities for his talents.

Advocating 'the Rights of my Country'

Some two years earlier, in October 1831, a large proportion of Sydney woke to the blinding pain of a collective hangover. Governor Ralph Darling was departing for England, and celebrations had gone on deep into the night. Some four thousand people converged on the mansion of Vaucluse House on the harbour's eastern shore. There the multitude got stuck into free food and drink and danced to the cheeky strains of 'Over the Hills and Far Away'. Heavy rain put paid to plans for illuminations and fireworks but could not dampen their spirits: the party at Vaucluse roared on. The editor of the *Sydney Gazette* despaired of conveying any idea of the pandemonium, the 'bawling, screeching, blaspheming, thumping, bumping, kicking, licking, tricking, cheating, beating, stealing, reeling, breaking of heads, bleeding of noses, blackening of eyes, picking of pockets and what not'.[47] An ox and half a dozen sheep were roasted and distributed to the populace. The beer and gin flowed like water. If the bacchanal at Vaucluse sounds like an antipodean version of the largesse the Fitzwilliams distributed from Wentworth House at times of rejoicing, this is no accident. The host of these Sydney revels was a man whose name carries a familiar ring.

Like many in the colony, William Charles Wentworth had a shady past. His father had escaped transportation by a hair's breadth and chosen exile instead, his mother was a convict, and young William had been born out of wedlock. Yet he also had powerful connections. D'Arcy Wentworth, his father, surgeon and sometime highwayman (arrested on Hounslow Heath with the proverbial black mask in his pocket) was distantly related to Earl Fitzwilliam. When D'Arcy managed to wriggle out of a series of charges, Fitzwilliam himself paid for his troublesome kinsman to depart for New South Wales in 1789. It marked the beginning of an extended patronage from the earl towards the antipodean Wentworths. Tall, broad-shouldered, coarse-featured and slovenly dressed, over the course of more than three decades William Charles would stride across colonial politics like a colossus. In 'selecting the Profession of the Law', he explained to Fitzwilliam in 1817, 'I calculate upon acquainting myself with all the Excellence of the British Constitution, and hope, at some future period, to advocate successfully the Rights of my Country to a participation in its Advantages'.[48]

In pursuit of this goal to make, as he put it, 'a new Britannia' in the antipodes, men like Wentworth had come up against Governor Darling, who found talk of the 'rights of Englishmen' in penal colonies to be 'absurd'. In this Darling was at one with Lieutenant Governor Arthur to the south. For both governors, convicts and emancipists had forfeited such rights by the crimes that had led to their transportation. By choosing to seek 'advantages' in a penal colony, as Darling put it, free emigrants too had chosen to 'voluntarily surrender' them.[49]

A wild and distant shore

Darling could not envisage, in the 'peculiar' system of a penal colony, any sense that the freedoms of the British constitution should hold sway. As he put it in a secret and confidential despatch to the Colonial Office in 1827, 'The evil of this place is the passion, which exists, that New South Wales should be the Counterpart of England'.[50]

By the late 1820s, though, Darling was fighting a rearguard action. For all the draconian measures that undoubtedly characterised penal societies, the germs from which a free colony would grow were already taking hold. The first independent newspaper in New South Wales, *The Australian*, was founded by none other than William Charles Wentworth, and his fellow Sydney barrister Robert Wardell in 1824. It was a strategic action in the battle for a species of public opinion that linked the empire together and included audiences from Sydney to London. In the absence of an elected colonial legislature, the press and the courtroom were the stages on which men of influence could enact their calls for constitutional change. 'The People are taught by the Papers', complained Darling, 'to talk about the rights of Englishmen and the free institutions of the Mother Country, Many of them forgetting their actual Condition'.[51]

Cases of seditious or criminal libel against their newspapers only allowed editors to just as publicly defend themselves in court with all the rhetoric of English liberty at their command. These courtroom pyrotechnics were of course then given top billing in their own papers, laid out for the benefit of the increasingly powerful reform lobby in London as much as for those in Sydney who were unable to squeeze into the court building itself. The courts were becoming, in Darling's own words, a 'theatre for vilifying the Governor and Government of the Colony, and holding up both to the Contempt and hatred of the Public'.[52] As historian Alan Atkinson puts it, Wentworth was blind 'to the most obvious and bloody feud in Australia'; that between the invading Europeans and the Indigenous inhabitants. Instead, it was the 'exclusives', that clique of patronage-dependent officials and self-interested landowners, who would play the villain in the drama of liberty being staged before British public opinion.[53]

Francis Forbes, the colony's Chief Justice, was sympathetic to the rights of the press, an attitude that caused great friction between him and Governor Darling. Darling was instructed by the Secretary of State to bring the colonial press, increasingly critical of the administration, under control. His methods were licensing laws and actions for seditious libel (a crime involving criticising officials with the aim of fomenting disaffection against government) but they would not prove easy to implement, in part because of Forbes's attitude. The editors of the *Australian* and the *Sydney Monitor* were soon in and out of court, but attacks on Darling's administration continued. The *Monitor* was a most irritating thorn in the government's flesh through the 1820s. Its editor, Edmund Smith Hall, proved remarkably adept at editing his paper while incarcerated, oscillating between the Supreme Court, where he was convicted for seditious libel, and the cell whence he returned to write more of the same.[54]

Edward Smith Hall, freeborn Englishman

Edward Smith Hall was a man not easily cowed: a poignant irony, given the role he is to play in John Dow's adventures. A self-declared 'radical' and 'reformer', Hall was much influenced by William Wilberforce in the years before he left Eng-

A wild and distant shore

land for New South Wales. Arriving in 1811, Hall contributed greatly to the richness of Sydney's public life, even when he wasn't editing the *Monitor* from gaol. His criticism of the power and privilege of the established church, for example, led to an 1828 confrontation with Archdeacon Thomas Hobbes Scott, head of the Church of England in Australia and one of Darling's cronies. When the *Monitor* launched a blistering attack on government privileges extended to the Anglican Church, with sideswipes at a man 'bred among politicians and merchants', Scott coolly decided upon an idiosyncratic revenge. He locked Hall, a widower, and his eight children out of their spacious pew in St James' Church and assigned them another in a 'cold and bleak' corner near the door. Nothing daunted, the agile Hall did a 'leap-frog' into his pew, forced the door and lifted his little daughters in after him. The beadles were outraged, but Hall taunted them from the pages of the *Monitor*: 'make not my Father's house a step-stone to worldly rank and etiquette'. Carpenters were called in to board up the disputed seats and constables were placed in the church to keep the peace. Many 'will doubtless be highly diverted with the running fight and the light infantry movements of the Knights of the Staff, and the Parishioner and his family', scoffed Hall, promising to camp in the aisles with his numerous family and warning that the crowds in church were sure to be prodigious: 'the charms of a game at *fisty-cuffs* in such a place, being more attractive even than Mr. Pearson's organ'.[55]

Matters then moved out of the church and into the Supreme Court, conveniently next door. Scott sued Hall for trespass, and got one shilling damages. Hall sued Scott for same, and won damages at £25. But Scott ultimately got off best when he sued Hall for criminal libel and won, making the editor the first to be convicted in the colony of libelling a public official. The fine was only twenty shillings, with imprisonment until it was paid, but Hall was required to enter into a good behaviour bond to the sum of £500 for the next twelve months.[56] Hall spent most of the following year in gaol, fighting criminal and seditious libel charges and producing the *Monitor* from his cell. But for all his bravado, he never fully recovered from the financial trials of 1829. Five years later, he would play an unexpected part in Dow's story when lack of funds drove the editor into the arms of a most unlikely political bedfellow: one James Mudie of Castle Forbes.

With Darling's departure in 1831, though, this dark future must have seemed improbable. 'HE'S OFF!' blazed from the windows of the *Monitor*'s offices in triumph, 'THE REIGN OF TERROR ENDED'.[57] Governor Richard Bourke, Darling's replacement, was widely anticipated as bringing a reversal in government policy. By the 1830s, with a two-party system largely in place in Britain, politics in the antipodes tended to be a more rough and ready mirror of the game at home. Those who had been Tories in the mother country coalesced around the 'exclusive' faction and sought to keep political power and social influence out of the hands of the 'emancipist' party. Darling had largely supported them. Emancipists included not only former convicts but also those who were their political allies, men who would have adhered to Whig or Radical factions in Britain.

For those, like Hall, who sought the rights of freeborn Englishmen at home and abroad, the new governor seemed a harbinger of a great change. Richard Bourke, who would hold the post from 1831 to 1837, was a Whig of reformist views, and the first liberal governor of New South Wales. Though the appointment had been made by the Tories, Bourke took office

A wild and distant shore

in Sydney just as Lord Grey's Whigs finally came out of opposition in London. The great Reform Act of 1832 was imminent.
The balance of power was about to shift – and John Dow's
fertile imagination was ready for it. The economy was boom-
ing, and there was many an opportunistic hope that a swindler
could use to his advantage.

'Pedigree and connections': colonial status anxiety

Dow's swindles were a frequent source of humour, at least for
those who had not suffered from them. The Clarkes were ridiculed in the Dumfries courtroom for being taken in. The anger
of those caught out in Sydney prompted similar amusement
during the 1835 trial for fraud: 'Mr Maclehose in giving his evidence completely lost his temper, and excited the laughter of
the whole court on many occasions … it was evident he had
been much disappointed in his *ci devant* Lordship.' The loss of
Francis Prendergast's turkeys to 'his Lordship's appetite' was
cause for ironic comment, and the *Herald*'s verbatim report of
James Roberts's testimony indicate how much his evidence was
enjoyed by the audience:

> I never saw a nobleman before – (*a laugh*) – I thought the
> prisoner appeared something above the common sort –
> (*repeated laughter*) … I don't think I would have taken his
> cheque, if I had not thought he was a Lord – (*a laugh*) – I
> really thought he was a Lord, *by the tremendous sway of gold
> chain he had about his neck.* – (*repeated laughter*) – I thought
> the *title* and his appearance sufficient guarantee for the
> payment of the money.

How self-conscious was this Sydney tittering? Everyone in the trial, from the judge down, seemed more than usually anxious to demonstrate that *they* could read the signs of rank and status correctly, that they knew the true nobility from the false. The laughter of spectators signalled assurance in the most public way possible that they were in on the joke. It was given an added edge by the widely acknowledged belief that in a convict society, people were not always what they seemed. 'Is it not a very usual thing', asked Dow during his 1835 trial, 'with persons who fall into *misfortune* and commit crime, in order to shield their family and connections from disgrace, to adopt an assumed name? is it not very common with prisoners in this Colony?'[58]

An Austrian baron, Charles von Hügel, included several diverting stories about Lascelles's imposture in his reminiscences of a visit to New South Wales between 1833 and 1834, and considered his anecdotes 'highly characteristic of the country in which it took place'.[59] Of course, we need look no further than Dow himself to see that imposture could flourish as much in Britain as it could in the colonies. Yet the idea that 'a change in hemispheres will reverse reputations' was common enough to add a distinct dimension to a trial about aristocratic identity in 1830s New South Wales.[60] When Dow was finally arrested for defrauding Roberts in January of 1835, the story of his career as a viscount was going to touch an entire society on the raw.

By the time Dow left Sydney on his tour of the interior in the early autumn of 1834, his adventures had left a trail of disappointed hopes. Knowingly or not, amongst the first was a kind of parody of the real Edward's clandestine romance. 'Lord Viscount Lascelles' had already been mentioned as a would-be poet in the Sydney press (the *Gazette* did not think much of his

A wild and distant shore

offerings).[61] Perhaps the women of Sydney would be less discerning. In April 1833 he eloped with Lilius Dickson, daughter of a fellow Scot; the engineer, miller and entrepreneur, John Dickson.

Dickson was a wealthy man, though his private life was somewhat irregular. He was, it was said, 'a notorious atheist', who had left a wife behind in Scotland. Lilius and her brothers and sisters were born of a long-standing liaison between Dickson and his convict 'housekeeper'. When Dickson found out about his daughter's intimacy with an aristocratic suitor, said Justice James Dowling (who presided over the subsequent court action), he 'flew into a rage, & struck his daughter with a chair & thereupon she left her father's house, & placed herself *for one night* under the protection of Lascelles'. In November 1833, Dow brought an action of *habeas corpus* in the Sydney Supreme Court to recover his alleged wife, using the name 'Edward Lord Viscount Lascelles eldest son of Earl Harewood'. No evidence of either marriage or cohabitation could be found, and the case was dismissed.

Lilius brings a rare whiff of sex into Dow's adventures. Most likely, though, his object was the usual financial one. 'It was understood & believed', wrote Dowling in his case notes, 'that nothing improper *in fact*, took place between the lady & Lascelles during this interval'. Whatever designs he might have had on the Dickson fortune, they failed. Still, the case provided a postscript for the Sydney gossips. Lilius was clearly not one to pine in thought. Justice Dowling was mortified to see her marry his own nephew not two months later. 'There being a cloud hanging about the personal reputation of *Lilius*', grumbled Dowling in his notes on the *habeas corpus* action, 'I could never reconcile it to my sense of respect for the honest & virtuous prejudices of the world, to regard her as a member of the Dowling family – however, I might have been disposed to get over pedigree & connexions'.[62]

Lord Harewood hears from Sydney

At the same time as he was romancing Lilius, Dow was weaving an even more elaborate scheme involving the family at Harewood itself. In March 1833, Sydney solicitor David Chambers was requested to call at a lodging house (whence Dow would later decamp leaving nine months rent unpaid) for the purpose of drawing up a power of attorney. Chambers's client described himself as 'Henry, Viscount Lascelles' and required the document to authorise his agent, Thomas Wilson, to apply for two annuities due from his father, the Earl of Harewood. Matters were to be arranged by one John Thomas Young, who would shortly leave the colony for England.[63] Chambers was immediately suspicious:

> from the first moment I saw him, I took him to be an
> impostor; I did not then tell him so to his face; I drew
> the document in the usual way, and read it to him; it
> commenced, 'Know all men by these presents, that I, *Henry*,
> commonly called Lord Viscount Lascelles'.[64]

At this point Dow made his second mistake, stopping Chambers to protest against the words 'commonly called', and insisting that as Lord Lascelles he was a 'Peer in his own right'. Evidently more familiar with the arcane naming practices of the British aristocracy than was Dow, Chambers 'attempted to explain to him that he could only bear the title of Lord Viscount Lascelles by courtesy'.

A wild and distant shore

The solicitor remarked that the annuities represented a very large sum of money to entrust to a stranger. Making reference to a handy copy of *Burke's Peerage*, he questioned his client minutely on the house of Harewood. Dow's 'answers were very unsatisfactory, and he seemed to know very little about the family', insisting that the eldest son of Lord Harewood was called Henry rather than Edward. (He may in some measure be excused. The innumerable Henrys and Edwards born to the Lascelles continue to inspire mistakes, including one in no less an authority than the *Oxford Dictionary of National Biography*.[65]) Dow, with commendable aplomb, assured Chambers that there 'must be some mistake in the book of English peerage'. Yet he also got the names, numbers and ages of his brothers and sisters wrong and seemed unfamiliar with the details of any members of the family save that of the third Lascelles son, MP William Saunders Sebright.[66] Chambers's suspicions were also aroused since his client appeared to be a much older man than Edward, born in 1796, ought to have been.

Business, however, is business, and the requisite letters and powers of attorney were duly drawn up. The London firm of Spottiswood and Robertson was directed to apply to the Earl of Harewood for the money. Chambers nevertheless took it upon himself to warn Young of his suspicions, and 'told him he was very unwise to think of leaving the Colony on so foolish an errand'. Notarial fees of £2 were paid, and Dow had gained not only the documents required, but also a valuable tutorial on the Harewood connections: 'he persevered to the last that his name was Henry', claimed Chambers, 'and it is only since that interview with me, and the production of "Burke's Peerage", that he has deemed it prudent to adopt the name of Edward'.[67]

In August 1833, Young arrived in England, bearing a variety of letters from the supposed viscount signed simply 'Lascelles' (the question of 'Edward' versus 'Henry' conveniently sidestepped). Soon after his arrival, they were duly despatched with suitably respectful covering letters from Young himself. Young was particularly anxious to hear from Lord Harewood. He wrote first on 25 August, from his lodgings near St Paul's Cathedral, enclosing a letter to his father from 'Lascelles', and following up the original letter with several others when delivery of the enclosure was delayed. The mails eventually obliged, and the earl received a letter from his long-lost son on 7 September.

'My Dear Father', wrote the supposed viscount from Sydney:

> This for the first time I take opportunity of addressing
> your Lordship since fulfilling the harsh penalty of the
> Law a Penalty tho, even of excilement bring with it a
> thousand disorders and at the same time thousand delights
> to a reflecting mind, such has it been to me the muse my
> favourite study has soothed in the hour of adversity and
> waned the harsh feelings of malignant fate.

After presumably drawing a deep breath at the conclusion of such a sentence, the letter continued in similar vein. It explained that the author would have written to his father earlier, but for the fact that he was 'aware that your Lordships malignity towards me can never be recalled'. 'What could I solicit from those who left me to spend a life of misery and drag out a weary existence even without the common necessaries by which Nature exist in a strange and savage land'? What indeed? The writer's imagination was evidently up to the task. Kindly consigning 'to the shades of oblivion' his parent's past short-

A wild and distant shore

comings, he (eventually) got down to brass tacks:

> Being in the Purgatorial Hell without the means of
> returning to my revered and much beloved country – I am
> compelled to transmit to a Power of Attorney to Mr Wilson
> and Messrs Spottiswood and Robinson [sic] to receive from
> your Lordship the full amount of my annuities which will
> amount to Thirty Thousand pounds Sterling.

He ended by saying that full instructions were held by 'Mr John
Thomas Young. If you have any good feeling towards me extend
it to Him.'[68]

Another letter, to the Marquess of Bute, written in Sydney
three days after the letter to Lord Harewood, was somewhat
more to the point:

> My dear Lord, The Bearer of this letter Mr John Thomas
> Young I beg to introduce to your Lordship as a Gentleman
> worthy of utmost attention he is a most ardent friend of
> mine and all the honours you bestow upon him will be
> confered upon me. I confide in your Lordship to procure
> him a grant of Land containing Four Thousand acres in any
> part of New South Wales he may think proper to select.[69]

Whatever other insults had been cast in his teeth during that
vitriolic election campaign of 1807, no-one had ever presumed
to call Henry Lascelles a fool. We really need go no further
than his explanation in seeking a reason for Dow's usurpation
of Edward's identity: 'the swindling attempt which had been
made in New South Wales must have had as its object to build
up credit in that country, as it is impossible that one shilling
could be obtained in this Country by the means resorted to'.[70]
Young and Dow *might* have been in collusion, a possibility that

certainly occurred to Lord Harewood, but all the evidence suggests that Young was Dow's victim rather than his co-conspirator. The prospect of Dow even attempting (let alone succeeding) to persuade the Lascelles family itself that he was Edward seems nil.

In Britain, a veil had very deliberately been cast over Edward's whereabouts, but his family knew perfectly well he was by this time firmly, though regrettably, ensconced with the Baroness Testa in Munich. We know also from the pointed letters Henry was getting offering news about his real son that, despite the Lascelles's best efforts, information of various sorts had leaked out. Edward's disgrace and disappearance was common enough knowledge across sufficiently diverse social circles to have come to the ears of a man like Dow. And yet, the countless mistakes made by Dow suggest that he probably had only the barest knowledge of the Harewood family or of what had happened to the real viscount.[71]

For Dow's purposes in the smaller world of the colonies, however, it was enough to know that Lord Lascelles had vanished from Britain. This, combined with the acknowledged practice, in literature as well as in life, for transportees to take on false names, was an important element to the deceit, and came up repeatedly in the court battles to follow. If 'Lascelles' had disappeared from Britain, he could plausibly reappear in the antipodes under a pseudonym. The entire elaborate ruse of the power of attorney was undoubtedly intended to swindle Young rather than to get any money out of Lord Harewood. Letters to Thomas Wilson in London indicate that Young was promised the sum of £1500 for his trouble, and was also lured with the prospect of going into both a distillery and a steamship business with 'Lascelles'.[72] Like the victims of John (or

A wild and distant shore

James) Colquhoun in Scotland, it was the story of Edward (or Henry) Lascelles's estrangement from his father and entitlement to both money and influence that made his story seem convincing.

Young's combination of naïveté and self-interest was fatal, despite the warnings he received from Chambers: 'the prisoner's representations had such an influence on his credulity', remembered the solicitor, 'that he could not consider him an impostor, and actually went to London'.[73] But if Dow had no real expectation of getting any money out of Lord Harewood, what were his motives in sending Young off to London? In his covering letter to Lord Harewood, Young hoped that matters would:

> be disposed for a speedy and amicable arrangement on
> which I am myself dependent for the fulfilling certain
> pecuniary engagements resulting from my acquaintance
> with Lord Lascelles, to meet which I have received an order
> on his Agents for fifteen hundred pounds which I trust your
> Lordship will see paid to me without any vexatious delay.

Lord Lascelles, explained Young to Lord Harewood, 'has sent me home for the purpose of assisting (if necessary) in the arrangements of his affairs, as well as to receive the sum of fifteen hundred pounds due to me by his Lordship, for which he has given me an order on his agents'. Young also mentioned to Spottiswood and Robertson that 'he had advanced money' to the impostor, presumably on the expectation that it and his £1500 would be paid once the annuity was secured.

Lord Harewood received the touching epistle from Sydney, together with Young's covering letter, on 7 September. His reply to Young, written the same day, was brief and to the point. The 'enclosure purporting to be from Viscount Lascelles is a gross imposition, as also the whole matter to which it relates'. The viscount had never been in New South Wales, wrote Lord Harewood, but as 'you state that you are about to return to Sydney, you may have an opportunity of dealing with the Impostor'.

Cold comfort indeed. Young immediately wrote back to Lord Harewood asking for any information he could give on the man who 'has so glaringly assumed the title of Visct Lascelles'. Young was given little to work with: 'I have no idea who the Impostor is' was the terse reply.[74]

Putting the Harewood hounds on the scent

Aided by his hardworking administrative staff, Lord Harewood was a meticulous man, as the carefully numbered and notated correspondence on both the false and the genuine Edward's scandalous affairs suggests. He was determined to have the matter cleared up. Having despatched the disappointing news to John Young, he instructed his agent, one Mr Nelson, to communicate both with Spottiswood and Robertson and with Wilson and to investigate the matter further. It was necessary to 'prevent the slightest degree of doubt attaching for a moment upon Edward', but the matter needed to be handled delicately.

The family had made careful efforts to cover up the circumstances of Edward's disappearance. Blackmail was a real possibility, as the anonymous letters Lord Harewood had already received indicate. Both Lord Harewood and Nelson, then, wanted to minimise any direct contact with unsavory characters. Nelson made concerted efforts to find out who the impostor might be. Initially he came up with several red herrings. Luckily for Nelson, indignant financial loss makes for

A wild and distant shore

determined archival research. Some two hundred years before I tracked Dow to that Dumfries courtroom, brushing off the thick layer of Edinburgh soot coating his trial record, Young had his own success amongst the transportation records of the Secretary of State.

Calling on Spottiswood and Robertson (after he had received the earl's assurances as to *their* respectability) Nelson ran into Young in their offices and was able to report to the earl that:

> at the Secretary of States Office, he [Young] had ascertained who the party was. He was well known there, & had been transported from Dumfries, under the name of John Dow alias John Colquhoun. Mr Young appeared very indignant but thoroughly satisfied there was no claim upon your Lordship nor any person at Sydney that was entitled to be called Lord Lascelles — Young is an Irishman, & I could not determine whether he was more a Fool or a Knave.

Robertson duly tramped off to the office of the Secretary of State himself, and a week or so later Nelson could report to his master, then evidently enjoying country pursuits:

> I saw Mr Robertson one day last week, he had been at the Secretary of States Office, & seen Mr Capper who manages the Convict concern there & who even from the writing sent to Spottiswood & Robertson was convinced the Scoundrel at Sydney was the man I mentioned to your Lordship, once he played a Game of Deception on a nephew of the late Duke of Buccleuys, another time, he was a relative of the Northumberland Family. I am much obliged to your Lordship & Lady Harewood for a Box of Game, arrived this morning.[75]

It was Nelson's opinion that 'there was not the slightest possibility that Young had it in his power to advance any money to His Principal Dow, alias Colquhoun', implying that the two were in it together. It seems more likely that Young did lend Dow money on the expectation of an inheritance, a pattern which fits the Colquhoun imposture and Dow's methods more generally. A similar arrangement of payment for letters delivered in England was also made with one James Maclehose, who had known Dow in Van Diemen's Land.[76]

It is unclear when John Thomas Young had first met the man calling himself Lascelles. Young had come free to the Australian colonies, but he was not a wealthy man. The two men both sought passage to England from Sydney in 1833, but while the ship's captain agreed to take 'Lascelles', he would not agree to their passage if Young should be of the party. 'Lascelles' later gave the captain a draft on a London bank to be redeemed by his father, Lord Harewood, in compensation for the trouble the negotiation had given. Needless to say, the captain never received a penny, but he was able to take a measure of revenge by filling in Lord Harewood's agent on Young's background. He took the precaution of making his information in confidence. 'I saw', wrote Nelson, 'he did not want to be brought into a squabble with a hot head Irishman'.[77]

<hr>

Young's motives for pursuing the matter further are unclear. Certainly he was incensed at the imposition and sought all in his power to expose Dow, for he would not have taken the trouble to visit the Secretary of State otherwise. But he probably also hoped to gain some assistance from Lord Harewood in his current distress. By January 1834, Young was in Bath, and

A wild and distant shore

still sending letters to Edward's father. He was anxious, so he said, to expose the impostor in Sydney. '[Y]ou will see by the accompanying newspaper', he wrote to the earl, enclosing a copy of the *Sydney Times*:

> that he is believed to be your Lordship's son on the faith
> of which (as in my case) he readily gets what ever he may
> want. I think if your Lordship would write to me what you
> may think fit on the subject recapitulating your former
> letters I would give every necessary publicity to same.

He requested that Lord Harewood frank his letters, and if possible return the newspaper that was sent in evidence: 'My circumstances have become so affected by the villainy of the Sydney Impostor that every shilling is an object to me 'till I get out of this expensive country'.[78] As a collection of colonial newspaper cuttings still lie in the storerooms of Harewood House, it seems that Young was not obliged. Nor is there any evidence that Dow's latest victim received any further correspondence from the earl. With Edward cleared, there was no need for his father to pursue the matter.

6

HIS LORDSHIP'S
TOUR DE FORCE

The whole community is rancorously divided into
parties on almost every subject.

Charles Darwin, *The Voyage of the Beagle*, 1839

Whether by the workings of Providence or by sheer dumb luck, John Larnach had escaped death in the Castle Forbes uprising. Now he would have his vengeance. Led by Aboriginal trackers to the rebels' encampment, Larnach and a group of mounted police ambushed them less than twenty miles from the homestead. Convicts absconding from their masters were an almost everyday occurrence in the colonies. Attempting to murder those masters was not. But if it was rather less than common, it was still in keeping with common perceptions. The Castle Forbes 'revolt' would not have caused quite such a stir in New South Wales had it not been for the highly charged political debate, no less heated than the reform struggles in Britain, then raging between two factions within the colony. And it was into this volatile drama that John Dow, still wearing the mask of

His lordship's *tour de force*

Viscount Lascelles but pursued by his swindled creditors, would step to deliver the next scene of his bravura performance.

The unnatural term of their lives

All the Hunter Valley rebels, now recaptured, already bore the marks of punishment scored into their flesh, the visible stigmata of their lives under the convict system. Many sentenced for crimes in Britain would find opportunities for a better life when fate sent them to the antipodes. For their children, born far from the desperation that had prompted many of their parents' crimes, the future would be even brighter. As their expanded horizons, as their greater political and economic rights pop up into our view, it can be easy to forget the physical violence that haunted their world. It was part of the apparatus of terror that the penal system was designed to underscore.

Flogging was suffered by men, rather than by women, and inflicted upon the bond and not the free. But its sights and sounds were part of the bloody reality of every man, woman and child in the colony. For all their sensationalism, perhaps it is worth remembering some of the more gruesome descriptions. The cat-o-nine tails, a whip made of nine to twelve greenhide leather strips, sometimes knotted at the end, could skin a man's back in twenty-five strokes. Witnesses said it sprayed gobs of flesh about for ants to carry off, and filled the victim's shoes with blood so that when released he squelched his way from the 'triangles' where he had been bound. In the summer, flies later laid their eggs in the lacerated flesh, and one was lucky if a 'humane companion' was on hand to extract the maggots. The pain was matched only by the violation and humiliation that flogging was designed to inflict.

It was ordered for all manner of offences: theft, absconding, failure to perform work, and that vague and commonly used charge, 'insubordination'. There was plenty of ways of getting back at a convict who complained of a master to the authorities. A 'sour look', claimed one critic of Mudie and his cronies, could be enough to earn one a flogging.[1] Until Governor Bourke changed the regulations in 1832, the highest numbers of lashes were spaced over several days to enable the victim to endure them: a practice, it should be said, that had been outlawed even in slave colonies as inhumane. Deaths from flogging were not unknown, though they were uncommon. Some prisoners prided themselves on their stoicism and refused to cry out. Most cracked. Their shrieks were an audible inducement to good behaviour, reportedly shaking the composure of witnesses both bond and free.

Flogging was generally the first tier of punishment. Worse recalcitrants were looped together in chain gangs, and sentenced to work on government labour projects for up to a year or more. Yoked to wagons laden with gravel and stone, they performed, as one who saw it remarked, 'all the functions of labour usually discharged by beasts of burden at home'.[2] The irons were riveted around each prisoner's ankles and could not be removed until they were struck off with a chisel. Specially designed trousers that buttoned all the way up the outside of each leg could be removed whilst the chains stayed in place.

Masters could not order the flogging of their own assigned servants; that was the task of the local magistrate. In Britain, local magistracies – justices of the peace – were just another of those paternal responsibilities accepted by members of the provincial gentry. In the colonies, they were appointed from

His lordship's *tour de force*

amongst the larger landowners, and the would-be gentry jealously guarded the status thus afforded. 'Respectability' was one supposed qualification for such an office; paternal magnanimity was not. If magistrates were prohibited from dealing out summary punishment to their own servants, they were authorised to invite a colleague to do so. Amongst the tight-knit group of pastoralist-magistrates on the Hunter, a friend or neighbour would usually oblige. The 'magistrates were so friendly to each other', said the convicts at Castle Forbes, 'no justice could be done them'. Since courthouses were few in remoter areas, judgements were usually given in private houses. A year before the Castle Forbes revolt, a notorious case in the Hunter Valley saw a guest sentence three assigned servants to floggings of a hundred lashes each whilst he was seated at dinner at their master's own table.[3]

The rebels crack

The six rebels at Castle Forbes – two English, four Irish – came to breaking point under this system.[4] As those who refused to join them well knew, a happy outcome for rebellion was remote. One of the Englishmen, John Perry, ran into the bush some days before the uprising began. Sentenced to life for sheep stealing when he was 23, Perry was assigned to Mudie early in 1832. By October 1833 he had suffered a total of two hundred lashes for offences ranging from stealing a pig to absconding. John Poole was a joiner, born in Dublin and transported for housebreaking in Lancaster in 1829. Upon arrival he was initially sent to a short-lived settlement in the Wellington Valley, an establishment for educated and higher-class convicts. Thereafter he found himself assigned at Castle Forbes.

Poole had the determination, skills and confidence to pro-test his treatment. He wrote to the Principal Superintendent of Convicts and the Director of Public Works complaining of the conditions at Castle Forbes, but the letters were intercepted by Larnach. Poole would later be described as 'a close minded man, and would scarcely tell his brother of any thing he was going to do'. But he told fellow convict James Browne that he was off to the bush. Browne tried to dissuade him. This was 'the first step to the gallows' he warned.[5] Poole would pay no heed.

The night before the rebellion began, he too had run off, along with two fellow Irishmen, James Riley and James Ryan. Riley, a carter and labourer, was originally sentenced to seven years for stealing snuffers and assigned to Mudie on arrival in New South Wales. In May 1832 he was found guilty of striking Larnach during an argument and sentenced to be worked in irons in Newcastle, before being returned to Castle Forbes. He too had accumulated more than two hundred lashes. Ryan was only seventeen, regarded as a 'boy' by the others. He had been transported the previous year for stealing bacon, but already had a hundred and fifty lashes etched into his back.

The last two rebels were Anthony Hitchcock, a brick-layer and fisherman from Essex, and David Jones, an Irish butcher, both transported for highway robbery. Just days previously, Jones and Hitchcock, together with another of Mudie's con-victs, Stephen Parrett, had been sentenced to labour in a chain gang for twelve months. The first act of the rebels, then, was to rescue them. The rebellion began on 5 November 1833, three days before 'Lord Lascelles' applied to the Sydney court for the return of Lilius Dickson. That the date was also the anniversary of the Gunpowder Plot was probably coincidental. Con-

His lordship's *tour de force*

stable Samuel Cook was taking Hitchcock, Jones and Parrett to nearby Maitland when he was challenged by a group of armed men. The constable deemed it prudent to give up without a fight. Parrett refused to join the gang, and urged young Ryan not to go. But Ryan was already guilty of having absconded. He knew the consequences for that. He was too afraid of what would happen to him if he went back to Larnach now.

It is all too easy (as was the case at the time) to paint Mudie as the villain of the Hunter Valley. But the 'cruelty' at Castle Forbes was more distinctive for the political mileage that would be made from it than for its unusual harshness.[6] Mudie would become one of the fiercest critics of 'special' treatment for educated convicts, but his relations with Poole, a favoured worker for whom he had once bought books and musical instruments, for example, were a not uncommon blend of patronage and violence. Now, however, any complexities in past personal relationships meant nothing. Once the rebels raised their hand against Larnach, their fates were sealed.

The dreadful sentence carried out

The six rebels were brought to trial at the Sydney Supreme Court on 9 and 10 December 1833. Convicts on capital trials were not usually provided with counsel, but an anonymous benefactor paid for Roger Therry, an Irish liberal and a vocal ally of Governor Bourke, to represent them. In their defence, the convicts pleaded that 'by the bad treatment, flogging, and bad provisions they had to endure, they were driven to desperation, and brought to this unhappy end'. Therry tried to bring conditions at Castle Forbes to the attention of the court to plead mitigation of sentence, but Chief Justice Sir Francis

Forbes, after some discussion, disallowed it. The judgement, like many in colonial courts, was a foregone conclusion. Several witnesses had seen the robbery at Castle Forbes and the attempted murder of Larnach. The guns too were produced in evidence, causing consternation when it was discovered they were still loaded.

Therry himself knew the case was hopeless. Later he said that the men declared they would prefer death to being returned to Mudie and Larnach. Poole (only twenty-two years old himself) pleaded repeatedly for the life of 'the boy Ryan', for, he said, 'they had forced him with them to prevent disclosures'.[7] It did no good. David Jones, against whom there was little evidence, was sentenced to exile on the living hell of Norfolk Island. The other five were all sentenced to death.

According to the solemn convention of the court, the Chief Justice then asked the men if they knew of any reason why the sentence of death should not be passed upon them. Hitchcock rose with dignity to his feet. It was to 'the unfortunate circumstance of his being assigned to the service of Major Mudie he attributed all his subsequent misfortune, and present unhappiness'. He had possessed, he told the court, 'an exemplary character before he went to Major Mudie; he had since been repeatedly flogged, by which, and by the unwholesome food he had subsisted on, his health had been ruined, and life itself, rendered burdensome'. He denounced the 'system of merciless infliction of the lash throughout the district of the Hunter River'.[8] He called for justice, and urged 'If the Court would but look at their bare backs, it would see their statement was not exaggerated'.

Poole echoed his friend's cry:

His lordship's *tour de force*

He was aware that anything he could urge in their behalf would be of but little avail — their doom was fixed: but he solemnly implored the Judge to cause an enquiry to be set on foot respecting the treatment of assigned servants at Major Mudie's, in order to prevent others from being forced into the unhappy situation in which they were then placed.[9]

Later Governor Bourke, explaining his decision to enquire into conditions at Castle Forbes, told the Secretary of State that, though nothing could excuse their 'violent and atrocious' actions, 'by the earnestness and apparent sincerity of their manner' in complaining of ill-treatment, the rebels had 'obtained in a very remarkable degree the sympathy of the Public'.[10]

Under the New South Wales Bushranging Act of 1830, the men should have been hanged within 48 hours. Hitchcock pleaded for some time in which they might compose themselves for eternity away from the noise and bad language of the prison yard. In company with another man convicted of highway robbery, Perry, Riley and young James Ryan were to hang on the public gallows behind Sydney gaol on 21 December. Attended by the ministers of their respective faiths, all appeared penitent and showed dignity and firmness in the face of death. The Sydney prison was located at the foot of a steep hill and formed a natural amphitheatre for spectators inside and out.[11] Last words were expected from the scaffold, but none of the Castle Forbes men could master their 'mental agony' enough to manage a word. Riley tried several times to speak, but failed. Perry 'prayed fervently, and appeared to feel all the horror natural to one in his appalling situation'. Ryan had sunk into a 'sort of simple listlessness … which did not leave him to the last'. The public remained convinced that the lad's life would be

Antipodes

spared at the last minute. There were loud and repeated cries for mercy from the watchers, to no avail.

The sheriff read the death warrants. The time for prayer elapsed, the men ascended the scaffold, and 'the fatal bolt was withdrawn'. Perry was lucky enough to die instantly. The others hung at the end of their ropes for several long minutes, convulsing their lives away before the horrified crowd. The courtyard rang with bitter curses called down upon the names of Mudie and Larnach. 'A greater degree of sympathy', wrote one observer, 'was manifested by the spectators for the melancholy end of the Hunter's River men, than any thing we have ever seen on similar occasions'. Feeling in the colony ran high. It was reported in the *Australian* that 'We have heard that Mr. Mudie has stated his opinion that no assigned servant is worth a farthing till he has received 300 lashes'. Riley's shirt slipped off as his body was cut down. One witness wrote to the paper: 'I was appalled at the spectacle his back presented, although it was nearly six weeks, since this man was last punished, his back was one continued sore, and exhibited ample proofs of the torture he had undergone'.[12]

Hitchcock and Poole had one more task yet to perform. Their deaths would underline the consequences of revolt to a restive population. They were loaded onto the steamboat *Sophia Jane*, taken to the Hunter district by sea, and then by horse cart to be executed at Castle Forbes itself. Now the authority of the law was played out in a chapter of accidents that would have been farcical had the circumstances not been so grim. The escort arrived so late that no official was present to meet the officer of the guard. They had to bivouac *en route* in the bush, arriving just in time for the execution that Saturday morning. Then there was no-one around to knock off the pris-

His lordship's *tour de force*

oners' irons. A convict friend of Poole tried, but he could not manage it without an anvil. The prisoners were duly marched more than a mile to a blacksmith's shop, and back again to the gallows erected in a paddock near Castle Forbes. No clergyman had been provided, so a local schoolmaster gave the men what comfort he could. With most of the staff at Castle Forbes assembled, the men ascended the scaffold in front of their friends and former fellows. In a state of near-collapse, speech was beyond them. This at least was one mercy: 'The prisoners were so much fatigued and exhausted, that they died without a struggle'. Months later, the gallows still stood in stark warning, presenting 'a dreary spectacle to travellers passing during the night'.[13]

The bull frog farmers of the Hunter Valley

Born around 1779, 'Major' James Mudie never attained the rank he affected in New South Wales, but was dismissed from the Royal Marines in 1810 whilst still a lieutenant. In his cups he was wont to boast of having successfully avoiding active service for years. An anonymous letter tipped off the War Office and an investigation revealed that Mudie was also defrauding the service with the connivance of his mistress, Mrs Scargill, an army widow. To avoid besmirching the reputation of the widow's fallen husband, the army did not subject Mudie to the public humiliation of a formal court martial.

With the loss of his army pay, however, Mudie next sought to make his fortune minting commemorative medals. These would honour the heroes and battles of the wars in which he had so assiduously avoided fighting. The venture went bankrupt, leaving Mudie with the nickname 'Major Medallion'. He was happy to appropriate the first half of this moniker when long-suffering friends arranged for his free passage to New South Wales. It was as a major that he arrived in Sydney in July of 1822, a widower accompanied by one step-daughter and three daughters of his own. On an estate named after his bene-factor, Sir Charles Forbes, Mudie presided over more than 4000 acres of the best land in the Hunter Valley.

The valley was fertile enough to support labour-intensive agriculture as well as the pastoralism more common in New South Wales, and Castle Forbes would soon yield a bountiful crop of wheat.[14] There was rich alluvial soil and the possibility of water-borne transport to Sydney. It was an attractive propo-sition for the wave of 1820s emigrants unleashed by the social unrest following the end of the Napoleonic wars. Or rather, it would be so long as they could prevail against the previous inhabitants. The first Europeans to grab land in the area were very different from the would-be gentry who followed. When Mudie arrived he was surprised to find around 2000 head of sheep and cattle already pastured there. Some who ran their livestock in the Hunter region had official permission to do so. Most did not. Squatting on Crown land at the edge of the settlement had become established practice. The land granted to Mudie was already occupied by Benjamin Singleton, son of a warehouse porter transported for seven years. Together with his family, Singleton had built stockyards, run livestock and planted crops. But with Mudie granted title on the land, he was summarily ejected. He was one of a group of small farmers of modest means, mostly former convicts and their kin, who had come into the valley a few years earlier, migrating from the Hawkesbury region to the south. Struggling, socially marginal and undercapitalised, they bitterly resented the well-connected

His lordship's *tour de force*

and cashed-up new arrivals.

When Singleton and his ilk had pushed north in search of land they were entering the country of the Kamilaroi. A loosely aligned group of peoples spread across the northern plains and speaking a related language, the Kamilaroi took their name from the negative term *kamil*. Consequently, as historian Roger Milliss puts it in his monumental study of the region's frontier wars, they were the 'nay-sayers'; the people 'who said No'.[15] And with Europeans and their livestock encroaching upon their land, the Kamilaroi soon made these sentiments known. By 1825 hostilities were in full swing, reaching a climax the following year. The spearing of stockmen and fencers was followed by reprisals. Lancelot Threlkeld, who ran a mission at Lake Macquarie, gave report of a man who had shot an intruder stealing corn from his paddock and hung the body from a tree, a cob of corn stuck between the teeth, until it rotted from the branch. The cycle of revenge killings spiralled into a general rising, and prominent landholders in the Hunter petitioned Darling for military assistance. The governor replied that they should defend themselves, criticising absentee landlords who chose to reside in Sydney rather than on their generous frontier landholdings. Nevertheless, troops were despatched, and the 'rebellion' soon crushed. Missionaries like Threlkeld, and government officials sympathetic to the injustices perpetrated against the Kamilaroi, reported gross abuses of power, and the murder of Indigenous prisoners in cold blood.

Having let slip the dogs of war, Darling now objected to the inevitable result. Despite the governor's attempts to get to the bottom of what had occurred, official investigations of the Hunter Valley atrocities were stymied by systematic obstruction on the ground. It was to become a well-established pattern on the Australian frontier over the course of the next century. The reports played down the causes of Kamilaroi discontent, glossed over the reprisals enacted by white posses, and exonerated those responsible for deaths in custody. Finally, however, Lieutenant Nathaniel Lowe was put on trial for having ordered the murder of a man known to Europeans as 'Jacky Jacky' who had been apprehended on suspicion of killing a stock-keeper. Ably defended by Robert Wardell and William Charles Wentworth, whose liberalism never extended to embrace Indigenous people, the court acquitted Lowe to scenes of public rejoicing in Sydney.[16] The 1826 resistance was crushed. It was the beginning of the end for the people who had said 'no' to Benjamin Singleton and his compatriots not five years earlier.

Singleton, ousted from Mudie's grant, later received land at a river crossing where sits the town that now bears his name. But his enmity for the newer emigrants remained undiminished. Emancipists and native-born colonists looked with outrage on these interlopers gobbling up huge chunks of the land they regarded as theirs by right. In a few short years, most of the land along the river had been granted as freehold to settlers with capital. The Hunter would develop into one of the most prosperous parts of the colony. With its large estates and bonded labour force, many compared it to the plantations of the American south. In unwitting echo of the Kamilaroi, whose land he had snatched away, Benjamin Singleton cried out in his turn that the 'Government had no right to give so much Land to Free Settlers and so little to those that are borne in the Country'.[17]

The new arrivals of the 1820s formed, in Governor Bourke's words, the 'little click of the Hunter River',[18] a tightly knit group of politically conservative would-be gentry. For the gov-

His lordship's *tour de force*

ernment-leaning *Sydney Gazette*, they were the 'bull frog farmers of the Hunter'.[19] Mudie and his like were happy to take advantage of the free labour provided by a penal system. They were equally determined to distinguish themselves from their emancipist neighbours, small-time farmers who were often ex-convicts or the children of convicts. The Hunter gentry complained that the older settlers fraternised with their assigned servants, eroding the social division between bond and free, and harboured escapees. Emancipists had little land of their own, so the grumbles went, but they ran their cattle where they would. When put in positions of authority (Singleton was made a district constable in 1823) they were prejudiced against the free settlers. It was these circumstances, suggests historian Sandra Blair, that probably inspired the general 'insubordination' of which masters in the district complained. The Hunter, riven with class tension, was an obvious flash point in the 'partisan brawl' that erupted during the time of Richard Bourke.[20] It was no accident that amongst the first shots of the war that ultimately ended transportation to New South Wales were those fired there.

The meticulous research of Sandra Blair into the Hunter Valley court records bears out what was commonly believed at the time. Discipline there was harsh, the convict population kept in check by systematic flogging. Mudie and his compatriots were a jittery lot, in both their judicial and their social authority. As relatively recent arrivals, they knew that they were considered beneath the ironically titled 'ancient nobility' of the colony. Centered around the Macarthur family, that social elite of former army officers and colonial officials had dominated the pecking order since the late eighteenth century.[21] The 'bull-frog farmers' had benefitted greatly from Darling's regime, but they viewed Bourke's liberal new order with loathing. Any initiatives the governor made to restrict the authority they wielded over their convict servants or to improve the civil rights of emancipists would be resisted. Hunter Valley settlers 'consider themselves a privileged Class', wrote Bourke:

> and were so during the late administration monopolizing land and convicts and wallowing in the favor of the Govt to which they gave their support in return … The Civil Servants and *Emigrant* Party are thus opposed to me, and my support is alone from the body of the People.[22]

Reform at home

Bourke's arrival coincided with a wind of change sweeping across both Britain and its antipodes. The Whigs would have liked to claim sole credit, but a growing liberalism within Tory circles meant that the new order was already well under way when the Whigs finally took power under Earl Grey in 1830. The new governor of New South Wales was well connected in these new circles of power. While cooling his heels awaiting his next colonial appointment, Bourke had began editing the correspondence of a distant relation, Edmund Burke, one of the heroes of the Whig pantheon (for all that he would inspire later generations of Victorian conservatives). The monumental four volumes would finally appear in 1844, his co-editor being none other than our old friend Lord Milton, by then Earl Fitz-william.[23]

After a struggle to the very end, Grey's Reform Bill finally passed on 4 June 1832. It by no means established true democracy. A property qualification to vote still applied. The ballot was still public. Women and workers remained disenfran-

His lordship's *tour de force*

chised. For some scholars, the changes represent no more than calculated self-interest amongst the propertied; 'a trick of the light' as one historian puts it, one that left aristocratic domination of political life unchallenged.[24] Nonetheless, contemporaries, wondering where it would lead, thought the change momentous.

Like other 'Young Whigs', Milton, who had hoped the Reformed Parliament would curb popular protest, viewed the extra-parliamentary agitation of the 1830s and 1840s with dismay.[25] There were definite gains for the disenfranchised in the legislation of 1832. The number of voters was substantially increased. The 'rotten' and 'pocket' boroughs were abolished. Parliamentary seats were redistributed to cover large towns, and populations which had not previously been represented gained new members. The Leeds merchant oligarchy found themselves 'rudely dethroned' by the post-reform bourgeois electorate.[26] Two years later, in a February by-election, it was possible for the one-time member of the Leeds Reasoning Society to take the step for which he had been fighting for some three decades. With a narrow majority over the rival Tory candidate, Edward Baines was elected MP for Leeds, 'the town which he had entered an apprentice, unknown to a single inhabitant'. 'It is well for the nation', wrote his filial biographer in 1851, 'that its institutions, notwithstanding a large admixture of aristocracy, permit it to draw its public servants from every walk of life'.[27]

The days of slavery were numbered also, despite the continued efforts in parliament of men like Henry Lascelles (now 2nd Earl of Harewood) to keep the system in place. In 1832 Henry chaired a public meeting held in the West Indian interest, arguing that there had been 'strong feelings of prejudice created in this country against all proprietors of West India property, as possessors of a slave population'. He claimed that the situation was not of the slave-owners' making. They had responsibilities towards the men and women they owned, and he likened this burden to a social duty to care for the poor. They were doing all they could to improve the lot of their slaves, and they were doing so while maintaining a vital sector of the nation's economy. Any ruination of the West Indian sugar interest would also injure the Mother Country.

Lord Harewood's speech at the City of London Tavern was punctuated by cheering. Those on his plantations, as Simon Smith's statistical analysis indicates, would have known otherwise: 'At the time the 2nd Earl rose to his feet to call for the continuation of slavery, the mortality rates on his West Indian estates still ranked among the highest of any recorded human population'.[28] In any event, the Lascelles were fighting with their backs against the wall. Wilberforce might have been anxious that the Reform Act went too far too fast, but the new electorate had brought immense pressure on the government to finally go the distance on the slave question.

The venerable 'Saint' was now more than seventy years old, and very frail. For one so long beset by bodily infirmities, it seemed a miracle his life had been extended thus far. Now he knew he was dying: 'I am like a clock which is almost run down'.[29] The Bill to abolish slavery throughout the British empire finally passed in July 1833. Perhaps Wilberforce had been waiting. He died within days of hearing the news that the battle was won.

His lordship's *tour de force*

Reform, and resistance, in the colonies

Convict transportation too was coming under increasingly heavy fire. Those promoting a new direction in emigration policy claimed that they could provide a better safety valve for Britain's economic and social pressure-cooker. Proponents of what was called 'systematic colonization' argued that, rather than granting land free to men of capital, the *sale* of Crown lands in the colonies could subsidise mass migration of 'deserving' poor out of Britain. Prominent amongst these theorists was Edward Gibbon Wakefield, whose thoughts on transportation and emigration were first inspired by a stint in Newgate, where he had been imprisoned for abducting a fifteen-year-old heiress. Wakefield argued that the Australian colonies were suffering from unregulated land grants and reliance on convict labour. If properly managed, they could be transformed into morally unexceptional, productive and closely settled colonies that would bring in sufficient revenue from the sale of Crown land. These greater concentrations of population would ensure a market for British manufactured goods overseas.

It was a plan neatly designed to relieve poverty and food shortage at home and to place the disposal of land more firmly under the control of imperial authorities abroad. It would curb the power of local oligarchies, whose mass land grab in the 1820s had belched forth such delusions of grandeur as the Major's. As these unbridled settler-capitalists pushed out the edge of settlement, there were increasingly pressing problems with financing the defence and administration of a greatly expanded empire.[30]

The new regulations of land sale were proclaimed by Darling in 1831 and revenue began to pour into government coffers.

Assisted emigration took off slowly at first, but as thousands took advantage of it, the days of the penal system were numbered. The colony more than doubled its settler population from around 46 276 in 1830 to 97 912 in 1838. If the proportion of convicts only slowly decreased during that same period (from 40.1 to 37.7 per cent), New South Wales would still be transformed by this 'flash flood of humanity'.[31]

If the highest offices in both New South Wales and Britain were now held by Whigs, if free emigrants were pouring into the colony in increasing numbers, the constitutional arrangements that had evolved for a penal system would still be slow to change. Vested interests would retard the process as far and as fast as they could. Bourke faced a hostile settler elite and colonial officials inherited from Darling's rule. Two generations of Colonial Office patronage had made him a Whig governor in the midst of High Tory counsellors.[32] Bourke was in favour of granting representative institutions to the colony, but at least two key battles had to be fought first. It was these that dominated the first years of his administration: the jury system, and the power of magistrates over convicts.

At a practical level, these questions arose from the particular challenges of administering justice in a penal colony. But they also reached far deeper, touching on fundamental questions about power and status. A penal colony was a constitutional no less than a social conundrum; a system in which free persons and convicts under sentence lived and worked side by side. As the demography of the colony began to shift from bond to free, how would these anomalies be resolved?

Convicts under sentence still accounted for around 40 per cent of the New South Wales population in 1830. Only a small proportion was incarcerated behind bars or worked in

His lordship's *tour de force*

road gangs. Even smaller numbers (those who had committed additional crimes in the colony itself) wore distinctive clothing. Most, therefore, were at large amongst the wider community, assigned as servants to free settlers, or to those who had already served out their sentences, or they were enjoying the privileges of 'tickets of leave' to work for themselves. In these circumstances, convict discipline presented obvious problems. Flogging was the most common mode of punishment (lockups were few and would deprive a master of a convict's valuable labour). Justices of the peace, like Mudie, were given large powers to deal out summary punishment.[33] They were the local government of the colony. As well as conducting the normal business of a magistrate for the free population, they presided over the musters of convicts, judged on their assignment to free settlers and on their eligibility for tickets of leave, heard complaints against them and set their punishments.

Holding a magistracy, then, was not only about status, but also about wielding power in very concrete ways. Mudie clung with tenacity to his office precisely because it set a seal of social approval on his own, somewhat dubious, antecedents. 'In the middling classes we find that the Magistracy is looked upon with jealousy', wrote the *Herald*. 'We apprehend the reason to be, that it is one of the only honorary distinctions in the Colony.'[34] Both juries and the power of magistrates were vital issues, as historian Alan Atkinson explains, 'at a time when law courts were the focus of community life. The right to sit in juries was a mark of authority and citizenship such as any respectable man might hope for.'[35] And herein lay the rub, for who was to be regarded as respectable in a penal colony? It was this question that fundamentally divided the emancipists and the exclusives.

Bourke was strongly in favour of the extension of civil juries, which would allow emancipists to participate, but he faced considerable opposition from his Legislative Council, packed with 'exclusives' appointed under Darling. The exclusives argued that former convicts would dominate juries just as they numerically dominated the colony, that they lacked the requisite social and moral authority to pass judgement on free emigrants, and that they were likely to favour their former compatriots in crime. Bourke was able to get the Jury Act of 1833 passed through the council by means of his casting vote, but only by conceding that in criminal cases the accused could have the option of being tried by either a civil or a military jury.

As well as pushing for jury reform, Bourke was disturbed by the ways magistrates exercised their power over assigned convicts, particularly in the more remote districts of the colony. His Summary Punishment Act, passed in 1832, restricted the power of magistrates by allowing no more than fifty lashes to be ordered for misdemeanours such as drunkenness, neglect of work, abusive language or 'insubordination'. Draconian as these measures sound, they were still an effective reduction on the severity of sentences magistrates could pass on their own authority. The Act was praised in liberal circles for restricting arbitrary tyranny, but it provoked vehement opposition from the conservative faction.

In August 1833, three days before John Young penned his first hopeful letter to Lord Harewood in England, Bourke received a petition from the Hunter Valley settlers complaining that his provisions reducing the powers of magistrates were endangering the community. A second petition sent directly to the King via the Colonial Office, which came to be known as the

His lordship's *tour de force*

'hole and corner petition', was passed privately from house to house in order that its blistering personal attack on the governor remain secret until it left Australia's shores. Three months later the petitioners' fears of convict insubordination seemed to take corporeal form with the outbreak at Castle Forbes, and the simmering conflict between the emancipist and exclusive political factions boiled over.

In April 1834, four months after the Castle Forbes rebels had swung from the gallows, the office of the *Sydney Gazette* printed an anonymous pamphlet entitled *Party Politics Exposed ... containing comments on convict discipline in New South Wales* signed by 'Humanitas, an Emigrant of 1821'. The *Gazette* was owned by Anne Howe, the widowed daughter-in-law of the paper's founder, George Howe, a printer initially transported for shoplifting. It was edited by an emancipated convict, Edward O'Shaughnessy, a minor Irish poet convicted for collecting taxes under false pretenses, possibly as a drunken prank, and by William Watt, a ticket-of-leave convict transported for embezzlement who would later marry Anne Howe.[36] Unsurprising, then, that the *Gazette* was a warm supporter of Bourke and a vehement critic of Mudie. It was an open secret in the colony that William Watt was the author of what became commonly known as the 'Humanitas' pamphlet. Watt's address 'To the British Nation' cried out against 'the wrongs of your persecuted, though criminal Brethren, languishing in the bitterest bonds of Slavery'. It reproduced much of the evidence in the Castle Forbes trial that testified of Mudie's and Larnach's cruelty, condemned the 'rabble of settlers on the Hunter' in the strongest terms, asserted the moral worth of the emancipists, and ended with a diatribe against the 'cabal' which was seeking to get rid of both Governor Bourke and Chief Justice Forbes by exerting influence in London.

The opposing newspapers were not long in responding. The *Herald* attacked the 'bad policy, bad faith and bad taste' of 'Humanitas and his allies' claiming 'it is want of power, on the part of this Convict writer and his faction, that *alone* prevents them from crushing all Emigrants and ruling the Colony at pleasure with a rod of iron'. That paper called for a 'Commission of Inquiry to determine that this shall no longer be a Penal Colony – that it has outgrown its early appointments, and is now fitted for the rights and privileges of British subjects of reputed character exclusively'.[37]

In September from the offices of the *Monitor* appeared the *Vindication of James Mudie and John Larnach from certain reflections ... relative to the treatment of them by their Convict Servants.* The pamphlet was printed by that fire-breather of the 1820s, Edmund Smith Hall. It was a significant *volte face* for the former radical, but such realignments within the rabidly partisan colonial press were not unknown. Hall had suffered financial disaster as a result of his long campaign against Darling. Although rescued by friends (William Charles Wentworth amongst them) he was facing creditors who threatened to foreclose on his presses. James Mudie was one of those who bought shares to save the paper, no doubt seeing the advantage of having a public mouthpiece under his own influence.[38]

Enter 'the Commissioner'

As this debate over convict discipline raged in the Sydney press, John Dow alias Lord Viscount Lascelles was making his progress around the interior of New South Wales, supposedly enquiring into the treatment of assigned servants. Events had provided

His lordship's *tour de force*

the perfect opening for a 'Government Commissioner' to take to the colony's roads and byways. We might be tempted to see some poetic justice in the spectacle of a former transportee, possibly the descendent of bonded Scottish miners, trying to ease the misery of assigned convict servants. Certainly he was known to tell outraged masters that their assigned servants deserved better treatment.[39]

Yet, like the prodigal heir, the character of government investigator (familiar to all in the colonies from the years of Bigge's investigations) was undoubtedly opportunistic, and Dow's motives self-interested. In January 1834, as his lordship was signing promissory notes for horses and wreaking havoc in Mrs Pendergrast's poultry yard, the real enquiries into conditions at Castle Forbes were being published daily in the Sydney papers. The status and treatment of assigned servants were the hottest issues of the moment. It was a sure bet that many would take the chance to entertain (and influence) such an important personage as a 'Commissioner appointed to receive and transmit to His Majesty the complaints of Assigned Servants'.[40] The role had definite advantages for one well versed in obtaining free board and lodging through false pretences. It was the perfect excuse to leave Sydney when creditors became too pressing, and to move on whenever the light of suspicion began to dawn.

We cannot be certain of Dow's precise movements, but the out-of-pocket horse-trader James Roberts later reported that when he went by appointment to Thompson's lodging-house in Prince Street, Sydney, he was told that 'Lord Lascelles' had left the bill unpaid and set out by stage-coach for Liverpool, a town about twenty miles to the south-west. In the guise of 'Commissioner', Dow seems to have continued on in that direction.

Reports of his progress were beginning to trickle into the press by the winter of 1834. On 31 July the *Herald* accused 'the writer ycleped "*Humanitas*"' of provoking class war between emigrant and emancipist, and called for the 'immediate necessity of a change of system, and of a COMMISSION OF INQUIRY to determine that this shall no longer be a Penal Colony'.[41] A week later, the authorities published a formal notice to deny that this much called-for commission was already at work:

> WHEREAS information has been received, that a person calling himself Lord Lascelles, in company with another whose name is unknown, has lately presented himself on the farms of Settlers in the Southern and Western parts of the Colony, and has given out that he is a Commissioner appointed to receive and transmit to His Majesty the complaints of Assigned Servants, and has thus deceived and misled divers persons; – His Excellency the Governor is pleased to notify that no such Commission is in existence, and that the whole proceeding is an imposture; and desires that Masters of Assigned Servants may warn them not to become the dupes of so absurd a fabrication.[42]

South-west of Sydney, in the county of Camden, domain of the powerful Macarthurs, Dow had found a congenial host in the shape of their hospitable but more socially marginal neighbour, Juan Baptiste Lehimaz D'Arietta. The Peninsula War (Napoleon's 'Spanish ulcer') had brought D'Arietta to New South Wales in 1821.[43] He was in good company. In a notable instance of jobs for the boys, being a Peninsula veteran seems almost to have been a prerequisite for senior administrators across the British empire between the 1820s and the 1840s.[44] D'Arietta had been attached in a contracting role to the commissariat

His lordship's *tour de force*

of the British Army, involved in the vital task of provisioning the campaign. Like Mudie, he arrived in the wave of post-war immigration, provided with letters of recommendation from William Morton Pitt, MP for Dorset. Having demonstrated sufficient capital as well as good connections, he was quickly granted 2000 acres on the Nepean River and assigned convicts to work it.

The estate was named Morton Park in honour of D'Arietta's distinguished patron. A fine house was built with a good aspect. A woman (thirty years his junior) was married. A son was born. Another dynasty of the New South Wales gentry seemed on its way. But D'Arietta always remained an outsider. His neighbours made fun of his broken English. He was popularly believed to have been a spy during the Napoleonic wars. He had married his mistress, Sophie Spearing, and their first child was born four months after the wedding. The Colonial Secretary found against him in a case in which D'Arietta was accused of trying to separate a convict from his wife in consequence of 'some private motives'.[45] There were rumours of another child born by a convict servant. Perhaps more important than all of these shortcomings, Morton Park was not a financial success. D'Arietta hovered on the brink of bankruptcy as the Macarthurs cast greedy eyes over his fertile acres.[46]

Life in the D'Arietta household could be volatile. On one occasion, or so report would have it, Sophie smashed a prize pumpkin over her husband's head in a fit of the sullens. '"Dios!", he cried, "What I do now for the pumpkin seed?"'[47] Having also been held up by bushrangers, D'Arietta was anxious about security. Surgeon Peter Miller Cunningham warned visitors to 'sound your horn' upon approaching the estate, 'unless you are heedless about having your coat-tails pulled off'. D'Arietta had surrounded himself with a slavering chain of guard dogs, complained Cunningham, 'pegged down to the ground at such exact mathematical distances, that two can just meet to lick each other's faces, and pinch a mouthful out of any intruder's hip'.

An acquaintance from Peninsula War days, George Boyes, who visited in 1824, found D'Arietta's limited and repetitive conversation somewhat wearing. Topics included the 'fidelity and the other good qualities of his dogs contrasted with the sloth, roguery, and ingratitude of his servants'; 'Mr. McArthur's horses destroying his Indian corn'; 'Mr. Morton Pitt M.P. for Dorsetshire'; 'His exploits with the Bush Rangers – together with what he would have done had there been occasion'. Nor was there any respite. Any chance of sentimental reverie inspired by the stillness of the night was broken 'by D.A.'s asking: "Wat is you tinking about?"' Boyes went so far as to calculate the number of minutes given over to each of the eight sole items of conversation: 'After my sufferings', he complained in a letter to his wife, 'Job's really appear tolerable'. Matters were not improved by the fact that 'De Arietta's whole range of the English language did not include above Fifty Words!'[48]

Dow, however, evidently found a host perfectly suited to his purpose. The kudos of entertaining an English lord, even incognito (as Dow purported to be travelling) would undoubtedly tempt a man struggling to establish himself amongst the local gentry. There was also, it seems, a scheme designed to appeal as much to his pocket-book as to his pride. In the wake of the government notice and debate in the press, D'Arietta wrote to the Colonial Secretary complaining that:

> sometime since I was imposed upon by the representations
> of this person calling himself 'Lord Viscount Lascelles'

His lordship's *tour de force*

and permitting him to reside for a considerable period on this Farm during which time he tampering with some of my most useful Men, promising to make the one 'a Lord Steward' another 'Gamekeeper' to His Lordship and Free Pardons to the whole, the consequence of which has been that these two Men have continued to annoy me in many ways, and I am apprehensive that they will do me some serious injury.

Clearly his dogs were insufficient protection from the enemy within. D'Arietta hoped to receive two replacements for Robert Pugh and Thomas Saunders who, the resident magistrate confirmed, 'have been very troublesome characters'. The marginal response was tetchy:

> Mr D'Arrieta may return the men as soon as he pleases — but after the indiscretion he has been guilty of in receiving such a Person into his House he can not expect that other men will be assigned him in their place. The [assigned] men sh[oul]d be shown the Govt Notice relating to this Lord Lascelles.[49]

D'Arietta's gullibility was the inspiration for a great deal of local gossip and derision. Austrian Baron Charles von Hügel noted that Dow had lived at Morton Park 'for two months and got money and anything he wanted' from D'Arietta. Von Hügel remarked that there were:

> several good stories … told about this affair, especially concerning the *impudence* of the Lord. According to one story, he gave Mr D'Arietta a letter to take to Sir Edward Parry, one of whose special friends he claimed to be, but who, he said, like his own family, wished him to remain

incognito here, as the commission he had been asked to carry out for the King of England required the greatest possible secrecy. On presentation of this letter, Mr. D'Arietta was to receive the money advanced to him. D'Arietta came to Sydney and found Sir Edward, whose departure had been unexpectedly delayed by one week. After reading the letter, Sir Edward gave it back to Mr D'Arietta, saying: 'I do not know this man'. Mr D'Arietta came back and began to tell the scamp how his mission to Sir Edward had fared, when he interrupted him saying that he could guess the end of the story, 'It was foolish of me not to remember that this was agreed on to prevent discovery'. Mr D'Arietta believed him and the fraudulent Lord Lascelles stayed there as long as it suited him.[50]

His host's protracted financial difficulties were a perfect opening for Dow's scheming. There was clearly some sort of swindle afoot that used the name of Sir Edward Parry, sometime Arctic explorer and then commissioner of the Australian Agricultural Company. At the height of the controversy in the Sydney press about the identity of the mysterious 'Lord Lascelles', the *Sydney Herald* published a letter to its editors: 'GENTLEMEN, I enclose the copy of an original document, said to be the production of "Lord Lascelles," as a specimen of His Lordship's *talents as a letter writer*, and to shew the consummate impudence of the fellow'. Filled with italicised grammatical and spelling errors, many of the names and places in the enclosed copy were tactfully omitted by the newspaper, but the letter signed 'Lascelles' is suggestively dated 'M_____, 13th April 1834', locating Dow at Morton Park at the time of writing. The letter was ostensibly addressed to 'J.E. Caldwell, Esq', whom the *Herald* noted was 'Not to be found'. It had originally enclosed another

His lordship's *tour de force*

letter ostensibly to be delivered to Sir Edward Parry, which, the *Herald* noted, was on opening found to be simply a blank.

It may well be that D'Arietta, having finally realised he had been duped, sent the 13 April letter to the *Herald* himself, omitting any mention of names that might bring down further ridicule on his head. Whatever its source, it is classic Dow, filled with references to other (probably imaginary) correspondence, complex instructions for powers of attorney and money that can be obtained from the Bank of New South Wales. In corroboration of von Hügel's account, an odour of secrecy spreads over the whole. There were fears of 'being detected', convoluted explanations of being unable to withdraw the money from the bank himself for 'it would have induced _____ to have made a *strick* and *dilligent* search, for the purposes of detaining me'. Edward Parry is mentioned in the letter as one of several agents with powers of attorney. The recipient was instructed to:

> arrange all my affairs with the most possible *despatch*; you
> shall find my horse and *gige* at my house in Princes street,
> take it and come along with Mr _____ who will convey
> to _____ , where I now am; bring with you eight hundred
> pounds in gold; give the usual per centage.

There were guarded instructions as to where an iron chest of valuables was hidden behind the skirting boards in Prince Street, and all preparations were to be made for a hasty departure, from sending 'my large dog, Trim, on board' to being sure of where the Captain would 'put in for me'.[51]

The press put 'Lord Lascelles' to work

As news of Dow's activities investigating convict conditions began to trickle in, the story was too good for the Sydney newspapers, locked in partisan conflict, to resist. There were factual reports and genuine speculation about the commissioner's movements and origins. But columns also soon filled with the elaborate and fantastical parodies so beloved by journalists of the period. In all of these, the editors cast 'Lord Lascelles' as a character in the political drama pitting emancipists against exclusives in the wake of the Castle Forbes revolt.

The link to the rebellion was made from the start. The correspondent from Argyle calling himself 'A Subscriber', who first alerted the Sydney reading public to the 'Government Spy's' progress through the Bathurst district, reported that 'Lascelles' was 'attended by a man servant ... formerly in the service of Major Mudie', and gave out that 'One or two of my neighbours think he may be an agent of the Hunterian party, sent across the country to tamper with our servants, and thereby cause them to be as insubordinate here, as they are represented to be in that quarter'. Three days later, another letter appeared in the *Monitor*, this time from 'Quid Nunc', who clearly had some knowledge of the 'Commissioner's real identity:

> the person who figures under that self-imposed title, arrived
> here from Van Diemen's Land in the schooner *Defiance*;
> and during my stay at Hobart did his duty as a prisoner of
> the Crown, by ringing the Penitentiary-bell at Launceston,
> attired in an orange-coloured dress, with a black cap, turned
> up like those of our *Sydney Prisoners*. At the expiration of his
> sentence, he determined to come to New South Wales, and
> turn not only Lord, but also poet. [52]

This was too good for the *Monitor* to let rest without comment. In his new role as Mudie's champion, Hall embarked upon an extended witticism about Lord Lascelles, linking him to the *Gazette* (which, we will recall, had earlier refused to publish his lordship's poetry) and poking fun at the predominantly emancipist settlers of counties Argyle and Bathurst:

> When his Lordship first honoured New South Wales with his presence, he was duly announced by his brother poet ... E. O'S. [Edward O'Shaughnessy] The latter extolled Lord L's verses, but rather objected to the *spelling*. His Lordship, in consequence, has honoured the latter literary character, with his distinguished patronage; and it is said, that in their 'feasts of reason and flow of soul,' ... they have often been assisted by that distinguished writer, the author of *Humanitas* [William Watt] ...
> At length his Lordship conceived the brilliant idea of *a tour*, to collect penal and prison *data*. The conception was received by his friends with rapture ... A clever amanuensis was found in an ex-mutineer of the establishment at Castle Forbes, and his Lordship and Secretary proceeded on their journey without delay. Lord Lascelles is given to pleasantry, and therefore proposed to his companion to quiz 'the natives' of Argyle, (particularly the *Country Justices* of that quarter, *new* as well as old) ... His Lordship has charmed all the *squatters* of the Southern confines of and beyond Argyle, by promising them respectively a section of land each.[53]

The *Gazette*, by contrast, considered that the '*monomania*' of those obsessed with insurrection had 'operated so powerfully as to summon a second Bigge into the field'. 'We are not surprised', its editor wrote on the same day as the above effusion from 'our sturdy antagonist the *Monitor*', 'that our near neigh-bours should have driven people crazy by the effect of their continual vapouring, and that "Lord Lascelles" should have taken the hint as Commissioner, upon an expedition which he was sure to meet with their good wishes, at least'.

The *Herald* took up the connection between the 'Commis-sioner' and 'Humanitas' as fact. The 'Convict Clique' had:

> dispatched an Emissary to foment disaffection among
> the Convicts in the southern districts of the Colony. This
> itinerant 'Humanitas' represents himself as a 'Commissioner'
> from the Home Government, empowered to investigate
> the grievances of the 'poor prisoners;' he undertakes to
> procure them satisfaction and redress, to release them
> from servitude, and to fix them upon grants of land of five
> hundred acres each.

We know from various complaints that Dow was given to making rash promises to convicts, and his activities were too good to pass up in making a political point. It was in the gov-ernment's real investigation into conditions at Castle Forbes that the *Herald* found the inspiration for the imposture:

> Taking this power from the [Hunter River] Magistracy,
> and conferring it upon an unknown and nondescript
> Commission [into Castle Forbes], was a proceeding fraught
> with bad consequences. The precedent, at all events, has
> not been disregarded by 'Lord Viscount Lascelles,' for as
> His Excellency thought fit to decline the services of the
> Magistracy in the Castle Forbes inquiry, the 'poisoned
> chalice has been returned to his lips,' by his Lordship's
> assuming the office of Commissioner of Inquiry, as

His lordship's *tour de force*

successor to Mr. Bigge, who, we believe, possessed the power of suspending the functions of the Anti-Emigrant Governor of that day [Lachlan Macquarie].[54]

The *Gazette* countered this broadside by declaring under the headline 'LORD LASCELLES' that 'A correspondent assures us that this impostor is in the pay of the "faction" that he was authorised to do their dirty work, in order to keep up discontent if possible', and that it was deeply unfair that they now 'call him a vagrant for obeying'. Its own elaborate parody saw the paper 'informed that bulky despatches were last night received, at a late hour, from the Secretary, and Commissioner of the "Insubordination Committee", Lord Viscount Lascelles', and gave a complete account of the minutes of the committee's meeting to draw up 'a critique of that villainous pamphlet by *Humanitas*', attended by 'Timothy Write-hard Crawler, Esq.' and 'Mr. Slyboots'. It was 'moved, seconded and carried that Lord Lascelles be condoled with on his "untoward" exposure, and admonished not to explain that this Committee had employed him'. The meeting congratulated:

> Messrs Jerry Sneak and Sturgeon of the 'Horrible' [Ward
> Stephens and Frederick Michael Stokes, proprietors of the
> *Herald*] ... on their obsequiency to the cause – and after
> congratulating themselves on the happiness the Committee
> felt in having two such obedient and silly gentlemen to
> drive, the Meeting broke up after sundry hahs and hems.[55]

Death of the tyrant doctor

With the doings of 'Lord Lascelles', both real and imaginary, providing inspiration for the Sydney editors, debate over public safety raged on. Then, as if to prove the prophets of doom correct, the colony was rocked by the murder of one of its most prominent citizens, Dr Robert Wardell, barrister and co-founder of the *Australian* newspaper. Wardell had been a passionate opponent of Darling in the courtroom and in print, and even on more archaic terrain. He fought two duels in the tempestuous 1820s, called out once by the governor's brother-in-law, the second time by the attorney general. All three men survived, although whether through good or bad marksmanship, history does not relate. Wardell's support for constitutional reform and emancipist rights did not preclude him, as magistrate, from insisting on the proper punishment of recalcitrant convict servants. Indeed, such was his reputation that he later featured by name in the 1839 poem, 'A Convicts Tour to Hell':

> You prisoners of New South Wales,
> Who frequent watchhouses and gaols
> A story to you I will tell
> 'Tis of a convict's tour to hell.

In that hell, so the verse continued, amongst those damned to torment for their persecution of convicts could be found 'Doctor Wardell', a 'dreadful yelling' issuing from his house.

It was from his earthly rather than his stygian abode that Wardell set out on 7 September 1834, mounted on his distinctive white horse. Soon after he came unexpectedly upon convict escapees John Jenkins, Thomas Tatterdale and Emanuel Brace. The three men had built a bark hut on Wardell's extensive property, and lived as bushrangers preying on the fringes of the colonial population. 'I am a man', was Jenkins' characteristically truculent response when Wardell asked for their names. 'You are only three poor runaways', replied the magis-

His lordship's *tour de force*

trate, 'you had better come along with me'. A muttered argument broke out. Jenkins whispered for Tatterdale to fetch the musket. Brace thought it were better to bear fifty lashes than risk their lives. But Jenkins was determined, and Tatterdale handed over the weapon. 'Oh, for God's sake don't do that', cried Wardell. 'By G_d I will!', was the reply.

Jenkins fired at close range. Brace didn't think the doctor had been hit, but Wardell knew better. 'Oh dear, I'm killed', cried he, as the horse wheeled round and galloped off in terror. Wardell's prediction proved accurate. Searchers found his body the next day. A surgeon surmised he had fallen from his horse through loss of blood and managed only a couple of steps before collapsing. He was forty-one. Meanwhile the convicts had made off across the river, Tattersdale almost drowning along the way. They remained hidden in the bush, but after a couple of days two of the men risked getting supplies from Sydney, for the constables did not know them. At the Sailor's Return, a tavern in the disreputable Rocks neighbourhood, Brace first learnt the identity of their victim when he read about Wardell's murder in the newspaper.

The men managed to remain at large for around five weeks, but were eventually captured when Tattersdale, looking for food in the kitchen of no less a victim than Justice Stephen, blundered into two mounted police baking their bread there.[56] Brace turned King's evidence to save his neck; Tattersdale and Jenkins were brought to trial before Wardell's friend and political ally, Chief Justice Francis Forbes. Faced with such overwhelming evidence, both men would hang. Called upon to say why sentence of death should not be passed upon him, Tattersdale was subdued, and asked only that Brace be required to attend the hanging.

Jenkins, on the other hand, caused a sensation, swore he had been given a 'bloody old woman' as counsel and that he would shoot every 'bloody bugger' in the court. He then broke free and knocked Tattersdale down. Later he admitted it had been a choice of being revenged on Tattersdale or seizing a constable's sword and going for the Chief Justice: 'then you would have had some fun'. A scene of total hysteria ensued with respectable citizens jostling with the 'mob'. As Forbes sat in 'mute astonishment', it took a dozen constables to restrain the raving Jenkins as the court was cleared amidst panicked cries that Jenkins too would escape, aided by the presence of 'many of the worst description of blackguards who infest Sydney'. 'My God, my God is he off, is he off?' Though Jenkins later sent his apologies to the Chief Justice for causing an uproar in court, he was bloodied but unbowed. Climbing the scaffold, he cheekily tugged on the rope that would hang him. 'Good morning my lads', he called to the crowd, 'as I have not much time to spare I shall only just tell you that I shot the Doctor for your benefit; he was a tyrant, and if any of you should ever take the bush, I hope you will kill every b——y tyrant you come across.'[57]

The 'Commissioner' run to ground

Meanwhile, the authorities were slowly closing in on Dow. Three days after the murder of Robert Wardell, the *Herald* reported:

Lord Viscount Lascelles – Who and what is this man? is the general enquiry. Suspicion follows him, and not without cause, is shrewdly surmised. Checks on the Banks of Australia and New South Wales, and orders on one 'E. Thomson, Esq.' have been briskly circulated; contributions

His lordship's *tour de force*

from the stables of the easily gulled ... settlers, and their
stores also have been pretty heavily levied on of late.[58]

Dow had spun a web of swindles across the community. Now
they were beginning to snag his own path. On 7 October 1834,
James Maclehose, who had known Dow in Launceston, wrote
a long letter to the *Sydney Times* under the title 'Death of Lascelles'. Maclehose made no mention of his own dealings with
Dow. (On a trip to London he had been given commissions
and letters to deliver by 'Henry, Viscount Lascelles'. It was a
similar arrangement to that made with Young, probably with a
similar object.[59]) Maclehose would later vent his spleen against
Dow's effrontery in court. For now he would not expose himself to ridicule. He wrote merely to caution the public against
'that highly polished personage, Lord Viscount Lascelles, Government Spy, Commissioner of Enquiry, and what is perhaps
nearer the truth, John Dow, alias Colquhoun'. He had seen letters from the Earl of Harewood explaining that his real son
was on the continent, and disclaiming all relationship with the
impostor. He gave details, that had clearly grown in the telling,
of Dow's arrest in Scotland: the impostor, he alleged, 'lived
in great splendour in Scotland, and carried on the practise
of swindling to the very great extent of some fifty thousand
pounds'. With the benefit of hindsight, Maclehose had this to
say about Dow's powers of persuasion:

> John Dow, *his Lordship*, is void of suavity of manners, and
> there is nothing indicated like pleasant features, instead
> of which there is something of a very peculiar cast in
> his countenance which supercedes it, aided by a lisping
> impediment of speech, which throws the person off his
> guard, and which assists him very much in his roguery.[60]

While visiting the camp of the missionary William Watson in the Wellington Valley, Dow was finally taken into custody on 20 August 1834 and examined at Bathurst. Under the title Lord Lascelles, Dow told Watson 'that he was on his way to the Hunter'. 'He expatiated at length', wrote Watson in his journal:

> on the British Parliament and animadrected on the conduct
> of His Excellency the Governor and the Legislative Council
> of this Colony. I knew that it was my duty 'not to speak evil
> of dignities' and on this principle I conducted myself. I said
> that I considered it more profitable to study the politics of
> the kingdom of Heaven than those of earthly potentates.[61]

Although Dow was examined, he was not charged, and it was only in January 1835 that he was finally tracked down and apprehended.[62] For all the varied confidence tricks that he had pulled off in New South Wales, it was for forging James Roberts's promissory note for £50 under the name Edward Lascelles that Dow was finally indicted for fraud.[63]

His lordship in the dock

On 1 May 1835, the *Australian* noted that:

> The Criminal Sessions commenced this morning with a
> heavy Calendar. The trial of the notorious John Dowe, alias
> Colquhoun, alias Luttrell, alias Lord Viscount Lascelles,
> will take place on Monday next; it is said, that *His Lordship*
> intends to object to the Jurisdiction of the Court, and claim
> a trial by his Peers, a novel question in this Colony will
> therefore be decided.[64]

When the trial got underway three days later, it soon hit a snag. The prisoner refused to plead 'on the ground that he was improperly described; he disclaimed the names of John Dow or Luttrel. The Court enquired of the prisoner what his name was, when he stated it to be Edward, Viscount Lascelles.'

The court responded that the law required the prisoner to put in an affidavit to that effect. Despite the warnings of Chief Justice Francis Forbes as to the serious consequences of perjury, the 'prisoner said that he cheerfully went forth to make that oath. Notwithstanding the combination of malignancy that had been arrayed against him, and the persecutions of the Press, he would do so with the tranquillity of an innocent conscience.'[65] As a result, the next day the court had to begin preliminary proceedings, Justice Burton presiding, by trying the prisoner 'on the issue of his name' before they could try the charge of forgery. Matters commenced at 11:30 in the morning before a capacity crowd. It would be 8:00 that night before sentence was handed down.

Never one to underestimate his claims, the prisoner requested he be tried by the chief justice, but to no avail. Asked whether he chose to be tried by a civil or military jury, Dow (as any man conscious of his high social status surely would) chose a jury of military officers. Before Mr Justice Burton, then, and a military jury, the prisoner offered the following defence:

> Gentlemen of the Jury – I stand before you now in a most
> awful situation, and therefore trust you will view my case
> and the extreme hardship of it. Gentlemen, I was not
> convicted in England; I was sent to these colonies unknown
> to my father, the Earl of Harewood; I arrived in this colony
> in the year 1826; a period of nearly nine years since, and
> during which time, the eldest son of the Earl of Harewood,
> Edward Viscount Lascelles, has never been heard of in
> the United Kingdoms; I arrived in V.D. Land without the

knowledge of my friends, destitute, pennyless, and without a friend – a convict, in a strange country and under the name of John Dow; but I distinctly assert I never went under the name of Dow, but for the stigma it would have cast upon my family, had it been known that a son of the Earl of Harewood was sent a convicted felon to V.D. Land. Gentlemen, it is perhaps within the knowledge of you all, if you have visited or resided in England within the last 9 years, that the eldest son of the Earl of Harewood was missing, and had been missing since the year 1826; now gentlemen, is it not reasonable to suppose had that son been dead or returned to his native land, the public prints would have noticed it?[66]

Dow went on to mention the notice of his arrival in the Van Diemen's Land newspapers, and he argued that these:

papers no doubt went to England, and such a paragraph must have met the eye of my father, the Earl of Harewood, as an extract from a V.D. Land paper, inserted in one of the English newspapers; and is it possible, gentlemen, to suppose if the Earl of Harewood had been aware the statement was incorrect, as an English Nobleman, and for the honour of his House, he would not have contradicted it by the most summary means in his power?

He also produced entries in the *Gazette* and the *Monitor* to prove the presence of Lord Lascelles in the colony. The solicitor general, in response, brought forth David Chambers, now Crown solicitor, who gave evidence as to the power of attorney he had drawn up in March 1833 and the mistakes Dow had made over the names Henry and Edward. He produced the letters he had received from Spottiswood and Robertson and, through them,

His lordship's *tour de force*

from Lord Harewood himself, confirming the prisoner to be an impostor, by name 'John Dow, who was convicted of swindling at Dumfries'.[67]

Philip Lander Fell, who had come out as a free passenger on board the *Woodman*, gave evidence, as did William Gunn, superintendent of the prisoner's barracks at Hobart Town and now conveniently on the mainland. Gunn's memory of his inmates was the stuff of legend: 'He has only to see a prisoner once, to be able to detect him in almost any disguise for years afterwards'. It was said he could 'call every prisoner in Van Diemen's Land by name, when he meets them', and give their exact history within the labyrinthine records of the penal system.[68] With such encyclopaedic knowledge at their disposal, it didn't take the members of the jury long. Without any deliberation, they pronounced the identity of the prisoner to be John Dow.

The way was now clear for the charges of forgery, this time before a civil jury. James Roberts told the sad tale of the dishonoured promissory note, how he had been impressed by a 'tremendous sway of gold chain' and afterwards made suspicious by the opinion of an opportune caller who had observed Dow and his 'secretary', now revealed to be a convict named Callaghan, upon the road. Roberts:

> remarked upon it as a singular thing, that a gentleman should be laughing and joking with his servant along the road, after leaving my house; I thought myself that it was not the way in which Lords usually conduct themselves towards their menial servants, and began to think that all was not right.

Francis Prendergast described the rapacious appetite of the haughty guest who insisted on dining alone in the parlour, while scraps were sent to the host and his wife in the kitchen: 'my wife told me about the turkeys; she said that upwards of a dozen of her finest turkeys had been destroyed; I am sure I saw you eat three or four myself'. The witness, laughed the *Herald*'s reporter, 'dwelt with peculiar feeling on the subject of the turkeys and other fowls which had fallen victim to his Lordship's appetite'. 'I trusted to your honour', said Prendergast bitterly to the prisoner in unconscious echo of Ambrose Clarke exactly a decade earlier, 'which is all I have ever received; I heard afterwards that you ran away'.[69]

The court again produced a string of witnesses who had known Dow in Van Diemen's Land. Philip Lander Fell again described in detail how Dow had claimed to be Lascelles on board the *Woodman*. Timothy Bentley, who had employed Dow as a clerk in the Engineer's department before he was dismissed for bad spelling and handwriting, testified that Dow had been gatekeeper at the lumber-yard (rather than its superintendant, as the prisoner claimed). William Gunn had traced the prisoner's history through the convict records for some reason he could not now recollect. James Maclehose knew Dow in Launceston, and had been persuaded to take letters from him to England.[70] All these men were familiar with the claims Dow had made to being Viscount Lascelles. All of them, bar the outraged Maclehose (who 'was recommended by His Honour to keep his temper within moderate bounds') were assiduous in explaining to the court that they had never believed it.

But the star witness was once more David Chambers, who told at length the story of the powers-of-attorney drawn up in 1833 and of the correspondence he had received from Spottiswood and Robertson:

His lordship's *tour de force*

informing me that the person who employed me must be an impostor. Those gentlemen wrote me stating, that having no faith in the Power of Attorney, they communicated immediately with the Earl of Harewood, who informed them that it was an imposture, as Lord Lascelles, whose name was Edward, was then at Munich.

Dow had been aware of Chambers's suspicions in 1833, remembered the Crown solicitor, and 'he took some pains to remove the impression which he saw I entertained'. In true Dow style, he showed Chambers a letter addressed to Lord Lascelles that he claimed had been written by the Marquess of Douro. Dow had never been afraid to aim high: the Marquess is better known to history as the Duke of Wellington, victor of Waterloo. It 'was badly written', remembered Chambers of this composition, supposedly penned by Britain's former prime minister; its:

orthography was extremely defective, and the whole composition abounded with vulgarisms; if anything had been wanting to confirm my suspicions as to his true character, that letter would have rendered it complete; from what I have seen of the handwriting of the prisoner, I can have no doubt that the said letter was written by him.[71]

'The house would close with the greatest éclat'

Dow cross-examined the witnesses brought against him with confidence and flair, and with due regard to the entertainment of his audience. To Timothy Bentley on the question of his occupation in Launceston:

you saw me near the gate! According to your idea of the duties of gatekeeper, I suppose if you happened to see the worthy Solicitor-General himself standing near the gate of the Lumberyard at Launceston, you would, of course, have set him down as a gatekeeper also! (*a laugh*).

And to David Chambers: 'look this way, Sir, don't be ashamed of yourself'. Even that severest of social critics and mouthpiece of the exclusives, the *Sydney Herald*, remarked:

> his head is remarkably well formed, and although he now appears squalid from imprisonment, there is a remarkable shrewdness developed in the *contour* of his features which bespeaks him the possessor of strong natural powers of mind. He appears to have had little or no education, as betrayed in the vulgarisms and mis-pronunciations with which his address to the Jury abounded; yet, on the whole, the tact with which he cross-examined the witnesses for the prosecution, and the ingenuity of his address, together with the manner of its delivery, exceeded the anticipations of the auditory, (he having a slight impediment in his speech,) and became a subject of general admiration.

For all his *sang froid*, the prisoner had little that was concrete to offer in his defence. Instead he launched with gusto into the tale which began this book, the melodrama I imagine appearing under the title 'The Lost Heir'. In it Henry Lascelles appears as a pasteboard villain who refused to use his influence to save his son from transportation. Those like 'my personal friend, the Marquis of Queensborough' (presumably Dow meant Queensberry) were similarly treacherous: 'fate had ordered it otherwise – he would not attend – I was convicted'. It was 'not necessary', said the prisoner coyly, 'for me to advert to the circumstances which led to my convictions – circumstances which induced me to abandon my legitimate name', but he was

His lordship's *tour de force*

advised 'to keep my rank as much a secret as possible, for the sake of my family'.

He cited the notices in the press and his correspondence with Governor Arthur under the name Lascelles as evidence that his true identity was accepted in the Australian colonies:

> does it not strike you, Gentlemen, as an extraordinary circumstance, that if I had presumed so flagrant an imposture, as the assumption of the character of heir apparent to the noble house of Harewood, without lawful authority, would I not, as prisoner of the Crown, have been instantly visited with punishment? Would not the noble Earl, my father, for the honour of his house, have exerted himself in some way to blot out the disgraceful stain, by production of proofs that I was not his son, the Lord Viscount Lascelles?

He claimed that the bad opinion of his character that pervaded in court was the fault of the Sydney press who had 'traced my footsteps with the keenest vigilance; it has followed me with unrelaxing vindictiveness'. Justice Burton eventually halted the orator, urging him to confine himself 'to argument upon facts – not on what you assume to be facts'.

Despite all the evidence ranged against him, the prisoner refused to admit that he was not Edward Lascelles. It had presumably been more difficult, confronted with his supposed father in the courtroom of Dumfries, to sustain the character of Colquhoun. On board the *Woodman* he had been threatened with a beating for denying the name of Dow. He had since discovered its uses. Because he *had* taken the name of Dow, he now argued, people would understandably know him under that name. This was a central pillar of his defence. It was widely known, claimed the prisoner, that Edward Lascelles had disappeared. The two men were therefore one and the same:

> Does not the evidence shew that the name of Dow was
> adopted to suit the object suggested by my misfortune?
> Does it not shew that I took early opportunities, after my
> departure from England, to disclaim that name and resume
> my own? … Who has been produced before you who ever
> saw Lord Viscount Lascelles – who can prove that I am not
> that man?

'Gentlemen', concluded the prisoner with unblushing sincerity, 'it is not my wish to work upon your feelings':

> I would avoid all attempts at interesting you in my
> misfortunes; were I so inclined, I could draw tears of
> sympathy from your eyes. If I have violated the laws of my
> country, which have been wisely framed for the comfort
> and protection of society, let me be visited by the hand of
> justice; none but cowards shrink from justice. Gentlemen,
> I am no coward; let me have rigorous justice – justice is all
> I require. God forbid I should endeavour to lead you astray.
> If the evidence leads you to my conviction, it is your duty
> to pronounce a verdict of guilty against me. You have sworn
> on the Gospel to do so; but I would once more entreat you
> to give it your most earnest consideration. Your verdict of
> guilty, consigns me to perpetual banishment, degradation,
> and misery. Gentlemen, I have done.

Justice Burton remained unmoved by this emotive appeal. He summed up by dwelling briefly on the law as regarding the offence of forgery: the question for the jury to consider was whether the prisoner had assumed a name which did not

269

His lordship's *tour de force*

belong to him, and whether the fraud could have been committed without the agency of that assumed name. He concluded by remarking that 'it had been clear to him, and it might have been observed by them, that the language of the prisoner was strongly tinctured with the accent of Scotland, and not of Yorkshire as he had represented'. Another clue was 'the style of the prisoners address – abounding as it did with such expressions as were common with vulgar and illiterate persons'. Both 'served to strengthen the assurance that the prisoner had assumed a character and name which did not belong to him'.[72]

It took the jury only a quarter of an hour to return a verdict of guilty. In passing sentence, Justice Burton 'strenuously imposed upon the prisoner the justice of the verdict against a man who would endeavour to traduce the honor of a noble house, by personating the name and character of the heir apparent'. Dow was sentenced to transportation to Van Diemen's Land 'for the term of his natural life'. Before an audience 'crowded to excess', the curtain had finally fallen.[73]

Dow was held in the bowels of the *Phoenix* prison hulk on Sydney harbour for close on four months. Housing up to 260 prisoners at one time, the *Phoenix* gave its name to Hulk Cove, the area of Sydney Harbour now known as Lavender Bay. Like the hulks that Dow had already experienced in Britain, the *Phoenix* was a holding pen. On board were convict witnesses giving evidence in court, invalids awaiting a ship to the Port Macquarie Invalid Station, and those like Dow under sentence of re-transportation. While they waited they were landed in shore parties to work on government projects: cutting timber, building fortifications, reclaiming land and working in the dockyards.

Dow was shipped back to Van Diemen's Land on 27 July

1835 together with five other convicts on board the brig *Siren*.[74]
It seems he had not completely given up his own attempts at
singing seductive songs for the unwary. One month before his
departure a letter from the Colonial Secretary to the principle
superintendent of convicts directed that he receive 'a number
of letters which the Superintendent of the Hulk reports to have
been brought on board by the Convict [Dow] ... and are considered to be of a very improper nature'.[75]

⟨⟨⟨⟩⟩⟩

Despite the truth behind at least some of the testimonies
in court, no-one in Sydney seemed any wiser as to who the
impostor actually was. The *Gazette*, while pronouncing him 'a
rogue', concluded that 'any further enquiry about him would
cost but ill-bestowed pains'. They probably suspected that there
was more to the disappearance of the real Edward than met the
eye. There were whispers about a Lascelles cover-up. The 'per-
tinency with which he [Dow] clung to his original assertion up
to the very latest moment', wrote the *Gazette*:

> combined with many other circumstances with which many
> persons even in this colony are said to be acquainted, raise
> a strong presumption that those parties who have altogether
> repudiated him in England, know something more of who
> and what he really is, than they had deemed it advisable to
> make known or to admit.[76]

For the *Hobart Town Courier*, reporting the outcome of the case
a month later, the reason for the prisoner's obstinacy lay elsewhere: 'We have no doubt that the idea that has taken so strong
a possession of his mind, though it led to the act of forgery
which amounted to a breach of the laws, is the fruit of insanity'.[77]

His lordship's *tour de force*

Was the man called John Dow mad? If so, it was a canny madness. Dow understood only too well how his world worked, where the weaknesses lay in its beliefs about status, and how best to exploit them. He would invariably suit his part to his audience, be it prodigal son or government official. It worked for some months in Scotland, until Patrick Miller took up his busy pen, and it worked for some years in New South Wales a decade later. In that Dumfries courtroom, Lord Hermand had urged Dow to 'reflect that he was going to a country where a more strict watch would be kept over his conduct'.[78] In fact, the antipodes offered generous scope for Dow's penchant for aliases. In a colony where 'criminals' and 'innocents' lived side by side, where social and political power were all too rapidly evolving, shrugging off one life and taking up another was part of marking out a new society. If anyone could understand the rules of that game, it was a serial impostor.

EPILOGUE:
THE PLAY IS PLAYED OUT

With Him the nations are as a drop of a bucket ... He
bringeth the princes to nothing: He maketh the judges of
the earth as vanity. He putteth down one and setteth up
another.

Herrick Pittsburgh, *God's Ways Unsearcheable*, 1865

In November 1841, Henry Lascelles, 2nd Earl of Harewood,
rode out to meet his death in the quiet lanes of Yorkshire. The
Lascelles were famous devotees of the hunting field. Henry
became Master of Foxhounds of the Bramham Moor Hunt in
1822 and kennelled the hounds at Harewood House for more
than twenty years. Thus was maintained 'at his sole expense,
the Harewood hunt in all its ancient reputation and splendour'.
It was, of course, a fitting pastime for one whose family had
fought so hard to establish themselves amongst the ranks of the
landed aristocracy.

Henry was in his seventy-fourth year, and had lost his wife
the previous February. His regular doctor, Francis Gibbs, testified that the earl had lately been in 'indifferent health' but was
so much better as to resume his usual exercise. Lord Harewood

followed the hunt until it ran a fox to ground at Grimston Hill, leaving as they tried to dig it out. Testifying before a coroner's inquest, Joshua Wilkinson, pupil of the local rector, saw Lord Harewood ride towards the village of Bramham in the gathering dark of a November afternoon. Shortly before he got there, the earl dismounted, and Joshua, no doubt hurrying home with a schoolboy's appetite for his tea, last saw the elderly gentleman standing palely by the hedge at the side of the lane, looking out over the fields.

It was dusk under a rising moon by the time that Stephen Shepherd, a whipper-in at Harewood House, came upon the earl collapsed upon the verge, his horse standing quietly by. All witnesses testified that he seemed to be 'quite dead', with no obvious marks of violence on his body. Shepherd and the Harewood huntsman William Bamford got their master's body to the Bay Horse Inn in Bramham. Surgeons were called. The medical men speculated that death 'was occasioned by the rupture of a blood vessel at the base of the brain', what we would call a stroke. The coroner's verdict put it more poetically: 'Died suddenly by the visitation of God'.[1]

Viscount Lascelles had assured his father from Munich that he, Edward, was 'not fitted for being at the head of a family in England'. I 'have always thought', wrote Edward of his brother, 'that Henry was infinitely better adapted to succeed you than myself in many respects'.[2] In the event, the question of succession never arose.

If it were true, as Dow claimed in May 1835, that Edward had completely vanished from the pages of the British press, this would not remain the case for long. In October 1835, the Sydney newspapers reporting the impostor's trial had arrived in Britain. Several publications picked up the 'remarkable' story

A Swindler's Progress

under headings like 'Soi-Disant Peer of the Realm Trans-ported'.[3] Though the reports did little more than summarise the legal proceedings contained in the *Sydney Herald*, the tale may have inspired the press to return to the story of the real Edward. Cryptic hints appeared in the *Times* some four months later:

> Viscount Lascelles, the eldest son of the Earl of Harewood,
> married some years ago Miss Louisa Rowley contrary, it was
> said at the time, to the wishes of his father. A separation
> between the parties took place some time afterwards,
> and the lady is since dead. His Lordship is now residing
> at Munich, where he is said to have formed a second
> matrimonial alliance.

Four days later, *The Satirist, and Censor of the Times* took up the story in characteristically cheeky vein, mocking the steely social ambitions of Edward's sister-in-law. As the anonymous letter sent to Lord Harewood from Vienna in 1830 attests, there had always been gossip about the hopes that Edward's disgrace must inevitably have raised in the breast of his younger brother:

> It has long been known that the Earl of Harewood intends
> depriving his eldest son of as much of the family estates as
> he possibly can. Lord Lascelles thought proper to marry one
> Louisa Rowley, who was a _____, that is, quite as virtuous
> a woman as the [notoriously debauched] Countess of
> Harrington; and consequently, he sullied our honourable
> peerage. Being a friend, we presume, to the lower orders, he
> has selected a second wife of not a very exalted rank, to the
> immense mortification of the second son, who being yoked
> to one of the aspiring daughters of the Marquis of Bath,
> has been panting for succession to the Peerage. As there is

apparently no salvation for the younger son in this world,
he had better turn his attention to the family motto [In God
only is salvation].[4]

The source of this *on dit* is obscure. So too is any information about Louisa Rowley, if, indeed, she had any existence outside the imagination. She may well have been a smokescreen put out by the Lascelles themselves to cover up the connection with Ann Elizabeth Rosser. If so, she proved a durable one.

Edward was settled in Wurzburg, on the northern edge of Bavaria, when a property settlement was signed between 'His Highborn Count Edward von Lascelles and Her Highborn Lady Philippine von Lascelles born Baroness von Lutzendorf' on 2 May 1838. Having each brought their property into common stock, his annual income was to pay their joint expenses. If they were ('contrary to expectation') to separate, she would still receive half of all his annual revenues and keep all accumulated property from their marriage. If either party died, he or she was to inherit the other's estate. Perhaps with one eye on the earl's views on this generosity to his son's former mistress, Edward and his wife appointed an executor in Wurzburg to prevent any 'judicial interference'.

A year later, in September 1839, the settlement was confirmed (bar an amendment about a reduction in their joint wealth) but Edward was too unwell to attend the court. The authorities were obliged to visit his residence where they found him 'in his Sitting Room out of Bed, unwell as it appeared but in perfectly sound mind'.[5] Three months later Edward was dead. For his sister-in-law Caroline, wife of William Saunders Sebright Lascelles, the death of the long-absent Edward was 'more of a shock than a sorrow', and it seemed 'odd, in the circumstances, to be wearing mourning'.[6] As had happened a generation earlier with the death of 'Beau' Lascelles, a second son called Henry was once more heir to the earldom. The dynasty's future again seemed to be firming. Henry boasted a suitable (and notoriously strong-minded) wife, and a growing brood of children. Their last child, the thirteenth, would be born just after the first had made the couple grandparents.[7]

By the end of 1839, news of Edward's death began to appear in the British press. The *Times* announced the 'melancholy event' on 17 December 1839, noting that the 'mortal remains of the deceased are to be interred in Germany'. Other papers seemed less well informed of his whereabouts. The *Leeds Mercury*, which should surely have known better, put it out that 'Lord L. had resided for some years on his father's estates in the West Indies'.[8] Again, it was a convenient rumour possibly started by the Lascelles themselves. The family appears to have been able to keep Edward's second marriage quiet, and Baroness Testa was absent from the obituary notices. So too was Ann Elizabeth Rosser. Numerous papers noted that Edward had married Miss Louisa Rowley in 1821, and that she was deceased.[9] The *Satirist* was moved to comment once more:

> The late Lord Lascelles was entirely excluded by his family. His marriage with Miss Louisa Rowley added no dignity to the family escutcheon, and had he lived to succeed to the title, he would have inherited as little as possible to support the dignity. The woman whom he married was an honest woman in every sense of the eye of the law, and, we doubt not, in propriety during her matrimonial career. How many of those flaunting about in fashionable life can be proved otherwise?

Three months later the same paper claimed, 'It is rumoured

277

Epilogue

that the family of Lord Harewood has been thrown into some consternation by the appearance of a youngster who claims to be the son of the late Lord Lascelles', but it could report nothing further.[10]

Edward had disappeared into garbled rumour and possibly deliberate misinformation. But with his steadier brother, Henry, later 3rd Earl of Harewood, the Lascelles lineage would indeed go from strength to strength. Three generations later, the Lascelles, whom in 1807 Fitzwilliam's supporters had labelled a 'Family Nobody knows', would reach out to the very apex of British society. Princess Mary, only daughter of King George V and Queen Mary, married a later Henry, Viscount Lascelles, in 1922. It was some two hundred years since the first Henry Lascelles had set out with his brothers from Yorkshire to Barbados. In due course Princess Mary's husband would take his place as the 6th earl, their son as the 7th. The princess played an important role in opening Harewood House to the public in the 1950s, and this royal lustre to the family history remains one of the drawcards for the visitors ('felicity hunters', as Repton may have been inclined to call them) who continue to flock to the estate.

'Whom the Gods would destroy they first make mad'

Notwithstanding those eight grandsons of Milton and Mary, all duly christened William Wentworth-Fitzwilliam, the Lascelles's archrivals of 1807 would prove less fortunate. In May 1948, the 6th Earl Fitzwilliam chartered a ten-seater plane and set off for the south of France. With him was his lover of almost two years, Kathleen 'Kick' Kennedy, sister of the more

A Swindler's Progress

famous Jack. He was married; she was Catholic. On a whim, the couple decided to lunch with friends in Paris while the plane refuelled. With bad weather approaching, the pilot was furious at the delay. Several hours later, despite his warnings, Fitzwilliam rashly insisted they go on. At ten thousand feet, the plane hit a ferocious storm and came down in the Ardèche mountains. Both passengers, the pilot and the co-pilot were all killed on impact. Kick's mother, the formidable Rose Kennedy, who had done all she could to separate the lovers, saw in the tragedy the hand of God.

Only two of the eight Williams had produced heirs. Now the 6th earl, at thirty-eight, had in turn died without a son, leaving only one branch viable. His father's cousin, Eric Spencer Wentworth-Fitzwilliam, a childless man in his sixties and known within the family as 'Bottle by Bottle', would inherit.[11] Eric held the title for only four years, presiding over a crumbling house, turned over to a College of Physical Education, and grounds requisitioned by the government and defaced by open-cast mining under Britain's recently nationalised coal industry. As the old man succumbed to his alcoholism, the two brothers who were his only heirs were locked in a legal row over the elder's legitimacy. The rival claimants were the sons of a chorus girl, children of an 1880s marriage kept deliberately obscure until well after the fact.

In 1818 the Lascelles had been warned of Ann Elizabeth Rosser's alleged plans 'of putting a spurious child to be hereafter Earl of Harewood'.[12] Now, in 1951, it was the Fitzwilliams who would finally fall victim to the consequences of a reckless and clandestine marriage. A court ruling decided in favour of the younger brother, who had no heirs, meaning that the judgement effectively ended their earldom. The last Earl Fitzwilliam

Epilogue

died in 1979, and the following decade his daughter put the gargantuan pile of Wentworth House up for sale. It had displayed the family's status for two and a half centuries, now the purpose for which it had been built was no more. Some years before his death, the last earl ordered the immolation of sixteen tons of family documents. They comprised most of Wentworth's twentieth-century historical record, and the pyres burnt for three weeks. It was, remembered one descendant, a kind of archival suicide: 'They wanted to destroy things, as they themselves had been destroyed'.[13] For all the aristocracy's continued hold on power and privilege, they could still be hoist by their own dynastic petard. Fate had ultimately reversed the outcomes of Edward's and of Milton's choices. 'Vanity of vanities, saith the Preacher, vanity of vanities; all is vanity'.

Exit the 'Major', pursued by a bear

On the far side of the world, Dow had departed from New South Wales. But the saga of Castle Forbes rumbled on. If Mudie was exonerated by the official investigation into conditions on his estate, now he overreached himself. William Watt, convict editor of the *Gazette*, was widely known to be the author of the 'Humanitas' pamphlet. Three months after Dow was finally convicted, in August 1835, Mudie launched a series of vindictive suits against Watt. He did his utmost to get the editor convicted of breaking the conditions of his ticket-of-leave, even stacking the Sydney bench with Hunter Valley magistrates. Governor Bourke was forced to act. He excluded Mudie, and several others involved in Watt's case, from the list of magistrates published in 1836. That Bourke commissioned William Charles Wentworth as Justice of the Peace in the same year

A Swindler's Progress

only underlined the point. In high dudgeon at this calculated insult, and his own loss of both caste and power, Mudie sold up and left the colony. In London he rushed into print with a vitriolic book designed to expose the excesses of Bourke's convict-loving administration.

The Felonry of New South Wales portrayed the colony as a sink of iniquity, a pandemonium of every imagined vice. Mudie's dubious past separated him from the educated 'gentlemen' convicts like Dow and Watt by only the narrowest of margins. Such felons had always disturbed any easy division of the population into two distinct classes, and it was their social pretensions that most enraged Mudie. He despised the word 'emancipist' and coined the word 'felonry' to include all past and present convicts. For him, the stain of transportation could never be washed out. It must be visited upon their children and their children's children. *The Felonry* caused a sensation. Copies from the period still bear their readers' affronted marginal notes, forests of exclamation points and cries of 'Nonsense', 'Bosh', 'Lie', 'Horrid Lie' and 'Proof? Proof?'[14]

There were nevertheless those in London willing to turn Mudie's wild accusations to political account. From 1837 to 1838, a parliamentary committee sat to investigate the system of transportation. It was chaired by the Radical parliamentarian Sir William Molesworth, Edward Baines's colleague and co-member for Leeds. Molesworth's committee was effectively a show trial, stacked with supporters of Wakefield's 'systematic colonisation'. For all that Mudie was widely regarded as a loose cannon (much of his evidence was so obviously biased that it was struck from the record) the events at Castle Forbes and his long feud with Governor Bourke meant he was willing to say exactly what members of the committee wanted to hear, and

Epilogue

in the most lurid possible terms at that. Transportation was an opportunity rather than a punishment for British felons, so the argument went, and it degraded the whole of colonial society, both felonry and free.

In the burst of emotion accompanying the abolition of slavery across the British empire, this other form of bonded labour was easily tarred with the brush of moral corruption. Against the loud opposition of many colonists, the system of transportation to New South Wales was abolished in 1840, just as systematic colonisation and assisted emigration were gaining pace. (It would continue in Van Diemen's Land until 1852.) In 1840 free people already outnumbered convicts by twelve to one in Sydney.[15] With transportation ended, the most serious stumbling block to a new constitution was removed; political change was now inevitable. Elected representative institutions were granted to New South Wales in 1842; responsible government, with a far wider franchise than Britain's, a decade later. As for Mudie's personal role in this drama, there was as yet one final scene to play.

The 'Major' had blackened the name of the entire colony, in the pages of *Felonry* as much as in the published evidence of the Molesworth Committee. Amongst his allegations were claims that settlers prostituted their wives to their convict servants, that 'unnatural crime' ran rampant, and that the convict-editor Watt 'actually ruled the colony' through a conspiracy with the governor. Now, with a breathtaking lack of insight, Mudie decided to move back to Sydney in 1840. Unsurprisingly, he found himself a pariah. Of all the people insulted in the pages of the *Felonry*, it was the son of the notoriously deaf Attorney-General John Kinchela ('not even the address or manners, or the language of a gentleman' according to Mudie's book) who cracked first.[16] John Kinchela junior, a pastoralist and magistrate from Bathurst, caught up with Mudie near the Sydney Bank in George Street a few months after the *Felonry*'s author landed. Having first made sure of his victim's identity, he laid into him with a riding crop. If a duel recognised the manly honour of both combatants, a horsewhipping was the proper action against a scoundrel. As the two men struggled, no-one was moved to intervene. On the contrary, an appreciative crowd gathered to witness the Major's come-uppance. Mudie, his hat dented, bleeding and covered with bruises, made it to a surgeon, but the deepest wound was to his pride. He brought a case of assault before the Supreme Court in late October, seeking damages of £1000.

Whether the defendant or the plaintiff was more on trial soon became a matter of opinion. In vain did Justice Willis repeatedly instruct counsel and jury to confine their attention to the evidence at hand. If the excited spectators crammed into the building had any doubts of the grandstanding that would follow, the choice of counsel for Kinchela soon put them to rest. Mudie faced cross-examination from his old adversary Roger Therry, defender of the Castle Forbes mutineers, the man he had denounced as the centre of the conspiracy between Watt and the government. Therry was not going to let a chance like this slip by; nor was the audience. At the conclusion of his opening remarks, 'some of the rabble', complained the *Herald*, 'testified their approbation by knocking with their hands and feet in the same way that is done at the Theatre'.[17] It was a good job, said Justice Willis, that he did not know who they were, or 'he would have taught them to respect the decency which ought to be observed in a court of justice'.

A few minutes was sufficient for the heartily entertained

Epilogue

jury to return a verdict of £50 damages. If the amount fell just short of calculated insult, those in court soon obliged. Before the indignant eyes of the authorities, a quick whip-around collected the sum from the riotous spectators and it was handed over on the spot. The honour of the colony was avenged. Mudie soon gathered up his family and departed once more for England. He died in obscurity in London, on the very eve of responsible government in New South Wales.

'Men at some time are masters of their fates'

Of all the characters in this story, it is John Dow whose end remains, fittingly, the most enigmatic. A year after the 1835 trial, under the title 'My Lord Lascelles', a 'Correspondent' to the *Sydney Gazette* facetiously complained:

> How unobservant are the Journals of the Sister Colony [Van Diemen's Land] not to enlighten us mortals to the northwards as to the fate of this 'Peer in his own right,' as he called himself, who quitted us to take up his residence there for his 'natural life'? Does he now sport with aldermanic complacency 'the swag' of gold chains around his neck, which caused him in this hemisphere more respect than did his title? Is he now lolling indolently at the Ship Inn luxuriating in turkies, ducks, fowls and hams, sending out to his landlord and lady the ribs and truck for him to feast upon ... has he the same *penchant* for purchasing horses, cattle, or in fact anything *tangible*, paying by his 'Lascelles' cheques on the Hobart Town Bank? Does the muse of Byron still inspire him, hoping at the same time that his orthography is corrected with his higher flights of fancy? And more than all, where, oh where is the magical

A Swindler's Progress

tin box? has that arcanum been yet penetrated – has the veil been torn aside, and admitted to vulgar eyes, the secret of the prison house? If so 'twere churlish of our southern contemporaries not to enlighten their readers on a subject which has caused so much caveling both here and in the Mother Country. His Lordship having exclaimed with Horace *Juvenis Partum* – it is but fair that we should know somewhat of his welfare.[18]

The *Gazette* was destined to remain disappointed. Tracing Dow's fortunes through the paperwork of the penal system throws up only scanty leads. When reconvicted in 1835, the clerks noted Dow's age as 38. It was now closer to that of the real Edward, rather than being (as in the convict register of 1826) that of a man some eight years younger.[19] Apparently the impostor had learnt the lessons from *Burke's Peerage* provided by David Chambers. Pinned down in the convict lists of 1835, his identity is a strange amalgam of noble and felon. His name is given as 'Dowe John alias Luttrell', his 'trade or calling' as 'Labourer'. This term didn't mean very much. As a frustrated clerk once complained: 'When I ask what their *trades* are, all the answer I can get from three-fourths of them is "A thief, a thief". Shall I put these down as *labourers*, sir?'[20]

Dow's birthplace is once more listed as 'Harewood, Yorkshire'. Interviewed as to his offence, the entry partially reproduces his reply: 'Forging the name of *Edward* Lascelles to a check, I don't recall how much, there were several, never was in custody in NSW before. I was transported to VDL by the ship Woodman in 1826 for 7 years.' His relations were duly noted as 'Father the Earl of Harewood – 4 Bros. Henry, William Sanders, Francis, Arthur. 3 Sisters. Caroline, Henrietta, Ann'. Dow clearly had gained some degree of familiarity with the Hare-

Epilogue

wood family tree, but his list is only partially correct and reads like a garbled version of the *Peerage*.[21]

Dow arrived once more in Van Diemen's Land on 4 August 1835.[22] How he spent the next few months is unknown. On 14 December, he was transferred to the secondary punishment settlement of Port Arthur, south-east of Hobart on the isolated Tasman Peninsula. Its terrors would be immortalised in the original convict gothic novel, Marcus Clarke's *For the Term of His Natural Life* of 1874. Exactly twenty years after the era of convict transportation ended in 1877 a fire gutted the penitentiary; wiped clean, some said, by the wrath of God. Its dark reputation was exploited for tourists from the very beginning, and tragically underscored there in 1996 when a gunman's killing spree left thirty-five people dead.

It is hard to dig beneath the patina of these horrific images. Port Arthur certainly had a perfect setting for its original purpose, close to Hobart, yet easily cut off from the rest of the island by a narrow sandy isthmus, less than a hundred yards wide, known as Eaglehawk Neck. Precautions against escape by land were formidable, though several inventive attempts were made. The ruse adopted in the 1830s by one Billy Hunt, a former strolling player with misplaced confidence in his own acting abilities, was one of the more ludicrous. Seeing a rather moth-eaten kangaroo hopping towards the Neck, one of the sentries observed audibly to his mates that he would take a shot at it. 'Don't shoot', yelped the beast, 'I am only Billy Hunt'. The marsupial was, it was said, 'happy to return to his lair in a whole skin'. The ground at Eaglehawk Neck was strewn with crushed shell to better reflect the light shed across it at night by lamp posts. Sentries were assisted by dogs chained, D'Arietta-style, at overlapping intervals across the neck, some

A Swindler's Progress

even tethered on platforms out to sea should any convict try and wade around the barrier. Though there were early complaints that the dogs were too mild-mannered, sufficiently fierce ones were soon signed up. By the early 1840s there was a phalanx: Caesar, Pompey, Ajax and Achilles (their less classical companions went by the names Ugly Mug, Jowler, Tear'em and Muzzle'em). As one observer wrote four years after Dow's arrival, 'Whether Port Arthur is, as called by some, an "Earthly Hell" or not, it has at all events its Cerberus'. A system of semaphores could flash a warning of convict escape before a man even reached the neck. Access to the peninsula was solely by water. The commandant kept a collection of captured escape craft on his own veranda, and it was popularly believed that the guards drew sharks closer to shore by dumping offal and blood off the beaches.[23]

Dow's 1835 sentence in Sydney had noted that he would not be sent to 'a penal settlement' (in other words a place of secondary punishment like Port Arthur) as his crimes in New South Wales had been committed as a free man, rather than as a convict.[24] Yet both Arthur and his Colonial Secretary, John Burnett, were eager to isolate the 'specials', those educated or higher-class convicts who so troubled men like Mudie, from the rest of the population. From 1833, the educated convicts of Hobart Town and Launceston were also sent to Port Arthur.[25] As historian Dulcie Denholm explains, for some 'it appeared to be the only place where they could be properly handled away from society'.[26] Into just such a category fell the subtle and plausible rogue named John Dow.

By the time Dow arrived, the institution was some five years old, and the earliest days of meagre rations and inadequate accommodation were over. In 1833 the discovery of coal

Epilogue

deposits nearby was a fortunate by-product of location (save for those who had to mine it). By 1835 there were almost a thousand prisoners on the peninsula. Apart from the extensive work required to build, expand and maintain the settlement, convicts undertook light manufacture such as shoemaking, tailoring, blacksmithing; they cut timber, made bricks and tiles, and cultivated land; and, their especial dread, they mined coal. Toward the end of Dow's time at Port Arthur, a flour mill and granary were under construction. According to instructions from Lieutenant Governor Arthur in 1832, prisoners wore distinctive yellow clothing issued to them before they left Hobart, their other clothing to be held there until they were released.[27]

We have almost no information on Dow's time at Port Arthur. His conduct record is once more a near blank, suggesting that he largely kept out of trouble. Despite his shortcomings in spelling and handwriting, he may still have been lucky enough to be employed as a clerk. If his conduct were good, he could expect to leave the labour gangs (where the death rate was formidable) after a probationary period, sooner if his skills were in demand. But the main purpose of Port Arthur was to produce goods that would offset its running costs. There were few opportunities to escape the punishingly hard physical labour that most endured. 'I will run your legs off, and have a dozen flogged before night, into the bargain. Come on, and I will show you what it is to work!' Thus did Linus Miller, an American prisoner labouring at the settlement during Dow's time, remember the words of his overseer: 'There's no such word as *can't* at Port Arthur'.[28]

The image of Port Arthur as a hell-on-earth was created very early, in part by a colonial press locked in a running battle with Lieutenant Governor Arthur over its own freedom

A Swindler's Progress

of speech. The penal settlement that carried his name was a useful image of Arthur as tyrant. Port Arthur had replaced an outpost of far more justified terror, that of Macquarie Harbour (from which the audacious Matthew Brady had escaped), and it took on its mythical status as well. When Marcus Clarke wrote his novel, he freely borrowed events from Norfolk Island and Macquarie Harbour and ascribed them to the settlement on the Tasman peninsular.[29]

A convict gothic melodrama, such as Dow was at such pains to enact before the Sydney courts, would leave his story here. What better punishment for a man so determined to keep shifting his identity, than to remain forever pinned down as a cipher within this chamber of horrors? Yet for all its fearsome reputation, Port Arthur was intended as a thoroughly modern system of total disciplinary surveillance. The cruelties of solitary confinement, lashings and shackles were as carefully controlled and rigidly monitored as the convicts themselves. And as such, for those deemed deserving, exit strategies *were* in place.

As New South Wales experimented with a new representative legislature, Dow was progressing slowly towards the end of his own incarceration. On 16 August 1843 he left Port Arthur, was placed under the control of the Principal Superintendent of Convicts in Hobart, and later that year obtained a ticket-of-leave. He was recommended for a conditional pardon in 1845, a status approved a year later.[30] He could not leave the colony or return to Britain, but so long as he abided by these conditions, he was at liberty to cast himself in yet another role. Mysterious to the last, he may even have managed as successful a reinven-

Epilogue

tion as had the colonial stage on which he played the part of Edward Lascelles. With his conditional pardon, John Dow was effectively a free man. And as such, he is free to disappear from our sight once more.

REFLECTIONS ON
A SWINDLER'S PROGRESS

It began with a bad case of footnote paranoia. And for that I blame the patriots. A month before winning the 1996 election, John Howard had declared his vision for the year 2000: Australians would be 'relaxed and comfortable' about their history. Eight years later, the country was embroiled in a localised variant of that broader debate known as the 'culture wars'. If the prime minister and his fellow travellers, three years into a second term, were feeling relaxed and comfortable, most Australian historians were finding things to be anything but. Those who had chronicled a legacy of violence against Indigenous peoples, the prime minister charged, were indulging in 'black armband' history.[1] In defence of the nation's reputation, critics were closing in on the footnotes of some of Australia's most esteemed scholars. It seemed they would check and re-check every reference until they had proven that frontier massacres had been exaggerated for sinister political ends.

As the flag of accuracy was waved across the battlements of the 'History Wars', I got increasingly twitchy. A soon-to-be released book with a hot pink cover called *Scandal in the Colonies* was unlikely to find itself in the history warriors' crosshairs. Nevertheless, perhaps I better just re-check a curious little story I'd used in the opening pages? An Austrian baron had related an anecdote about Australia that seemed to exemplify everything I wanted to say about status and empire. And it was funny to boot. What better vignette with which to open a study of colonial re-invention? After all, how many convict-cum-viscounts do you come across, even 'in the trade'?

The page proofs were rolling off the press. It was at this spectacularly inopportune moment that I decided to dig a little further into my traveller's tale. Baron Charles von Hügel recounted an amusing story he had heard on his visit to the antipodes. It seemed to him to encapsulate the topsy-turvy, looking-glass world of a penal colony: a former convict had made a pretty good living defrauding others while passing himself as 'Lord Lascelles'. As I did my last-minute check, the sources suddenly multiplied. The swindler jumped from passing anecdote to detailed legal archive. He now had an implausible-sounding name, John Dow, a host of irritated victims, and a fascinated public at his trial. I was at first horrified (too late to include all this in the book!) but increasingly absorbed. It was clear that the story still underlined the point I had made in *Scandal in the Colonies* – that the antipodes was a place for social reinvention, albeit usually of a less mendacious and spectacular type. The obsessive concern with respectability in cities like Sydney was in part a response to just such sneers made by Baron von Hügel and his ilk: that the tale was 'highly characteristic of the country in which it took place'.[2]

A Swindler's Progress

This is true, so far as it goes, but it is of course only half the story. Looking back, I see now just how far the fog of my ignorance still enveloped me. I knew only that a swindler had used the name of Edward Lascelles to his own ends. The prisoner had never admitted his guilt, claiming to be Lascelles right to the end, but the evidence seemed against him. To ape a viscount in the colonies had obvious advantages. It wasn't necessary for there to be an original. So the first question to ask was this one: if the prisoner wasn't a viscount, was the identity merely his own invention? I knew nothing, then, of the real Lascelles of Harewood House, not even how to pronounce their name (it rhymes with 'tassels'). And then came the epiphany. Edward Lascelles was not only a real viscount, he was a viscount with a scandalous past. More to the point (at least for my purposes) he came from a family who had backed their rise into the aristocracy with money made through slavery in the West Indies. It was, to quote from Tom Stoppard's wonderfully apposite play, *Arcadia*, 'one of those moments that tell you what your next book is going to be'.[3]

I could see only the barest outline of the story at this stage. But it was enough. An impostor had disconcerted an entire society that was itself on the make. And he had chosen as his model a man whose family had reinvented itself no less profoundly than had the colonists of New South Wales. This story of imposture and social opportunism bound together people, places and ideas right across the British imperial world.

For someone who had spent more than a decade studying the question of imperial identities, it was perfect. I was in the midst of what has been called 'the transnational turn', a movement within history writing that questioned whether the 'nation' was the proper topic of analysis. What is 'British' or

Reflections on *A Swindler's Progress*

'Australian' or 'West Indian' history?[4] How meaningful were such concepts to people in the late eighteenth and early nineteenth centuries? How useful are they now? Von Hügel had presented his impostor as the tale of a brazen felon duping a series of gullible provincials. A historian tracing a national story might have used this anecdote to show how far 'we' had moved on. Reading his account, I could imagine it as an obscure, somewhat entertaining footnote in a book that charted the emergence of Australian egalitarianism from a too-slavish regard for the social hierarchies of the mother country. Yet a growing literature on transnational biography and imperial networks showed just how easily lives slip between the boundaries once taken for granted by historians.[5] As one biographical thread is pulled, national frameworks which appear comfortably stitched-up are apt to unravel.

I began my work, then, with Dow telling a lie in a Sydney courtroom. As I followed the entangled stories of John Dow and Edward Lascelles, of how the lie came to be told, and of the tragedy that enabled the lie, I found myself crossing the globe in multiple directions. In this tale about forged identities I could see a broader story emerging. The real significance of John Dow's adventures in New South Wales was only revealed when I realised that this ostensibly isolated incident was a chapter in a sprawling saga of opportunism and imposture which reached right across the British empire and linked the eighteenth and nineteenth centuries.

In this obscure and unlikely tale, I saw a new way to understand and to write of some of the key events that had transformed Britain and its empire over that time. The disputes in which the Lascelles family were engaged in Yorkshire, and in which Dow was embroiled in New South Wales, were part

A Swindler's Progress

of the way in which the British world was convulsed in this period by debates about the proper nature of politics. We could see these shifts as much in the anxiety over an impostor as we could see them in the expansion of the electoral franchise. The right to act within the public sphere in both Britain and the colonies was claimed and defended by rhetoric that emphasised particular models of identity for men. The move in Yorkshire politics from Earl Fitzwilliam to Edward Baines, after all, took place within a single generation. Feeding in to this identity crisis were issues such as wealth (and its source), demeanour (which could be racialised as 'civilisation') and social influence.

For a historian, an impostor's importance lies precisely in how he (in this instance) is able to lay bare the assumptions of his own society. Unlike that more famous impostor of historical scholarship, Natalie Zemon Davis's 'Martin Guerre', John Dow never tried to make his model's *lives* his own. He never sought to take the place of their persons, but to make use of the position that a viscount or a baronet's son could command in society.[6] What was so disturbing to contemporaries about Dow's concoctions was that they demonstrated just how far supposedly firm social hierarchies could be reduced to ephemera. By self-consciously performing their claim to a distinct identity, impostors drop clues in the historical record as to how status was made manifest, disputed and endorsed. Impostors reveal the expectations of their audience at the same time as they subvert them, demonstrating how status differences were experienced in everyday encounters. Impostors and confidence men and women are likely to flourish at precisely those moments when social hierarchies are most fluid.[7]

Who, then, is the swindler in the title of this book? The

Reflections on *A Swindler's Progress*

impostor's performance is an extreme version of more wide-spread behaviour by the socially ambitious. Very little, as we have seen, really separated a man like John Dow from someone like James Mudie. Impostors unmasked put the status of others at risk; they showed up how much everyone else's status identity was fragile. While there is of course a very real difference between impostors and people with new titles, we can also draw an analogy between imposture, performance and social climbing. All, from the wealthiest aristocrat to the most desperate convict, were vulnerable. The Lascelles family rose to power during a time when England was experiencing acute anxiety about the colonial origins of new wealth. The debates of the 1807 Yorkshire election are incomprehensible otherwise. Dow was performing the peer in a community disturbed by its reputation as a place where criminals could rise to the first rank. And he was doing so in the wake of a convict rebellion and a bitter wrangle between rival political factions. When Dow successfully persuaded people of his aristocratic status, he laid bare in uncomfortable ways how far social boundaries were permeable rather than fixed; he exposed how much the elite might be merely the invention of their own ambition.

As I began my hunt for Dow and the Lascelles, scholars of empire were calling for histories that recognised that developments in British and colonial societies were part and parcel of the same process. The problem was: how to write it? How could this miracle of synthesis be achieved in anything like a readable manner? How could you *show* it was happening? And how could you show what it was like to be caught up in these interconnected events? Here I had the story of two men: of one who had come to vanish, and another who had stolen that identity to pursue his own ends. But their fates were part of

A Swindler's Progress

far bigger events. Without the Lascelles's dynastic ambitions, Edward would never have had to disappear. And those ambitions were crucially bound up in how Britain was transformed as the *ancien régime* gave way to the modern era. Dow was an opportunist, busily exploiting every possible fissure opened up to him by his surroundings. And the biggest fissure of colonial society in the 1830s was the question of convict transportation. Without those debates, Dow's role as 'Commissioner' would never have been possible.

Perhaps it was all the tales Dow told in court. Perhaps it was the years I had spent as detective, unravelling the web of secrets and lies told by and about both the impostor and his model. For long periods of time I had shared the confusion felt by Dow's victims. I had followed false leads. (No, Edward had *not* married Harriet Wilson's sister.) I had come across unexpected windfalls. (Without some well-timed advice, I would never have realised the implications of Dow's connection with Scottish coalminers.) Like the readers of Sydney's newspapers some two hundred years before me, I had even found myself possessed by the hunger to know what was inside a mysterious 'tin box'. In this instance, however, it was another tin box – of papers at Harewood House including letters chronicling the hidden story of Edward's disappearance. It would take several years before I could look inside. As I waited, as I continued the work, it became increasingly clear to me that what I was writing needed to be told not as analytic history but as a narrative, and as a mystery story at that.

This was less a biography of Dow and the Lascelles than a biography of their times. I would follow my characters where their stories led into my broader concerns. I would pause and explore those events when they seemed particularly notewor-

Reflections on *A Swindler's Progress*

thy, even if their wider significance had escaped my protagonists at the time. The danger, of course, would be that the connection between the personal and the social stories would become too contrived. But as the research unfolded, there seemed an almost spooky match between my characters and my research agenda. If the West Indian connection had led me into the Dow and Lascelles story, I never anticipated that I would find it so populated with the key issues and personalities of the era.

Is narrative simply a way for historians to smooth over the mess that is the past; to re-arrange it into comfortingly familiar patterns that have beginnings, middles and ends? And yet, for all our scholarly suspicion of the neatening effects of stories, they still possess a powerful explanatory energy. What was it like to be buffeted by those forces that were transforming so profoundly the British imperial world in the late eighteenth and early nineteenth centuries? Those caught up in them would not live their lives according to the synthesising arguments of scholars. Rather, they would act according to the dictates of narrative and plot: finding opportunities, being thwarted, experiencing greed, hope, despair. To follow these twists and turns is to highlight the way their world was changing. It is luck and chance and swindles and lies and unexpected opportunities that direct lives and fates. The path these take is a path made possible by the shifts that encompass the 'age of liberty' and by the advantages and disappointments that the new world order would bring.

A Swindler's Progress

'The speech for the defence'

Like many historians, I've had a lot of conversations over the years trying to explain to outsiders what precisely it is that I do; suggesting to the curious (or the polite) that whatever that task is, it's not predominantly about discovering new facts. That being so, the Gods of history appear to have plotted an intricate revenge. It might seem at best politically inadvisable, at worst naïve, to admit to how much pleasure I have found in the years spent uncovering the facts buried at the heart of this book. The fates of Edward Lascelles and John Dow were the least of these mysteries. Far more challenging was the way their life histories took me to places and topics about which I was woefully ignorant. As the 'two viscounts' swept me along in their wake, the endless questions to long-suffering colleagues began: Scottish coalminers were *what*!? What the hell are gig mills and shearing frames? Or plumpers? Or wapentakes? And who exactly could vote in Britain before the 1832 Reform Act? Those embarking on transnational history know that it notches up even more than the usual number of debts incurred by all historical research: like a vampire, you prey on the experts of the new fields you move into; you plead with institutions to give you grants to travel to far-flung archives; and you force yourself on long-suffering hosts who put you up once you get there. All of this means that the acknowledgements you write quickly take on a tone of grovelling (but unrepentant) apology.

After I came across the imposture of John Dow, many people, sometimes from the most unexpected quarters, helped me uncover the story that lay behind it. The first to do so was Richard North, then editor of the University of Sydney

Reflections on *A Swindler's Progress*

alumni magazine. Without his local knowledge of Yorkshire and his journalist's nose for a story, I would never have got in touch with Harewood House so quickly. Greg Manning read Richard's story, and contacted me with the news that he was descended from Ann Elizabeth Rosser's younger sister, who had ended up in Australia when her husband was transported. Not only did Greg provide me with his research on the Rossers and Cookes, he also regaled me with wonderful anecdotes about a 'certain sense of eminence' that had been transmitted successively through the family down the years. If his grandmother's generation were proud of their family connections to the house of Harewood, any memory of what that connection actually entailed had long since been selectively erased.

I received unfailingly courteous and helpful attention from the archivists and curators of all the institutions listed in the bibliography. Special mention must be made of the staff (both past and present) at Harewood House, and I am grateful for the kind permission given by the Earl and Countess of Harewood and Trustees of the Harewood House Trust to reproduce items in their collection. Melissa Gallimore and Terry Suthers, former director of the Harewood House Trust, gave endless help in accessing the collection and discussed the Lascelles with me in eager conversations over many years. Sue Page and Heather Griffiths kindly dealt with image reproduction at very late notice.

It was through Harewood House that I first made contact with the extraordinary Karen Lynch, whose name is mentioned with such justifiable passion in so many acknowledgements written by scholars working on this period. If Karen had not, with the utmost generosity, made available to me her research on Edward Lascelles, this book would quite literally have been impossible to write. I have relied almost entirely on Karen's work for the documents about Edward's marriage. Other instances in which I am indebted to her research are noted specifically in the footnotes. I am also very grateful for the expertise of Bruce Kercher on colonial law, Iain Duffield and Hamish Maxwell-Stewart on Scotland and Tasmania, Patrick Eyres on the Fitzwilliams, and Jim Walvin, Douglas Hamilton and Simon Smith on the Lascelles and the West Indies.

At the University of Sydney, for their financial and other support over the course of this project, I would like to acknowledge the then Dean of the Faculty of Arts, Stephen Garton, the past and present Heads of School, Richard Waterhouse and Duncan Ivison, and the past and present Chairs of Department, Shane White and Robert Aldrich. I received painstaking and inventive research assistance from Rhiannon Davis and James Drown. James's later copyediting not only solved the usual problems, it also made me laugh out loud. My thanks go to him for slipping in a reference to Shakespeare's most famous stage direction. I have learnt tremendously from my fellow historians in the Australian area: James Curran, Penny Russell, Richard Waterhouse and Richard White. Sophie Loy-Wilson and Amanda Kaladelfos, part-time teachers whose dedication goes above and beyond the call of duty, made it possible for me to deliver the manuscript to the publishers in the midst of end-of-semester marking chaos.

Over the years I discussed the book endlessly with many colleagues and friends, and I am fortunate to work in a department where those two categories are harder to pull apart than at any other institution I know. The 'Not the Twentieth Century' writer's group – Penny Russell, Cindy McCreery, Michael McDonnell and Frances Clarke – have performed repeated

Reflections on *A Swindler's Progress*

academic alchemy on this and on all my work. I must pay especial tribute to Penny Russell, not only for her brilliant insight
into the art of writing, but also for the support, guidance and
leadership she gives to us all. Martin Thomas lent the writing group his house in the Blue Mountains, where we planned
works of staggering genius for one another around the kitchen
table. (This being far easier to accomplish than writing one's
own.) Robert Aldrich, by persuading me to write a 10 000-word
history of the British Empire, helped me see that it was possible to be both authoritative and succinct. Clare Corbould was
a meticulous and inspiring reader. That she was thwarted in her
valiant efforts to eradicate the passive voice is my fault alone.
Kate Fullagar gave crucial advice on plot structure and how to
use 'characters'. Emma Christopher endlessly talked over questions of readership and market. James Curran expanded my
knowledge of the Australian vernacular. Ever since Iain McCal-
man launched *Scandal in the Colonies* in 2004, he has been a tireless supporter of everything I have done. From the very start
he saw more clearly than anyone else, including me, what this
book was about. And he fought for it every step of the way.

John Hirst, Liz McKenzie, Robert Ross, and Nigel Worden
were all incisive readers. (Nigel Worden accomplished a literary feat by writing his review in rhyming couplets using fridge
magnets.) After I had repeatedly tried and failed, Tony Moore
came up with a brilliant title. Peter Denney suggested sub-
lime images and epigraphs from his research on landscape.
David Cannadine not only encouraged me to write this book
for an audience beyond the academy, his belief in the project
also helped immeasurably with finding a publisher who had
that same vision. It took precisely thirty seconds of enthusiastic
telephone conversation to prove that Phillipa McGuinness was

A Swindler's Progress

that publisher. My thanks go to Kathleen McDermott, and to all at UNSW Press and Harvard University Press.

I was fortunate to have friends to host me during my frequent research trips to Britain. In London: Kezia Lange (kindred spirit for more than twenty years), Rob Pavey and my godson Samuel Pavey; Sarah Mee and the late, and sorely missed, Diana Mee. In Yorkshire: Marianne and Rob Louw and family; Andrew Thompson and Sarah Lenton and family. All my hosts entered into my obsession with Dow and the Lascelles with extraordinarily good grace. When I imagined who would be reading the story, it was of them that I thought.

This book is for all my family, especially my siblings and best mates Carey and David, and above all for my parents, Jock and Liz McKenzie, to whom it is dedicated. When I was barely walking, they embarked on several years of working, studying and travelling around the world. They were young, and they were brave enough to think that leaving home with a small child and no money was simply a minor inconvenience. And so they took me on their adventures, and they soon learnt that they could keep a toddler quiet in any museum, or gallery or historic site they wanted to visit if only they told her endless stories about the people who once lived there. They set my feet on the path, and in the home straight they lent me the two things which are surely guaranteed to get any book finished: an isolated cottage and a golden Labrador whose greatest joy in life is to be taken for walks along the beach in front of it. I know of no better place to write than that wild African shore, no better way to calm creative doubt than to strain against that wind, and no better companion than Amber McKenzie, literary critic extraordinaire. For that, and for their many other gifts to me, this book is but small recompense.

Reflections on *A Swindler's Progress*

NOTES

Abbreviations

AOT	Archives Office of Tasmania
BL	British Library
F(M)	Fitzwilliam (Milton) Collection, Northamptonshire Record Office
HH	Harewood House, West Yorkshire
HRA	*Historical Records of Australia*
ML	Mitchell Library, Sydney
NAS	National Archives of Scotland
NYCRO	North Yorkshire County Record Office
SRNSW	State Records, New South Wales
WWM	Wentworth Woodhouse Muniments, Sheffield Archives
WYAS	West Yorkshire Archive Service, Leeds

Prologue

1 *Sydney Herald*, 14 May 1835; *Monitor*, 6 May 1835.
2 ML A1206, 1210, 1211, 1214: Bigge Report Appendix, p 5162.
3 *Herald*, 14 May 1835.
4 *Monitor*, 6 Aug 1834.
5 Roger Therry, *Reminiscences of Thirty Years' Residence in New South Wales and Victoria*, Sampson, Low, Son & Co, London, 1863, p 168.
6 *NSW Government Gazette*, 6 Aug 1834; *Monitor*, 9 Aug 1834; *Herald*, 4 Sept 1834; *Australian*, 12 Aug 1834; *Gazette*, 9 Aug 1834; *Herald*, 2 April 1835; *Monitor*,

6 Aug 1834; *Herald*, 12 Feb 1835.

7   Roger Milliss, *Waterloo Creek: The Australia Day massacre of 1838 ~ George Gibbs and the British conquest of New South Wales*, UNSW Press, Sydney, 1994, p 8.

8   *Herald*, 14 May 1835.

9   *Herald*, 7 May 1835.

Part One: Arcadia

1   Memoir of Humphry Repton, BL, Add MSS 62112, pp 90, 94.

2   Robert Isaac Wilberforce and Samuel Wilberforce, *The Life of William Wilberforce by his sons, Robert Isaac Wilberforce and Samuel Wilberforce*, John Murray, London, 1838, vol 3, pp 55–56.

3   Diary of William Wilberforce, Bodleian Library, Ms Don e 164 MSS Wilberforce, c 35, 15 July 1802.

4   Memoir of Humphry Repton, pp 90, 92.

5   Mary Mauchline, *Harewood House*, David and Charles, London, 1974, p 114.

6   Memoir of Humphry Repton, pp 94–96.

7   Wilberforce and Wilberforce, *Life of William Wilberforce*, vol 3, p 331.

8   John Jewell, *The Tourist's Companion, or the History and Antiquities of Harewood in Yorkshire, Giving a particular description of Harewood House, Church, and Castle: with some accounts of its environs, selected from various authors, and containing much information never before published*, B Dewhirst, Leeds, 1819, p 34.

9   Memoir of Humphry Repton, p 97.

1 Et in Arcadia ego

1   Tom Stoppard, *Arcadia*, Faber & Faber, Boston/London, 1993, pp 13, 27.

2   John Jewell, *The Tourist's Companion, or the History and Antiquities of Harewood ...*, B Dewhirst, Leeds, 1819, p 8

3   *A Collection of the Speeches, Addresses, and Squibs produced by all Parties during the Late Contested Election for the County of York*, Edward Baines, Leeds, 1807, pp 39–40.

4   SD Smith, 'Henry Lascelles 1690–1753', *Oxford Dictionary of National Biography*; Carol Kennedy, *Harewood: The Life and Times of an English Country House*, Hutchinson, London, 1982, pp 32–33.

5   SD Smith, *Slavery, Family and Gentry Capitalism in the British Atlantic: The World of the Lascelles 1648–1834*, Cambridge University Press, Cambridge, 2006, p 71; Kennedy, *Harewood*, p 34.

6   Douglas Hamilton, 'Private enterprise and public service: Naval contracting in the Caribbean c1720–50', *Journal of Maritime Research*, April 2004.

7   Smith, *Slavery, Family and Gentry Capitalism*, pp 138, 62.

8   Smith, *Slavery, Family and Gentry Capitalism*, pp 87–88. The quote is from a letter from James Abercromby to Robert Dinwiddie, the Lascelles's old adversary in the customs dispute.

9   Kathryn Cave, Kenneth Garlick and Angus Macintyre (eds), *The Diary of*

Joseph Farington, 16 vols, Yale University Press, New Haven/London, 1978–1984: vol 8, p 3073; vol 2, p 570.

10 Smith, *Slavery, Family and Gentry Capitalism*, p 53

11 James Raven, *Judging New Wealth: Popular Publishing and Responses to Commerce in England 1750–1800*, Clarendon Press, Oxford, 1992, pp 201, 202–203.

12 Mary Mauchline, *Harewood House*, David and Charles, London, 1974, p 33.

13 Carol Kennedy, *Harewood: The Life and Times of an English Country House*, Hutchinson, London, 1982, pp 54–55.

14 Karen Lynch, 'Some Lascelles ladies', in Ruth Larsen, *Maids & Mistresses: Celebrating 300 Years of Women and the Yorkshire Country House*, Yorkshire Country House Partnership, Yorkshire, 2004, p 54.

15 See Lynch, 'Some Lascelles ladies'; Haillie Rubenhold, *Lady Worsley's Whim: An Eighteenth-Century Tale of Sex, Scandal and Divorce*, Chatto & Windus, London, 2008.

16 Francis Ferrand Foljambe (Aldwark) to John Hewett, 28 Jan 1779, Notts Archives, DD/FJ/11/1/4/33-34 ; Andrew Warde (Hooton) to his uncle John Hewett, 6 Feb 1779, Notts Archives DD/FJ/11/1/4/43-44 . My thanks to Karen Lynch for providing these references.

17 David Cannadine, 'The making of the British upper classes', in his *Aristocracy: Grandeur and Decline in Modern Britain*, Yale University Press, New Haven/London, 1994, p 29.

18 Kennedy, *Harewood*, p 42.

19 Peter Mandler, *The Fall and Rise of the Stately Home*, Yale University Press, New Haven/London, 1997, p 8.

20 *Diary of Joseph Farington*, vol 5, 29 Aug 1801, p 1599.

21 Jewell, *Tourist's Companion*, pp 17–31.

22 The provisions of Henry Lascelles's will laid down that the estate would be inherited by the children of his younger half-brother Edward, rather than by the children of his elder brother, George.

23 Mark Girouard, *Life in the English Country House: A Social and Architectural History*, Yale University Press, New Haven, 1994.

24 From 'The price of the county', *Leeds Mercury*, 16 May 1807.

25 *The Times*, 29 Nov 1841; 2 June 1807.

26 William Hague, *William Wilberforce: The Life of the Great Anti-Slave Trade Campaigner*, Harper Perennial, London, 2008, pp 36, 369; Lady Bessborough to Lord Granville Leveson Gower, 4 June 1807: Countess Castalia Granville (ed), *Lord Granville Leveson Gower (First Earl Granville): Private Correspondence 1781–1821*, John Murray, London, 1916, vol 2, p 251.

27 James Boswell, *Life of Johnson*, Oxford University Press, Oxford 1980, p 1292.

28 Robert Isaac Wilberforce and Samuel Wilberforce, *The Life of William Wilberforce by his sons, Robert Isaac Wilberforce and Samuel Wilberforce*, John Murray, London, 1838, vol 1, p 54.

29 EA Smith, *Whig Principles and Party Politics: Earl Fitzwilliam and the Whig Party 1748–1833*, Manchester University Press, Manchester, 1975, p 80; Boyd Hilton, *A Mad, Bad and Dangerous People? England 1783–1846*, Oxford University Press,

Oxford, 2006, p 43.

30   Wilberforce, *Life of William Wilberforce*, vol 3, p 316

31   The Fitzwilliams held titles in both the Irish and United Kingdom peerages.
     The first was an earlier creation, making the 4th Earl simultaneously the
     2nd Earl, the 5th simultaneously the 3rd and so on. It was customary within
     the family to count their earldoms according to the Irish honours, though
     historians tend to use the British peerage.

32   The house was known as 'Wentworth Woodhouse' until the time of the first
     Marquess of Rockingham, and again after 1835, but during this time it was
     correctly styled 'Wentworth House': Smith, *Whig Principles*, p 51, n 2.

33   Geoffrey Howse, *The Wentworths of Wentworth: The Fitzwilliam (Wentworth) Estates
     and the Wentworth Monuments*, Trustees of the Fitzwilliam Wentworth Amenity
     Trust, Wentworth, 2002, p 25.

34   Catherine Bailey, *Black Diamonds: The Rise and Fall of an English Dynasty*,
     Penguin, London, 2008, pp xx–xxi.

35   Fitzwilliam to Laurence, 29 April 1807, Northamptonshire Record Office,
     F(M), 515/2.

36   Lady Bessborough to Lord Granville Leveson Gower, 4 and 6 June 1807, in
     Granville (ed), *Granville Leveson Gower Correspondence*, p 251.

37   Frank O'Gorman, *Voters, Patrons, and Parties: The Unreformed Electoral System of
     Hanoverian England 1734–1832*, Clarenden Press, Oxford, 1989, p 36.

38   These population figures include the township of Leeds as well as out-
     townships within the Leeds borough: RG Wilson, *Gentlemen Merchants:
     The Merchant Community in Leeds 1700–1830*, Manchester University Press,
     Manchester, 1971, pp 202, 207.

39   Wilson, *Gentleman Merchants*, pp 228, 247, 169.

40   Mrs Mary Hale to Mrs Elizabeth Hale, 2 May 1801, in TH Lewin (ed), *The
     Lewin Letters*, Archibald Constable & Co, London, 1909, vol 1, p 83; 'Diary of
     William Wilberforce', Bodleian Library, Ms Don e 164 MSS Wilberforce,
     c 35, 15 July 1802 (cf Wilberforce, *Life*, vol 3, pp 55–56, where this remark was
     edited out of the account of his 1802 visit).

41   D Fraser, 'The life of Edward Baines: a filial biography of the "The Great Liar
     of the North"', *Northern History*, 31 (1995), p 209.

42   Edward Baines (jun), *The Life of Edward Baines, Late MP for the Borough of Leeds*,
     Longman, London, 1851, pp 7–8, 27.

43   Baines, *Life of Edward Baines*, p 45.

44   Wilson, *Gentleman Merchants*, p 172.

45   Wilberforce, *Life of William Wilberforce*, vol 3, p 284.

46   James Vernon, *Politics and the People: A Study in English Political Culture c 1815–
     1867*, Cambridge University Press, Cambridge, 1993, pp 85–86.

47   EA Smith, 'Earl Fitzwilliam and Malton: A proprietary borough in the early
     nineteenth century', *English Historical Review*, 80(314), 1965, pp 51–69.

48   Quoted in Frank O'Gorman, *Voters, Patrons, and Parties: The Unreformed Electoral
     System of Hanoverian England 1734–1832*, Clarendon Press, Oxford, 1989, p 59.

49   Marmeduke Spencer to J Ingham, 22 May 1807: WYAS, WYL250/6/3

Harewood Papers, Local Affairs, Elections, bundle 9.

50 *Leeds Intelligencer*, 8 June 1807.

51 *York Herald*, 30 May 1807.

52 *A Poetical Description of Mr Hogath's Election Prints: In Four Cantos* ~ *Written Under Mr Hogarth's Sanction and Inspection*, T Caslon, London, 1759.

53 Robt Cattle's Statement of Expences &c incurred at the general election for the County of York, 1807, on account of the Hon Hy Lasscelles: WYAS WYL, box 5, p 72.

54 Henry Vavasour to Henry Lascelles, 22 Oct 1806; WJ Bethell to Henry Lascelles, undated 1806: WYAS, WYL250/6/3, Harewood Papers, Local Affairs, Elections, bundle no 9.

55 Robert Isaac Wilberforce and Samuel Wilberforce (eds), *The Correspondence of William Wilberforce*, John Murray, London, 1840, p 76.

56 Charles Holmes to Henry Lascelles, 29 Oct 1806; H Cholmley to Henry Lascelles, 23 Oct 1806: WYAS, WYL250/6/3, Harewood Papers, Local Affairs, Elections, bundle 9.

57 Hilton, *Mad, Bad and Dangerous People?*, pp 53–54; Hague, *Wilberforce*, p 28.

58 Quoted in Hague, *Wilberforce*, p 86.

59 James Walvin, 'Freedom and slavery and the shaping of Victorian Britain', *Slavery and Abolition*, 15(2), 1994, pp 246–59.

60 Chistopher Leslie Brown, *Moral Capital: Foundations of British Abolitionism*, University of North Carolina Press, Chapel Hill, 2006, p 47.

61 Peter Cochrane, *Colonial Ambition: Foundations of Australian Democracy*, Melbourne University Press, Melbourne, 2006, p 11.

62 Linda Colley, *Britons: Forging the Nation 1707–1837*, Yale University Press, New Haven/London, 1992.

63 Brown, *Moral Capital*, p 387.

64 Eric Williams, *Capitalism and Slavery*, Deutsch, London, 1964, p 66.

65 Randle Jackson, *The Speech of Randle Jackson, Esq Addressed to the Honorable the Committee of the House of Commons* ..., C Stower, London, 1806, p 28.

66 EP Thompson, *The Making of the English Working Class*, Penguin, Harmondsworth, 1968, p 555.

67 Pat Hudson, *The Genesis of Industrial Capital: A Study of the West Riding Wool Textile Industry c1750–1850*, Cambridge University Press, Cambridge, 1986, p 37.

68 *Considerations Upon a Bill ... respecting the Woollen Manufacture*, C Stower, London, 1803.

69 *Report from the Committee on the Woollen Manufacture of England*, (orig 1806), Irish University Press Series of British Parliamentary Papers, Industrial Revolutions Textiles, 2, Shannon, 1968.

70 Derek Gregory, *Regional Transformation and Industrial Revolution: A Geography of the Yorkshire Woollen Industry*, Macmillan, London, 1982, p 124.

2 The price of the county

1 William Hague, *William Pitt the Younger*, Harper Perennial, London, 2005,

pp 26, 427.

2   Quoted in Hague, *Wilberforce*, p 325.

3   *Report from the Committee on the Woollen Manufacture of England*, Irish University Press Series of British Parliamentary Papers, Industrial Revolutions Textiles, 2, Shannon, 1968 , pp 8, 10.

4   *Leeds Mercury*, 25 July 1807.

5   *Leeds Mercury,* 1 Nov 1806; HH, political pamphlets, 1807; *Leeds Mercury,* 30 May 1807.

6   *Leeds Intelligencer*, 15 June 1807; 'WY' to Henry Lascelles, undated letter, WYAS, WYL 250/6/3 Harewood Papers, Local Affairs, Elections, bundle 9; Robert and SamuelWilberforce, *The Life of William Wilberforce by his sons*, John Murray, London, 1838, vol 3, p 279; J Whiteley to Henry Lascelles, WYAS, WYL 250/6/3, Local Affairs, Elections, bundle 9.

7   *Times*, 8 Nov 1806; 'Diary of William Wilberforce', 2 Nov 1806, Bodleian Library, Ms Don e 164 MSS, Wilberforce, c 35.

8   Wilberforce, *Life of William Wilberforce*, vol 3, pp 316, 317.

9   Diary of the Revd Richard Hale, NYCRO, ZFM Chaloner Papers Mic1419, pp 52–53. (My thanks to Karen Lynch for providing this reference.)

10   French Laurence to Fitzwilliam, 3 May 1807, F(M) 72/1.

11   Fitzwilliam to French Laurence, 29 April 1807, F(M), 515/2; A Bill of the Fare at Wentworth House on the 4th May 1807 being the Birthday of Lord Viscount Milton when his Lordship came of Age, F(M), 72/2.

12   *York Herald*, 9 May 1807; *Times*, 5 June 1807.

13   *Correspondence of Edmund Burke*, quoted in EA Smith, *Whig Principles and Party Politics: Earl Fitzwilliam and the Whig Party 1748–1833*, Manchester University Press, Manchester, 1975, p 108.

14   Frank O'Gorman, *Voters, Patrons, and Parties: The Unreformed Electoral System of Hanoverian England 1734–1832*, Clarendon Press, Oxford, 1989, p 117.

15   *Leeds Mercury*, 9 May 1807.

16   Eliza Ryvers, *Ode to the Right Honourable Lord Melton, Infant Son of Earl Fitzwilliam*, London, 1787.

17   Smith, *Whig Principles and Party Politics*, p 113

18   Georgiana, 5th Duchess of Devonshire to Lady Spencer, 6 Dec 1805, Chatsworth MSS, quoted in Smith, *Whig Principles*, p 283; Herbert Maxwell (ed), *The Creevey Papers: A Selection from the Correspondence and Diaries of the late Thomas Creevey*, John Murray, London, 1903, pp 166–67; Queen Charlotte to Lady Harcourt, July 1794, in EW Harcourt (ed), *The Harcourt Papers*, James Parker, Oxford, 1880, p 44.

19   John Gore, *Thomas Creevey's Papers*, Penguin, London, 1985, p 276.

20   The information on Milton and Lady Milton came to Farington from the portrait painter William Owen: Kathryn Cave et al (eds), *The Diary of Joseph Farington*, vol 14, Yale University Press, New Haven/London, 1984, pp 4853, 4921–22.

21   Gore, *Thomas Creevey's Papers*, p 276; Milton to Lady Fitzwilliam, 30 Sept 1816, F(M), 85/24.

22 *Leeds Mercury*, 23 May 1807.

23 Jonathan Gray, *An Account of the Manner of Proceeding at the Contested Election for Yorkshire in 1807*, York, 1818, p 24.

24 Wilberforce, *Life of William Wilberforce*, vol 3, pp 324, 316, 334–35.

25 Gray, *Account of the … Election for Yorkshire*, p 37.

26 EA Smith, 'The Yorkshire elections of 1806 and 1807: A study in electoral management', *Northern History*, 2, 1967, p 81, n 81.

27 Gray, *Account of the … Election for Yorkshire*, p 18.

28 Edward Baines (jun), *The Life of Edward Baines, Late MP for the borough of Leeds*, Longman, London, 1851, pp 65–66; *Leeds Mercury*, 23 May 1807.

29 O'Gorman, *Voters, Patrons and Parties*, pp 255–56.

30 Gray, *An Account of the … Election for Yorkshire*, pp 12, 31.

31 ED Cuming (ed), *Squire Osbaldeston: His Autobiography*, John Lane, London, 1926, pp 1, 11 Smith, *Whig Principles and Party Politics*, p 327.

32 Mary Milton to Lady Fitzwilliam, 11 May 1807, F(M), 72/12.

33 Smith, 'The Yorkshire Elections of 1806 and 1807', p 80; Cuming, *Squire Osbaldeston*, p 12.

34 Milton to unnamed recipient, 19 Nov 1807, F(M), 72/78.

35 *York Herald*, 16 May 1807.

36 Mary Milton to Lady Fitzwilliam, 11 May 1807, F(M), 72/12; Mary Milton to Lady Fitzwilliam, 18 May 1807, F(M), 72/17.

37 Cuming, *Squire Osbaldeston*, p 12; *Times*, 5 June 1807.

38 Wilberforce, *Life of William Wilberforce*, vol 3, p 330.

39 James Vernon, *Politics and the People: A Study in English Political Culture c 1815–1867*, Cambridge University Press, Cambridge, 1993, p 132.

40 *A Collection of the Speeches, Addresses, and Squibs produced by all Parties during the Late Contested Election for the County of York*, Edward Baines, Leeds, 1807, pp 35, 19.

41 Mary Milton to Lady Fitzwilliam, 11 May 1807, F(M), 72/12; Mary Milton to Lady Fitzwilliam, 18 May 1807, F(M), 72/17.

42 HH, Political Pamphlets.

43 Fitzwilliam to Grenville, 20 Jan 1806, 27 Jan 1806, 1 Feb 1806, BL Add 58955.

44 Mary Milton to Lady Fitzwilliam, 11 May 1807, F(M), 72/12.

45 Milton to Fitzwilliam, 23 May 1807, F(M), 72/29.

46 Wilberforce, *Life of William Wilberforce*, vol 3, p 327.

47 *Leeds Intelligencer*, 8 June 1807.

48 Wilberforce, *Life of William Wilberforce*, vol 3, pp 325–26.

49 Baines, *The Life of Edward Baines*, p 63.

50 *Leeds Mercury*, 30 May 1807; *York Herald*, 30 May 1807.

51 'Milton's Minority', WWM, E221, Election Handbills.

52 *A Collection of the Speeches, Addresses, and Squibs produced by all Parties during the Late Contested Election for the County of York*, Edward Baines, Leeds, 1807, p 29.

53 HH, political pamphlets, 1807; *Collection of Speeches*, pp 34–35.

54 *Collection of Speeches*, p 70.

55 *Collection of Speeches*, p 72.

56   Linda Colley, *Britons: Forging the Nation 1707–1837*, Yale University Press, New Haven/London, 1992, p 360.

57   Smith, *Whig Principles*, p xii.

58   HH, political pamphlets, 1807; *Collection of Speeches*, p 42.

59   *Collection of Speeches*, pp 18, 99; *Leeds Mercury*, 13 June 1807; *Collection of Speeches*, p 70.

60   *Leeds Mercury*, 13 June 1807.

61   Wilberforce, *Life,* vol 3, p. 331

62   Milton to Fitzwilliam, F(M), 72/21, 72/34, 72/42, 72/47, 72/51, 72/55, 72/59; *Leeds Intelligencer*, 1 June 1807.

63   WWM T/16/1, Mary Milton to Mrs Sanderson, 7 June 1807

64   *York Herald*, 6 June 1807, 13 June 1807; *Leeds Mercury*, 13 June 1807; *Times*, 9 June 1807, *Leeds Mercury*, 13 June 1807; *Leeds Mercury*, 13 June 1807; *York Herald*, 13 June, 20 June 1807; *Collection of Speeches,* p. 98.

65   Wilberforce, *Life of William Wilberforce*, vol 3, p 332.

66   Wilberforce, *Life of William Wilberforce*, vol 3, pp 330, 337.

67   Lady Bessborough to Lord Granville Leveson Gower, 4 June 1807, in Countess Castalia Granville (ed), *Lord Granville Leveson Gower (First Earl Granville), Private Correspondence 1781–1821*, John Murray, London, 1916, vol 2, p 251.

68   William Hague, *William Wilberforce: The Life of the Great Anti-Slave Trade Campaigner*, Harper Perennial, London, 2008, p 206.

69   James Raven, *Judging New Wealth: Popular Publishing and Responses to Commerce in England, 1750–1800*, Clarendon Press, Oxford, 1992, p 231.

70   Diary of the Richard Hale, p 53 (thanks again to Karen Lynch for the reference).

71   Smith, 'Yorkshire elections', pp 83–84.

72   Wilberforce, *Life of William Wilberforce*, vol 3, p 330.

73   *Leeds Mercury*, 30 May 1807.

74   Philip Harling, *The Waning of 'Old Corruption': The Politics of Economical Reform in Britain 1779–1846*, Clarendon Press, Oxford, 1996.

75   Robert Worthington Smith, 'Political Organization and Canvassing: Yorkshire Elections Before the Reform Bill' *The American Historical Review*, 74:5, (1969), pp 1538–1560; Robert Worthington Smith, 'Political organisation', p 1540; EP Thompson, *The Making of the English Working Class*, Penguin, Harmondsworth, 1968, p 571.

76   'No Coalition', WWM, E221, Election handbills.

77   HH, political pamphlets, 1807.

78   *Leeds Mercury*, 16 May 1807, 30 May 1807

79   *Leeds Mercury*, 16 May 1807.

80   Lord Harewood to Spencer Perceval, 7 Dec 1809, BL, Add 38244.

81   Chistopher Leslie Brown, *Moral Capital: Foundations of British Abolitionism*, University of North Carolina Press, Chapel Hill, 2006, p 47.

82   David Cannadine, 'The making of the British upper classes', in his *Aristocracy: Grandeur and Decline in Modern Britain*, Yale University Press, New Haven/London, 1994, p 30.

83   Lord Harewood to Spencer Perceval, 7 Dec 1809, BL, Liverpool Papers, vol
      55, Add 38244; see also Lord Harewood to 2nd Earl of Liverpool, 2 Oct 1809
      (vol 54, Add 38243); Spencer Perceval to Lord Harewood, 13 Dec and 22 Dec
      1809, (vol 2, Add 38191); Lord Harewood to Spencer Perceval 24 Dec 1809
      (vol 55, Add 38244); 2nd Earl of Liverpool to Lord Harewood, 1 Aug 1812 (vol
      139, Add 38328); Lord Harewood to 2nd Earl of Liverpool, 3 Aug 1812 (vol 60,
      Add 38249). My thanks to Karen Lynch for these references.
84   Letterbook of Henry Lascelles, WYAS, WYL250/6/4 Harewood Papers,
      Local Affairs, Elections.
85   *Leeds Mercury*, 22 August 1812.

Part Two: Ruin and disgrace

1   Jane Austen, *Mansfield Park*. Published in 1814, *Mansfield Park* was begun in 1812.
2   This London residence of the Earls of Harewood, also confusingly named
     'Harewood House', was demolished in 1908.
3   Edward James to Henry, 2nd Earl of Harewood, 4 Sept and 7 Oct 1826: HH.
4   Edward Harcourt (ed), *The Harcourt Papers*, James Parker, Oxford, 1880, vol 4,
     p 10.
5   Kathryn Cave, Kenneth Garlick and Angus Macintyre (eds), *The Diary of
     Joseph Farington*, 16 vols, Yale University Press, New Haven/London, 1978–
     1984: 25 Jan 1796 (vol 2, p 482); 14 Nov 1795 (vol 2, p 403).
6   He matriculated at Oxford (Christ Church), 21 Oct 1813, aged 17, but did not
     take a degree.
7   Henry Stooks Smith, *An Alphabetical List of the Officers of the Yorkshire Hussars
     from the Formation of the Regiment to the Present Time*, London, 1853.

3 Harewood at bay

Epigraph from *Devil's Cub*, by Georgette Heyer, reprinted with permission of The
Ampersand Agency Ltd acting on behalf of the Estate of Georgette Heyer. *Devil's
Cub*, Copyright © Georgette Heyer, 1932. Published in the UK by Arrow Books.
1   Ann Elizabeth Rosser to Edward Lascelles, 18 Aug 1818; 21 Aug 1818; 6 Aug
     1818; 12 Oct 1818 and 30 Sept 1818: HH. (Unless otherwise noted, all letters
     cited in this chapter are in this collection.)
2   Anthony Fletcher, *Gender, Sex and Subordination in England 1500–1800*, Yale
     University Press, New Haven/London, 1995, p 342.
3   John Tosh, 'The Old Adam and the New Man: Emerging themes in the
     history of English masculinities 1750–1850', in Tim Hitchcock and Michele
     Cohen (eds), *English Masculinities 1660–1800*, Longman, London and New
     York, 1999.
4   Undated memorandum by Lord Harewood's agent giving 'substance of an
     anonymous letter to the Earl of Harewood dated Bristol 6th Nov 1818 and
     received by Him on the 12th of the same month'.
5   Marriage certificate of Edward Lascelles: Bristol Record Office, St James.
     (My thanks to Karen Lynch for this reference.)

6 Sherrard to Henry Lascelles, 28 Nov 1818.

7 Lawrence Stone, *Road to Divorce: England 1530–1987*, Oxford Uniersity Press, Oxford, 1990, p 129.

8 Sherrard to Henry Lascelles, 5 Dec 1818.

9 Henry Lascelles to Edward Lascelles, 26 Nov 1818.

10 Sherrard to Henry Lascelles, 9 Dec 1818.

11 William Lascelles to Henry Lascelles, 18 July 1819.

12 Lynch, Karen, 'Some Lascelles ladies', in Ruth Larsen (ed), *Maids & Mistresses: Celebrating 300 Years of Women and the Yorkshire Country House*, Yorkshire Country House Partnership, Yorkshire, 2004, pp 57–58.

13 Articles of separation, 14 Dec 1818; Ann Elizabeth Rosser to Harris, 4 Jan 1819.

14 Undated anonymous letter to Henry Lascelles, received 11 Jan 1819.

15 Edward Lascelles to Henry Lascelles, 29 Jan 1819

16 Lawrence Stone, *Family, Sex and Marriage in England 1500–1800*, Weidenfeld & Nicolson, London, 1977, and Randolph Trumbach, *The Rise of the Egalitarian Family: Aristocratic Kinship and Domestic Relations in Eighteenth-Century England*, Academic Press, New York, 1978; and for a summary of the views of their critics see Robert Shoemaker, *Gender in English Society 1650–1850: The Emergence of Separate Spheres?* Longman, London, 1998, pp 90–91.

17 Amanda Vickery, *The Gentleman's Daughter: Women's Lives in Georgian England*, Yale University Press, New Haven/London, 1998, p 41.

18 John Habakkuk, *Marriage, Debt, and the Estates System: English Landownership 1650–1950*, Clarendon Press, Oxford, 1994, p 147.

19 Lawrence and Jeanne C Fawtier Stone, *An Open Elite? England 1540–1880*, Clarendon Press, Oxford, 1984; Trumbach, *Rise of the Egalitarian Family*, pp 84–87; David Thomas, 'The social origins of marriage partners of the British Peerage in the eighteenth and nineteenth centuries', *Population Studies 26*, 1972, pp 99–111.

20 Leonore Davidoff, *The Best Circles: Society, Etiquette and the Season*, Croom Helm, London, 1973, p 23.

21 Later generations are a striking contrast: see Catherine Bailey, *Black Diamonds: The Rise and Fall of an English Dynasty*, Penguin, London, 2008.

22 Ruth Larsen, 'Dynastic domesticity: The role of elite women in the Yorkshire country house 1685–1858', PhD thesis, University of York, 2003.

23 Henrietta Frances, Lady Duncannon, to Georgiana, Lady Spencer, 6 May 1786, in Vere Brabazon Ponsonby, 9th Earl of Bessborough, with A Aspinall, *Lady Bessborough and her Family Circle*, John Murray, London, 1940, p 38.

24 Georgiana, 5th Duchess of Devonshire, to Lady Spencer, 6 Dec 1805, Chatsworth MSS, quoted in EA Smith, *Whig Principles and Party Politics: Earl Fitzwilliam and the Whig Party 1748–1833*, Manchester University Press, Manchester, 1975, p 283; Lady Bessborough to Granville Leveson Gower, 6 Dec 1805, in Countess Castalia Granville (ed), *Lord Granville Leveson Gower (First Earl Granville), Private Correspondence 1781–1821*, John Murray, London, 1916, vol 2, p 144.

25 Fitzwilliam to Milton, 15 June 1817, F(M) 88/31.

26 Mary Milton to Milton, 22 July 1817, F(M) 88/42; 23 July 1817, 88/43; 23 July 1817, 88/43; 30 August 1817, 89/33; 25 July 1817, 89/6.

27 Mary Wentworth-Fitzwilliam to Milton, 27 July 1817, F(M) 89/10.

28 Mary Milton to Milton, 26 July 1817, F(M) 89/7.

29 Mary Milton to Milton, 8 Aug 1817, F(M) 89/24; William Charles Wentworth-Fitzwilliam to Milton, 8 Aug 1817, 89a/24.

30 This reckoning includes children who died shortly after birth and is based on peerages published in the 1830s.

31 *Derby Mercury*, 10 Nov 1830.

32 William Wilberforce to Milton, 6 Nov 1830, WWM G68/1.

33 *Derby Mercury*, 1 Dec 1830.

34 Carles Percy to Ralph Sneyd, 19 Dec [1818], Keele University, Sneyd Papers, SC 12/10. My thanks to Karen Lynch for this reference.

35 Lady Cawdor to Mary Stewart Mackenzie, National Archives of Scotland, Seaforth Papers, Correspondence of Mary Stewart Mackenzie, GD/46/15/17/24. My thanks to Karen Lynch for this reference.

36 Herbert Maxwell (ed), *The Creevey Papers: A Selection from the Correspondence and Diaries of the late Thomas Creevey, MP*, John Murray, London, 1903, vol 1, p 294.

37 Death notice of William Rosser, Hereford and Dore Registration District, 1851, no 425 (my thanks to Greg Manning for this reference and for genealogical information on the Rosser and Cooke families); Flexney to Henry Lascelles, 13 April 1819; Townend to 'Hunt' (Flexney), 28 June 1820.

38 *Hereford Chronicle*, 28 July 1838.

39 *Hull Packet*, 14 July 1823

40 Miss MA Yeoman to Revd R Hale, York, 14 August (no year); Yeoman to Emily Hale, 30 Aug 1819; Sherrard to Henry Lascelles, 21 April 1819.

41 Townend to 'Hunt' (Flexney), 15 July 1819; Flexney to Henry Lascelles, 13 April 1819.

42 SD Smith, *Slavery, Family and Gentry Capitalism in the British Atlantic: The World of the Lascelles, 1648–1834*, Cambridge University Press, Cambridge, 2006, p 185.

43 Edward Lascelles to Henry Lascelles, 11 April 1819; Henry Lascelles to Edward Lascelles, 15 June 1819; William Lascelles to Henry Lascelles, 18 July 1819.

44 Russell to Henry Lascelles, 29 July 1820.

45 *John Bull*, 7 Feb 1825.

46 John Russell, *A Tour in Germany, and some of the Southern Provinces of the Austrian Empire, in the years 1820, 1821, 1822*, 2 vols, A Constable & Co, Edinburgh, 1824, vol 1, p 1.

47 *La Belle Assemblée*, 1 Aug 1824; *John Bull*, 7 Feb 1825.

48 Russell, *A Tour in Germany*, vol 1, p 6; vol 2, pp 78–79, 283.

49 Russell to Henry Lascelles, 28 Jan 1822.

50 *A Tour in Germany*, vol 2, p 326.

51 Russell to Henry Lascelles, 28 Jan 1822 (since the 1st Earl had died in 1820, Henry was now 2nd Earl of Harewood, and Edward was Viscount Lascelles).

52 Russell to Henry Lascelles, 14 June 1821.

53 Russell to Henry Lascelles, 26 Aug 1821; Russell to Henry Lascelles, 28 Jan 1822.

54 Sir Robert Gordon (1791–1847), *Oxford Dictionary of National Biography*.

55 John Russell to 2nd Earl of Harewood, 28 Jan 1822.

56 John Russell to 2nd Earl of Harewood, 28 Jan 1822.

57 Stone, *Road to Divorce*, pp 182, 156–57, 163.

58 Edward Lascelles to 2nd Lord Harewood, 5 Sept 1831; Anon to 2nd Lord Harewood, recd Nov/Dec 1830.

59 *Maitland Mercury*, 12 June 1873.

60 2nd Earl of Harewood to Edward Lascelles, 24 Aug 1831.

61 Edward Lascelles to 2nd Earl of Harewood, 5 Sept 1831.

62 Edward Lascelles to 2nd Earl of Harewood, 5 Sept 1831; Edward Lascelles to 2nd Earl of Harewood, 12 Feb 1832.

63 Edward Lascelles to 2nd Earl of Harewood, 5 Sept 1831.

64 2nd Earl of Harewood to Edward Lascelles, 20 Sept 1831.

65 Edward Lascelles to 2nd Earl of Harewood, 11 Sept 1831.

66 2nd Earl of Harewood to Edward Lascelles, 16 Oct 1831.

67 Maud Mary Lyttelton Wyndham Leconfield, Baroness Leconfield and John Gore, *Three Howard Sisters: Selections from the writings of Lady Caroline Lascelles, Lady Dover and Countess Gower 1825 – 1833*, John Murray, London, 1955, p 52.

68 Edward James to Henry, 2nd Earl of Harewood, 4 Sept 1826; 7 Oct 1826.

69 James Adams to NL Fenwick, 28 Sept 1826, encl in Fenwick to 2nd Earl of Harewood, 30 Sept 1826.

4 The lost heir

Epigraph from *Murder at the Vicarage* (1930) © Agatha Christie Ltd, A Chorion Company, all rights reserved.

1 *Dumfries Weekly Journal*, 3 May 1825.

2 Lord Advocate's Department, High Court Precognitions, NAS, AD14/25/123, pp 32–37.

3 James Hamilton (ed), *A Memoir of Lady Colquhoun*, James Nisbet, London, 1850, pp 50–51, 61.

4 Janet Colquhoun (ed), *The Works of Lady Colquhoun of Rossdhu*, James Nesbit, London, 1852, p 22.

5 28 April 1816, quoted in *Memoir of Lady Colquhoun*, pp 50–51.

6 *Dumfries Weekly Journal*, 3 May 1825.

7 Lord Advocate's Department, High Court Precognitions, NAS, AD14/25/123.

8 Jennine Hurl-Eamon, 'The Westminster impostors: Impersonating law enforcement in early eighteenth-century London', *Eighteenth-Century Studies*, 38(3), 2005, pp 461–83.

9 Lord Advocate's Department, High Court Precognitions, NAS, AD14/25/123.

10 *Oxford English Dictionary Online* (2nd edn, 1989), Oxford University Press,

Oxford, 2007.

11 John Stevenson, *Letters in Answer to Dr Price's Two Pamphlets on Civil Liberty* ...,
    G Burnett/Richardson and Urquhart, London, 1778, p 175.

12 Robert Bald, *A General View of the Coal Trade of Scotland* ..., A Neill and Co/
    Oliphant & Brown, Edinburgh, 1808, pp 72–73.

13 Stevenson, *Letters in Answer to Dr Price's Two Pamphlets on Civil Liberty*, p 171.

14 Baron F Duckham, *A History of the Scottish Coal Industry*, vol 1, *1700–1815*, David
    & Charles, Newton Abbot, 1970.

15 Bald, *A General View of the Coal Trade of Scotland* ..., p 72.

16 Quoted in Duckham, *A History of the Scottish Coal Industry*, p 280.

17 Lord Advocate's Department, High Court Precognitions, NAS, AD 14/25/123.

18 High Court of Justiciary, NAS, JC 26/467.

19 *Dumfries & Galloway Courier*, 19 April 1825.

20 *Dumfries Courier*, 26 April 1825; *Dumfries Weekly Journal*, 3 May 1825.

21 *Dumfries Courier*, 26 April 1825; High Court of Justiciary, NAS, JC 26/467.

22 *Dumfries Weekly Journal*, 3 May 1825.

23 Jorgen Jorgensen, *A Shred of Autobiograhy*, Sullivan's Cove, Adelaide, 1981, p 44.

24 Robert Hughes, *The Fatal Shore: A History of the Transportation of Convicts to
    Australia 1787–1868*, Collins, London, 1988, p 139; Dan Sprod, *The Usurper:
    Jorgen Jorgenson and his Turbulent Life in Iceland and Van Diemen's Land 1780–1841*,
    Blubber Head Press, Hobart, 2001, p 537.

25 Jorgensen, *A Shred of Autobiograhy*, pp 44–45.

26 Alphabetical record book of convicts arriving in VDL, vol D, 1804-1830, AOT,
    CON 31/9, no 393.

27 Peter Cunningham, *Two Years in New South Wales*, Angus and Robertson,
    Sydney, 1966, p 290.

28 Jorgensen, *A Shred of Autobiograhy*, p 46.

29 *Hobart Town Gazette*, 6 May 1826

30 *Woodman* Appropriation List, AOT, MM 33/5.

31 Sprod, *The Usurper*, p 539; Jorgensen, *A Shred of Autobiograhy*, p 48.

32 Frank Clune and PR Stephenson, *The Viking of Van Diemen's Land: The Stormy Life
    of Jorgen Jorgensen*, Angus and Robertson, Sydney, 1954, pp 328–29; Jorgensen,
    A Shred of Autobiograhy, p 49.

33 AGL Shaw, *Convicts and the Colonies: A Study of Penal Transportation from Great
    Britain and Ireland to Australia and Other Parts of the British Empire*, Melbourne
    University Press, Melbourne, 1977, p 123.

34 Cunningham, *Two Years in New South Wales*, pp 293, 300.

35 *Sydney Herald*, 14 May 1835.

Part Three: Antipodes

1 CMH Clark, *A History of Australia*, vol 2, *New South Wales and Van Diemen's Land
   1822–1838*, Melbourne University Press, Melbourne, 1968, pp 205–206.

2 Roger Therry, *Reminiscences of Thirty Years' Residence in New South Wales and
   Victoria*, Sampson, Low, Son & Co, London, 1863, pp 164–65.

3   *Monitor*, 21 Jan 1834.

4   James Mudie, *Vindication of James Mudie and John Larnach from Certain Reflections on their Conduct ...*, ES Hall, Sydney, 1834, p x.

5   Mudie, *Vindication*, p 50; Sandra Blair, 'The revolt at Castle Forbes: A catalyst to emancipist emigrant confrontation', *Journal of the Royal Australian Historical Society*, 64(2), 1978, p 99.

6   *Monitor*, 21 Jan 1834; *Party Politics Exposed, In a letter addressed to the Right Honorable The Secretary of State for the Colonies ...*, Anne Howe, Sydney, 1834, p 51; *Monitor*, 31 Jan 1834.

7   Clark, *History of Australia*, vol 2, p 211.

5 A wild and distant shore

1   *Hobart Town Gazette*, 6 May 1826; Jorgen Jorgensen, *A Shred of Autobiograhy*, Sullivan's Cove, Adelaide, 1981, p 51.

2   Alphabetical registers of male convicts, AOT, CON 23/1, no 395; see also Indent of the ship *Woodman*, ML, A 1059, p 188 ; *Woodman* Appropriation List, AOT, MM 33/5.

3   *Hobart Town Gazette*, 29 April 1826.

4   Hamish Maxwell-Stewart, *Closing Hell's Gates: The Death of a Convict Station*, Allen & Unwin, Sydney, 2008, pp 183–86; Lloyd Robson, *A History of Tasmania*, vol 1, Oxford University Press, Melbourne, 1983, p 143.

5   James Boyce, *Van Diemen's Land*, Black Ink, Melbourne, 2008, pp 169, 119.

6   Robson, *History of Tasmania*, vol 1, pp 81–82; 89, 101; Kirsty Reid, *Gender, Crime and Empire: Convicts, Settlers and the State in Early Colonial Australia*, Manchester University Press, Manchester, 2007, p 30; Boyce, *Van Diemen's Land*, p 78.

7   Reid, *Gender, Crime and Empire*, p 74.

8   David Cannadine, *Ornamentalism: How the British Saw their Empire*, Penguin, London, 2002, p xx.

9   Edward Baines (jun), *The Life of Edward Baines, Late MP for the borough of Leeds*, Longman, London, 1851, p 64; Lord Fitzwilliam, hand-written note on copy of *Leeds Mercury*, 14 June 1817, encl in Fitzwilliam to Grenville, 19 June 1817, Dropmore Papers: Correspondence between 2nd Earl Fitzwilliam and Lord Grenville 1791–1823, BL, Add 58955.

10   John Stevens, *England's Last Revolution: Pentrich 1917*, Moorland, Buxton, 1977, p 15.

11   Baines, *Life of Edward Baines*, p 90; Edward Baines, *History of the Reign of George III, King of the United Kingdom of Great Britain and Ireland*, Longman, Leeds, 1820, p 42.

12   EP Thompson, *The Making of the English Working Class*, Penguin, Harmondsworth, 1968, p 530, 87.

13   Anon, *Spies and Bloodites!!! The Lives and Political History of those arch-fiends Oliver, Reynolds, & Co. Treason-Hatchers, Green-Bag-Makers, Blood-Hunters, Spies, Tempters, and Informers-General to His Majesty's Ministers. Including a complete Account of all their Intrigues, Snares, Plots, Plans, Treasons, and Machinations, in the Metropolis,*

Manchester, Birmingham, Leeds, and various Parts of the Country, laying open the whole of their Transactions with Government, &c &c, John Fairburn, London, 1817, p 1.

14 Bernard Porter, *Plots and Paranoia: A History of Political Espionage in Britain 1790–1988*, Routledge, London/New York, 1992, p 41.

15 Stevens, *England's Last Revolution*, p 47.

16 Thompson, *Making of the English Working Class*, p 727.

17 Baines, *History of the Reign of George III*, pp 79, 82.

18 Lord Sidmouth to Mr Parker, 31 May 1817, F(M) 88/26; Fitzwilliam to Milton (unsubscribed), 18 June 1817, F(M) 88/35 ; Fitzwilliam to Milton, 19 June 1817, F(M) 88/36.

19 Fitzwilliam to Grenville, 19 June 1817, Dropmore Papers, BL, Add 58955.

20 Robert Reid, *The Peterloo Massacre*, Heinemann, London, 1989, p 183.

21 Reid, *Peterloo Massacre*, p 197.

22 Memoir of Humphry Repton, BL, MSS Add 62112, pp 153–54.

23 Geoffrey Howse, *The Wentworths of Wentworth: The Fitzwilliam (Wentworth) Estates and the Wentworth Monuments*, Trustees of the Fitzwilliam Wentworth Amenity Trust, Wentworth, 2002, p 32; Catherine Bailey, *Black Diamonds: The Rise and Fall of an English Dynasty*, Penguin, London, 2008, pp 181–82.

24 Marlow, *Peterloo Massacre*, p 193.

25 EA Smith, *Whig Principles and Party Politics: Earl Fitzwilliam and the Whig Party 1748–1833*, Manchester University Press, Manchester, 1975, pp 346, 354.

26 Fitzwilliam to Grey, 24 March 1822, quoted in Smith, *Whig Principles*, p 368.

27 Peter Mandler, *Aristocratic Government in the Age of Reform: Whigs and Liberals 1830–1852*, Clarendon Press, Oxford, 1990, p 16.

28 Quoted in Smith, *Whig Principles*, p 223.

29 Mandler, *Aristocratic Government in the Age of Reform*, pp 87–96.

30 Zoe Laidlaw, *Colonial Connections 1815–1845: Patronage, the Information Revolution and Colonial Government*, Manchester University Press, Manchester, 2005, p 103; JM Bourne, *Patronage and Society in Nineteenth-Century England*, Edward Arnold, London, 1986.

31 Stuart Macintyre, *A Concise History of Australia*, Cambridge University Press, Cambridge, 1999, p. 53; Evans, 'Creating 'an Object of Real Terror'' in Martin Crotty and David Roberts (eds), *Turning Points in Australian History*, UNSW Press, Sydney, 2009.

32 *Gazette*, 9 August 1834.

33 Fletcher, *Ralph Darling*, p 103; Clark, *History of Australia vol 2*, p 35

34 Clark, *History of Australia vol 2*, pp 13–14.

35 Hirst, *Convict Society and its Enemies*, p 200.

36 Hartwell, *Economic Development of Van Diemen's Land*, pp 31, 70.

37 Macintyre, *Concise History of Australia*, p 59.

38 Boyce, *Van Diemen's Land*, pp 198–206.

39 *Sydney Gazette*, 7 May 1835.

40 Conduct Record, AOT, CON 31/9.

41 Edward Curr, *Van Diemen's Land*, London, 1824, quoted in Diane Phillips, *An*

Eligible Situation: The Early History of George Town and Low Head, Karuda Press, Canberra, 2004, p 42.

42 Dow to Arthur, 29 Jan 1828, AOT, CSO 1/244, pp 46–47.

43 Dow to Arthur, 29 Jan 1828, AOT, CSO 1/244, pp 60–61; Phillips, Eligible Situation, pp 48–51.

44 Robson, Van Diemen's Land, vol 1, p 289.

45 Dow to Arthur, 23 March 1828, AOT, CSO 1/244, pp 50–52.

46 Hobart Town Courier, 23 May 1834; 5 June 1835.

47 Gazette, 20 Oct 1831; Brian Fletcher, Ralph Darling: A Governor Maligned, Oxford University Press, Melbourne, 1984, p 292.

48 William Charles Wentworth to Fitzwilliam, 15 Jan 1817, F(M) 88/4; John Ritchie, The Wentworths: Father and Son, Melbourne University Press, Melbourne, 1997.

49 Darling, memo on proceedings, and Address voted by a public meeting, in Darling to Horton, 4 Feb 1827, CO 323/49, quoted in Hazel King, Richard Bourke, Oxford University Press, Melbourne, 1971, p 146.

50 Darling to Hay, 'Secret and Confidential', 9 Feb 1827, HRA, 1:13, p 99.

51 Darling to Hay, 'Secret and Confidential', 9 Feb 1827, HRA, 1:13, p 99.

52 Darling to Goderich, 10 Oct, 1828, HRA, 1:13, p 548.

53 Alan Atkinson, The Europeans in Australia: A History, vol 2, Democracy, Oxford University Press, Oxford, 2004, p 64.

54 Bruce Kercher, Outsiders: Tales from the Supreme Court of New South Wales 1824–1836, Australian Scholarly, Melbourne, 2006, p 134; RB Walker, The Newspaper Press in New South Wales, Sydney University Press, Sydney, 1976, p 16; Erin Ihde, A Manifesto for New South Wales: Edward Smith Hall and the Sydney Monitor 1826–1840, Australian Scholarly, Melbourne, 2004.

55 Monitor, 5 July 1828; 12 July 1828.

56 Kercher, Outsiders, p 133.

57 Fletcher, Ralph Darling, p 292.

58 Sydney Herald, 14 May 1835.

59 Charles von Hügel, New Holland Journal, November 1833–October 1834, trans and ed Dymphna Clark, Melbourne University Press, Melbourne, 1994, p 298.

60 Lucy Duff Gordon, Letters from the Cape, ed Dorothea Fairbridge, Oxford University Press, London, 1927, p 47.

61 Gazette, 9 March 1833.

62 Ex parte Lascelles, in re Dickson, Dowling, Proceedings of the Supreme Court, vol 83, SRNSW, 2/3266.

63 'Lascelles' [John Dow] to Thomas Wilson, March 1833, ML, Doc 79.

64 Sydney Herald, 14 May 1835.

65 The ODNB's entry for Henry, 2nd Earl of Harewood, describes him as 'Beau' Lascelles and also mentions the likeness to George IV possessed, in fact, by Edward, his elder brother.

66 Gazette, 7 May 1835.

67 Sydney Herald, 14 May 1835.

68 'Lascelles' [Dow] to 2nd Earl of Harewood, 22 March 1833, HH.

69 'Lascelles' [Dow] to Lord Bute, 25 March 1833, encl in Lady Sheffield to 2nd Earl of Harewood, (nd, recd 25 Sept 1833), HH.

70 2nd Earl of Harewood to (no direction), 11 Sept 1833, copy of letter, HH.

71 Apart from the mistakes made before David Chambers, Dow's letters made reference to Lascelles estates and relations that had no basis in reality: 'Lascelles' [John Dow] to Thomas Wilson, March 1833, ML, Doc 79.

72 'Lascelles' [John Dow] to Thomas Wilson, March 1833; 'Lascelles' [John Dow] to Thomas Wilson, 20 March 1833; 'Henry, Viscount Lascelles' [John Dow] to Thomas Wilson, 12 April 1833: ML, Doc 79.

73 *Sydney Herald*, 14 May 1835.

74 John Thomas Young to 2nd Earl of Harewood, 25 Aug 1833; 6 Sept 1833; Spottiswood and Robertson to 2nd Earl of Harewood, 11 Sept 1833; 2nd Earl of Harewood to John Thomas Young, 7 Sept 1833 (copy) and 13 Sept 1833 (copy): HH.

75 2nd Earl of Harewood to Nelson, 14 Sept 1833 (copy); Nelson to 2nd Earl of Harewood, 10 Sept 1833; Nelson to 2nd Earl of Harewood, 16 Sept 1833, quoting letter from the Earl to Nelson, 12 Sept 1833; Nelson to 2nd Earl of Harewood, 10, 11, 13 and 16 Sept 1833, and undated (recd 24 Sept 1833): HH.

76 *Sydney Herald*, 14 May 1835.

77 Nelson to 2nd Earl of Harewood, 16 Sept 1833, HH.

78 Young to 2nd Earl of Harewood, two letters, 4 Jan 1834, HH.

6 His lordship's *tour de force*

1 Robert Hughes, *The Fatal Shore: A History of the Transportation of Convicts to Australia 1787–1868*, Collins, London, 1988, p 428; *Party Politics Exposed, In a letter addressed to the Right Honorable The Secretary of State for the Colonies...*, Anne Howe, Sydney, 1834, p 7.

2 Roger Therry, *Reminiscences of Thirty Years' Residence in New South Wales and Victoria*, Sampson Low Son & Co, London, 1863, pp 41–42.

3 *Monitor*, 28 Jan 1834; *HRA*, 1: 16, pp 719–723.

4 The background and punishment records of the Castle Forbes mutineers can be found at Sue Wiblin and David Roberts, 'The Castle Forbes Affair: Records of the 1833 Convict Revolt in the Hunter Valley, NSW Australia', <www.une.edu.au/arts/ACF/cf1833/>.

5 *Monitor*, 28 and 21 Jan 1834.

6 John Hirst, *Convict Society and Its Enemies*, Allen & Unwin, Sydney, 1983, p 183.

7 Therry, *Reminiscences*, p 168; *Herald*, 12 Dec 1833.

8 Therry, *Reminiscences*.

9 *Australian*, 13 Dec 1833.

10 *HRA*, 1:17, p 543.

11 Bruce Kercher, *Outsiders: Tales from the Supreme Court of New South Wales 1824–1836*, Australian Scholarly, Melbourne, 2006, p 85.

12 *Australian*, 23 Dec 1833; 13 Dec 1833; *Gazette*, 24 Dec 1833.

13 *Herald*, 30 Dec 1833; 31 March 1834.

14 W Allan Wood, *Dawn in the Valley: The Story of Settlement in the Hunter River Valley to 1833*, Wentworth, Sydney, 1972, p 207.

15 Roger Milliss, *Waterloo Creek: The Australia Day Mssacre of 1838, George Gibbs and the British Conquest of New South Wales*, UNSW Press, Sydney, 1994, p 21.

16 Wood, *Dawn in the Valley*, pp 128–34; Milliss, *Waterloo Creek*, pp 61–66; Kercher, *Outsiders* pp 31–38.

17 Quoted in Sandra Blair, 'The revolt at Castle Forbes: A catalyst to emancipist emigrant confrontation', *Journal of the Royal Australian Historical Society*, 64(2), 1978, p 97.

18 Bourke to Richard Bourke jnr, 26 Sept 1834, Bourke Papers, vol 6, ML, A1733, pp 37–40.

19 *Gazette*, 8 April 1834.

20 Wood, *Dawn in the Valley*, pp 35–36; Blair, 'Revolt at Castle Forbes', p 97.

21 Sandra Blair, 'The felonry and the free? Divisions in colonial society in the penal era', *Labour History*, 45, 1983, p 10; Blair, 'Revolt at Castle Forbes', p 98

22 Bourke to Spring-Rice, 'Confidential', 12 March 1834, Bourke Papers, vol 9, Correspondence with Lord Montague 1823–1855, ML, A1736, pp 209–216.

23 Hazel King, *Richard Bourke*, Oxford University Press, Melbourne, 1971, pp 130–31.

24 CA Bayly, *Imperial Meridian: The British Empire and the World 1780–1830*, Longman, London/New York, 1989, p 236. In the short term at least, the power of the landed interest was actually increased: Boyd Hilton, *A Mad, Bad and Dangerous People? England 1783–1846*, Oxford University Press, Oxford, 2006, p 435.

25 Peter Mandler, *Aristocratic Government in the Age of Reform: Whigs and Liberals 1830–1852*, Clarendon Press, Oxford, 1990, pp 94–96.

26 Hilton, *Mad, Bad and Dangerous*, p 163.

27 Edward Baines (jun), *The Life of Edward Baines, Late MP for the borough of Leeds*, Longman, London, 1851, p 177.

28 SD Smith, *Slavery, Family and Gentry Capitalism in the British Atlantic: The World of the Lascelles, 1648–1834*, Cambridge University Press, Cambridge, 2006, pp 280–281, 311–316, 307. Smith notes that his basis for comparison excludes the effects of warfare, plague or famine.

29 William Hague, *William Wilberforce: The Life of the Great Anti-Slave Trade Campaigner*, Harper Perennial, London, 2008, p 500.

30 Bayly, *Imperial Meridian*, p 238.

31 Peter Cochrane, *Colonial Ambition: Foundations of Australian Democracy*, Melbourne University Press, Melbourne, 2006, p 25. The figures are from King, *Richard Bourke*, p 212.

32 The observation belongs to Chief Justice Francis Forbes: CMH Clark, *A History of Australia*, vol 2, *New South Wales and Van Diemen's Land 1822–1838*, Melbourne University Press, Melbourne, 1968, p 214.

33 King, *Richard Bourke*, pp 212, 145–46.

34 *Herald*, 11 Aug 1834.

35 Alan Atkinson, *The Europeans in Australia, A History*, vol 2, *Democracy*, Oxford University Press, Oxford, 2004, p 62.

36 Blair, 'The felonry and the free', p 4.

37 *Herald*, 31 July 1834.

38 RB Walker, *The Newspaper Press in New South Wales*, Sydney University Press, Sydney, 1976, p 22; Lloyd Robson, *A History of Tasmania*, Oxford University Press, Melbourne, 1983, vol 1, p 304; Sandra Blair, 'The "Convict Press": William Watt and the *Sydney Gazette* in the 1830s', *Push from the Bush*, 5, 1979, pp 104–105.

39 *Herald*, 4 Sept 1834.

40 *NSW Government Gazette*, 6 Aug 1834.

41 *Herald*, 31 July 1834.

42 *Government Gazette*, 6 Aug 1834.

43 Judith Keene, 'Surviving the Peninsula War in Australia: Juan D'Arrieta ~ Spanish free settler and colonial gentleman', *Journal of the Royal Australian Historical Society*, 85, 1999, p 37.

44 Zoe Laidlaw, *Colonial Connections 1815–1845: Patronage, the Information Revolution and Colonial Government*, Manchester University Press, Manchester, 2005.

45 Petition of Samuel McCrea, 21 Dec 1825, SRNSW, COS 4/1791.

46 Keene, 'Surviving the Peninsula War'.

47 Susan Ballyn and Lucy Frost, 'A Spanish convict, her clergyman biographer, and the amanuensis of her bastard son', in Lucy Frost and Hamish Maxwell-Stewart (eds), *Chain Letters: Narrating Convict Lives*, Melbourne University Press, Melbourne, 2001, p 102.

48 Peter Cunningham, *Two Years in New South Wales*, Angus and Robertson, Sydney, 1966, pp 61–62; Peter Chapman (ed), *The Diaries and Letters of GTWB Boyes*, vol 1, *1820–1832*, Oxford University Press, Melbourne, 1985, pp 180–82.

49 SRNSW, Colonial Secretary: letters received re convicts, box 4/2239, letter 34/7602.

50 Charles von Hügel, *New Holland Journal, November 1833–October 1834*, trans and ed Dymphna Clark, Melbourne University Press, Melbourne, 1994, pp 398–99.

51 *Herald*, 1 Sept 1834.

52 *Monitor*, 6 Aug 1834; 9 Aug 1834.

53 *Monitor*, 9 Aug 1834.

54 *Gazette*, 9 Aug 1834; *Herald*, 11 Aug 1834.

55 *Gazette*, 12 Aug 1834; 14 Aug 1834.

56 Kercher, *Outsiders*, p 88.

57 *Herald*, 10 Nov 1834, *Australian*, 11 Nov 1834.

58 *Herald*, 4 Sept 1834.

59 *Herald*, 14 May 1835.

60 *Sydney Times*, 7 Oct 1834.

61 Journal of William Watson, 19–20 Aug 1834, in Hilary M Carey and David Roberts, 'The Wellington Valley Project: Papers relating the Church Missionary Society mission to Wellington Valley, New South Wales 1830–

1842', <www.newcastle.edu.au/group/amrhd/wvp/>.

62 31 Jan 1835, SRNSW, Colonial Secretary: letters received re convicts, 4/2289.3, letter 35/790.

63 SRNSW, Supreme Court, informations and other papers, 'John Dow or John Luttrell, alias Lord Viscount Lascelles, Forgery, 5 May 1835', Information no 18/1835.

64 *Australian*, 1 May 1835.

65 *Herald*, 7 May 1835.

66 *Gazette*, 7 May 1835.

67 *Gazette*, 7 May 1835.

68 Linus Miller, *Notes of an Exile to Van Diemen's Land*, Fredonia, New York, 1846, pp 285–86.

69 *Herald*, 14 May 1835.

70 The *Herald* gives his name as 'John' Maclehose, but the letter he wrote to the *Sydney Times* about the imposture is signed 'James Maclehose'.

71 *Herald*, 14 May 1835.

72 *Herald*, 14 May 1835.

73 *Gazette*, 7 May 1835.

74 Pheonix Hulk, Transportation book 1834–1837, SRNSW, 4/4535; Assignment lists and associated papers, AOT, CON 13/7.

75 Alexander McLeay to FA Hely, 27 June 1835, SRNSW, Colonial Secretary's correspondence: Letters sent re convicts, 4/3681, p 148

76 *Gazette*, 7 May 1835.

77 *Hobart Town Courier*, 5 June 1835.

78 *Dumfries Weekly Journal*, 3 May 1825.

Epilogue

1 Carol Kennedy, *Harewood: The Life and Times of an English Country House*, Hutchinson, London, 1982, p. 67 – 68; *Times*, 29 Nov 1841; *Times*, 27 Nov 1841.

2 Edward Lascelles to 2nd Earl of Harewood, 11 Sept 1831, HH.

3 *Belfast News-Letter*, 2 Oct 1835; *Jackson's Oxford Journal*, 3 Oct 1835; *Hampshire Telegraph and Sussex Chronicle*, 5 Oct 1835; *Manchester Times and Guardian*, 10 Oct 1835; *Caledonian Mercury*, 19 Oct 1835.

4 *The Times*, 20 Jan 1836; *The Satirist, and Censor of the Times*, 24 Jan 1836.

5 Prob 11/2000, National Archives, London. My thanks to Karen Lynch for this reference.

6 Maud, Baroness Leconfield and John Gore (eds), *Three Howard Sisters: Selections from the writings of Lady Caroline Lascelles, Lady Dover and Countess Gower 1825–1833*, John Murray, London, 1955, p 52.

7 Karen Lynch, 'Some Lascelles ladies', in Ruth Larsen (ed), *Maids & Mistresses: Celebrating 300 Years of Women and the Yorkshire Country House*, Yorkshire Country House Partnership, Yorkshire, 2004, p 59.

8 *Times*, 17 Dec 1839; *Leeds Mercury*, 28 Dec 1839.

9   *Times*, 17 Dec 1839; *Newcastle Courant*, 3 Jan 1840; *Leeds Mercury*, 4 Jan 1840; *The Satirist*, 12 Jan 1840.

10   *The Satirist*, 12 Jan 1840; 12 April 1840.

11   Catherine Bailey, *Black Diamonds: The Rise and Fall of an English Dynasty*, Penguin, London, 2008, pp 420–25, 433.

12   Anon to Henry Lascelles, undated (recd 11 Jan 1819), HH.

13   Bailey, *Black Diamonds*, pp 437–49, xxiii.

14   James Mudie, *The Felonry of New South Wales*, (orig Whaley & Co, London, 1837), facs edn, ed Walter Stone, Melbourne, 1964.

15   Peter Cochrane, *Colonial Ambition: Foundations of Australian Democracy*, Melbourne University Press, Melbourne, 2006, p 20.

16   Mudie, *Felonry*, pp 105, 147.

17   *Herald*, 28 Oct 1840.

18   *Gazette*, 14 June 1836.

19   AOT, CON 16/1, no 1013, pp 10–11.

20   Peter Cunningham, *Two Years in New South Wales*, Angus and Robertson, Sydney, 1966, pp 301–302.

21   AOT, CON 16/1, no 1013; *Burke's Peerage*, pp 1311–1312.

22   Conduct record, AOT, CON 35/1, no 1013, p 162.

23   Thomas Lempriere, *The Penal Settlements of Van Diemen's Land*, orig 1839, Royal Society of Tasmania, Hobart, 1954, p 69; Maggie Weidenhofer, *Port Arthur: A Place of Misery*, Oxford University Press, Melbourne, 1981, pp 106, 109–110; Robert Hughes, *The Fatal Shore: A History of the Transportation of Convicts to Australia 1787–1868*, Collins, London, 1988, p 406.

24   *Herald*, 14 May 1835.

25   Weidenhofer, *Port Arthur*, pp 18–19; Ian Brand, *Penal Peninsula: Port Arthur and its Outstations 1827–1898*, Regal, Launceston, 1990, p 18; CMH Clark, *A History of Australia*, vol 2, *New South Wales and Van Diemen's Land 1822–1838*, Melbourne University Press, Melbourne, 1968, p 275.

26   DA Denholm, 'Port Arthur: the men and the myth', *Historical Studies*, 14(55), Oct 1970, p 415.

27   Brand, *Penal Peninsula*, p 10.

28   Hamish Maxwell-Stewart, 'The rise and fall of John Longworth: Work and punishment in early Port Arthur', *Tasmanian Historical Studies*, 6(2), 1999, pp 96–114; Linus Miller, *Notes of an Exile to Van Diemen's Land*, Fredonia, New York, 1846.

29   Denholm, 'Port Arthur', pp 419–23.

30   AOT, CON 31/9, no 393; CON 35/1, no 1013, p 162.

Reflections on *A Swindler's Progress*

1   Liz Jackson's interview with John Howard, on 'An average Australian bloke', *Four Corners*, ABC TV, first broadcast 19 Feb 1996. The phrase 'black armband history', much-used by Howard, was coined by historian Geoffrey Blainey

in 1993: see Stuart Macintyre and Anna Clark, *The History Wars*, Melbourne University Press, Melbourne, 2003, p. 3.

2   Charles von Hügel, *New Holland Journal, November 1833–October 1834*, trans and ed Dymphna Clark, Melbourne University Press, Melbourne, 1994, p 298. Afficionados will appreciate the irony that this book was edited by Dymphna Clark, wife to Australia's most well-known historian. On the battles over Manning Clark's reputation, see Macintyre and Clark, *The History Wars*, pp 50–71.

3   Stoppard, *Arcadia*, p 27.

4   See Antoinette Burton, 'Who needs the nation? Interrogating "British" history', in C Hall (ed), *Cultures of Empire: Colonizers in Britain and the Empire in the Nineteenth and Twentieth Centuries*, Manchester University Press, Manchester, 2000.

5   Amongst a vast literature, see Catherine Hall, *Civilising Subjects: Colony and Metropole in the English Imagination 1830–1867*, Routlege, Chicago/London, 2002; Zoe Laidlaw, *Colonial Connections 1815–1845: Patronage, the Information Revolution and Colonial Government*, Manchester University Press, Manchester, 2005; David Lambert and Alan Lester (eds), *Colonial Lives Across the British Empire: Imperial Careering in the Long Nineteenth Century*, Cambridge University Press, Cambridge, 2006; Tony Ballantyne and Antoinette Burton (eds), *Gender, Mobility and Intimacy in an Age of Empire*, University of Illinois Press, Urbana Champaign, 2008.

6   Natalie Zemon Davis, *The Return of Martin Guerre*, Harvard University Press, Cambridge, 1983; Jennine Hurl-Eamon, 'The Westminster impostors: Impersonating law enforcement in early eighteenth-century London', *Eighteenth-Century Studies*, 38(3), 2005, pp 461–83; Thomas Kidd, 'Passing as a pastor: Clerical imposture in the colonial Atlantic world', *Religion and American Culture*, 14(2), 2004, pp 149–74.

7   Karen Halttunen, *Confidence Men and Painted Women: A Study of Middle-Class Culture in America 1830–1870*, Yale University Press, New Haven, 1982.

REFERENCES

Archival sources: United Kingdom

National Archives of Scotland

High Court of Justiciary
Lord Advocate's Department, High Court Precognitions

Bodleian Library

Ms Don e 164 MSS, Wilberforce, c 35: Diary of William Wilberforce

British Library

Add MSS 27337: Correspondence and Papers of James Gillray
Add MSS 38244, 38243, 38191, 38244, 38328, 38249: Liverpool Papers
Add MSS 58955: Dropmore Papers
Add MSS 62112: Memoir of Humphry Repton

Harewood House, West Yorkshire

Political pamphlets
Papers relating to Edward Lascelles

Northamptonshire Record Office

Fitzwilliam (Milton) Collection

Sheffield Archives

Wentworth Woodhouse Muniments
  (The Wentworth Woodhouse Muniments have been accepted in lieu of
  Inheritance Tax by HM Government and allocated to Sheffield City Council)

A Swindler's Progress

West Yorkshire Archive Service, Leeds

Harewood Papers

Archival sources: Australia

State Records, New South Wales

Dowling, *Proceedings of the Supreme Court of New South Wales*
Correspondence, Colonial Secretary's Office
Phoenix Hulk Transportation Book
Supreme Court, informations and other papers

Archives Office of Tasmania

Convict Appropriation Lists
Convict Conduct Registers
Convict Indents
Correspondence, Colonial Secretary's Office
Description Lists of Convicts
Index of Convicts Locally Convicted or Transported to Other Colonies

Mitchell Library, Sydney

Bonwick Transcripts: Appendix to the reports of John Thomas Bigge
A 1733, A 1736: Sir Richard Bourke Papers
A 1206, A 1210, A 1211, A 1214: NSW Governor's Despatches
Doc 79: Papers relating to John Dow

Published primary sources: Newspapers and Magazines

United Kingdom

Belfast News-Letter
Caledonian Mercury
Derby Mercury
Dumfries & Galloway Courier
Dumfries Weekly Journal
Hampshire Telegraph and Sussex Chronicle
Jackson's Oxford Journal
John Bull
The Hull Packet and Original Weekly Commercial, Literary and General Advertiser

References

La Belle Assemblée, or, Bells Court and Fashionable Magazine
Leeds Intelligencer
Leeds Mercury
Manchester Times and Guardian
Newcastle Courant
The Satirist, and Censor of the Times
The Times
York Herald

New South Wales and Van Diemen's Land

Australian
Hobart Town Courier
New South Wales Government Gazette
Sydney Gazette
Sydney Herald
Sydney Monitor
Sydney Times

Websites

Sue Wiblin and David Roberts, 'The Castle Forbes affair: Records of the 1833 convict revolt in the Hunter Valley, NSW Australia', <www.une.edu.au/arts/ACF/cf1833/>

Hilary M Carey and David Roberts, 'The Wellington Valley Project: Papers relating the Church Missionary Society mission to Wellington Valley, New South Wales 1830–1842', <www.newcastle.edu.au/group/amrhd/wvp/>

Books, pamphlets and articles

Anon, *A Collection of the Speeches, Addresses, and Squibs produced by all Parties during the Late Contested Election for the County of York*, Edward Baines, Leeds, 1807

Anon, *Considerations Upon a Bill Now Before Parliament, for Repealing (In Substance) the whole Code of Laws respecting the Woollen Manufacture of Great Britain: And for Dissolving the Ancient System of Apprenticeship, by the Abrogation of the Laws relating thereto, as far as they respect the Clothing Trade, in certain Counties, mentioned in the said Bill*, C Stower, London, 1803

Anon, *Party Politics Exposed, In a letter addressed to the Right Honorable The Secretary of State for the Colonies; Containing Comments on Convict Discipline in New South Wales; and Embodying a Particular Analysis of the Published Evidence Taken at Castle Forbes by Commissioners Plunkett and Hely, Respecting the Treatment of Assigned Convict Servants by an Emigrant of 1821*, Anne Howe, Sydney, 1834

Anon, *A Poetical Description of Mr Hogarth's Election Prints: In Four Cantos. Written Under*

Mr. Hogarth's Sanction and Inspection, T Caslon, London, 1759

Anon, *Spies and Bloodites!!! The Lives and Political History of those arch-fiends Oliver, Reynolds, & Co. Treason-Hatchers, Green-Bag-Makers, Blood-Hunters, Spies, Tempters, and Informers-General to His Majesty's Ministers. Including a complete Account of all their Intrigues, Snares, Plots, Plans, Treasons, and Machinations, in the Metropolis, Manchester, Birmingham, Leeds, and various Parts of the Country, laying open the whole of their Transactions with Government, &c &c*, John Fairburn, London, 1817

Baines, Edward, *History of the Reign of George III, King of the United Kingdom of Great Britain and Ireland*, Longman, Leeds, 1820

Baines, Edward (jun), *The Life of Edward Baines, Late MP for the borough of Leeds*, Longman, London, 1851

Bald, Robert, *A General View of the Coal Trade of Scotland, Chiefly that of the River Forth and Mid-Lothian, as connected with the supplying of Edinburgh and the North of Scotland with FUEL; to which is Added An Inquiry into the conditions of these women who carry coals under ground in Scotland, known by the name of Bearers*, A Neill and Co/Oliphant & Brown, Edinburgh, 1808

Bessborough, Vere Brabazon Ponsonby, 9th Earl of Bessborough, with A Aspinall, *Lady Bessborough and her Family Circle*, John Murray, London, 1940

Boswell, James, *Life of Johnson*, Oxford University Press, Oxford, 1980

Cave, Kathryn, Kenneth Garlick and Angus Macintyre (eds), *The Diary of Joseph Farrington*, 16 vols, Yale University Press, New Haven/London, 1978–1984

Chapman, Peter, *The Diaries and Letters of GTWB Boyes 1820–1832*, vol 1, Oxford University Press, Melbourne, 1985

Colquhoun, Janet, *The Works of Lady Colquhoun of Rossdhu*, James Nesbit, London, 1852

Cuming, ED (ed), *Squire Osbaldeston: His Autobiography*, John Lane, London, 1926

Cunningham, Peter Millar, *Two Years in New South Wales*, Angus and Robertson, Sydney, 1966

Duff Gordon, Lucy, *Letters from the Cape,* ed Dorothea Fairbridge, Oxford University Press, London, 1927

Gore, John, *Thomas Creevey's Papers*, Penguin, London, 1985

Granville, Countess Castalia (ed), *Lord Granville Leveson Gower (First Earl Granville), Private Correspondence 1781–1821*, John Murray, London, 1916

Gray, Jonathan, *An Account of the Manner of Proceeding at the Contested Election for Yorkshire, in 1807, chiefly relating to the Office of Sheriff*, York, 1818

Hamilton, James, *A Memoir of Lady Colquhoun*, James Nisbet, London, 1850

Harcourt, Edward William (ed), *The Harcourt Papers*, James Parker, Oxford, 1880

Historical Records of Australia, Government Printer, Sydney, 1914–1925

Hügel, Charles von, *New Holland Journal, November 1833–October 1834*, trans and ed Dymphna Clark, Melbourne University Press, Melbourne, 1994

Jackson, Randle, *The Speech of Randle Jackson, Esq Addressed to the Honorable the Committee of the House of Commons, Appointed to consider the State of the Woollen Manufacture of England, on behalf of the Cloth-Workers and Sheerman of the Counties of Yorkshire, Lancashire, Wiltshire, Somersetshire and Gloucestershire. Published by them from the short-hand copy of Mr Gurney*, C Stower, London, 1806

Jewell, John, *The Tourist's Companion, or the History and Antiquities of Harewood in*

Yorkshire, Giving a particular description of Harewood House, Church, and Castle: with some accounts of its environs, selected from various authors, and containing much information never before published, B Dewhirst, Leeds, 1819

Jorgensen, Jorgen, *A Shred of Autobiograhy*, Sullivan's Cove, Adelaide, 1981

Leconfield, Maud Mary Lyttelton Wyndham, Baroness Leconfield and John Gore, *Three Howard Sisters: Selections from the writings of Lady Caroline Lascelles, Lady Dover and Countess Gower 1825 – 1833*, John Murray, London, 1955

Lempriere, Thomas James, *The Penal Settlements of Van Diemen's Land*, orig 1839, Royal Society of Tasmania, Hobart, 1954

Lewin, TH (ed), *The Lewin Letters*, 2 vols, Archibald Constable & Co, London, 1909

Maxwell, Herbert (ed), *The Creevey Papers: A Selection from the Correspondence and Diaries of the late Thomas Creevey, MP*, John Murray, London, 1903

Miller, Linus W, *Notes of an Exile to Van Diemen's Land*, Fredonia, New York, 1846

Mudie, James, *The Felonry of New South Wales*, (orig Whaley & Co, London, 1837), facs edn, ed Walter Stone, Melbourne, 1964

——, *Vindication of James Mudie and John Larnach from Certain Reflections on their Conduct ... Relative to the Treatment by them of their Convict Servants*, ES Hall, Sydney, 1834

Report From the Committee on the Woollen Manufacture of England with Minutes of Evidence and Appendix, Irish University Press Series of British Parliamentary Papers: Industrial Revolutions Textiles, 2, Shannon, 1968

Russell, John, *A Tour in Germany, and some of the Southern Provinces of the Austrian Empire, in the years 1820, 1821, 1822*, 2 vols, A Constable & Co, Edinburgh, 1824

Ryvers, Eliza, *Ode to the Right Honourable Lord Melton* [sic], *Infant Son of Earl Fitzwilliam*, London, 1787

Smith, Henry Stooks, *An Alphabetical List of the Officers of the Yorkshire Hussars from the Formation of the Regiment to the Present Time*, London, 1853

Stevenson, John, *Letters in Answer to Dr Price's Two Pamphlets on Civil Liberty, &c with some remarks on the parliamentary debates of last session, as they appeared in the News-Papers: Also Copies of Four Letters, concerning the Slavery of the Colliers, Coal-Bearers, and Salters in Scotland*, G Burnett/Richardson and Urquhart, London, 1778

Therry, Roger, *Reminiscences of Thirty Years' Residence in New South Wales and Victoria*, Sampson, Low, Son & Co, London, 1863

Walker, George, *The Costume of Yorkshire, Illustrated by a Series of Forty Engravings, being facsimiles of original drawings, with descriptions in English and French*, T Bensley, London, 1814

Wilberforce, Robert Isaac and Samuel Wilberforce (eds), *The Correspondence of William Wilberforce*, John Murray, London, 1840

Wilberforce, Robert Isaac and Samuel Wilberforce, *The Life of William Wilberforce by his sons, Robert Isaac Wilberforce and Samuel Wilberforce*, John Murray, London, 1838

Secondary sources

Atkinson, Alan, *The Europeans in Australia, A History*, vol 2, *Democracy*, Oxford University Press, Oxford, 2004

Bailey, Catherine, *Black Diamonds: The Rise and Fall of an English Dynasty*, Penguin, London, 2008

Ballantyne, Tony and Antoinette Burton (eds), *Gender, Mobility and Intimacy in an Age of Empire*, University of Illinois Press, Urbana Champaign, 2008

Ballyn, Susan and Lucy Frost, 'A Spanish convict, her clergyman biographer, and the amanuensis of her bastard son', in Lucy Frost and Hamish Maxwell-Stewart (eds), *Chain Letters: Narrating Convict Lives*, Melbourne University Press, Melbourne, 2001

Bayly, CA, *Imperial Meridian: The British Empire and the World 1780–1830*, Longman, London/New York, 1989

Blair, Sandra, 'Patronage and prejudice: Educated convicts in the New South Wales press 1838', *Push from the Bush*, 8, 1980, pp 75–87

——— , 'The "Convict Press": William Watt and the *Sydney Gazette* in the 1830s', *Push from the Bush*, 5, 1979, pp 99–119

——— , 'The felonry and the free? Divisions in colonial society in the penal era', *Labour History*, 45, 1983, pp 1–16

——— , 'The revolt at Castle Forbes: A catalyst to emancipist emigrant confrontation', *Journal of the Royal Australian Historical Society*, 64(2), 1978, pp 89–107

Bourne, JM, *Patronage and Society in Nineteenth-Century England*, Edward Arnold, London, 1986

Boyce, James, *Van Diemen's Land*, Black Ink, Melbourne, 2008

Brand, Ian, *Penal Peninsula: Port Arthur and its Outstations 1827–1898*, Regal, Launceston, 1990

Brown, Chistopher Leslie, *Moral Capital: Foundations of British Abolitionism*, University of North Carolina Press, Chapel Hill, 2006

Brown, Richard, *Church and State in Modern Britain 1700–1850*, Routledge, London/New York, 1991

Burton, Antoinette, 'Who needs the nation? Interrogating "British history"', in C Hall (ed), *Cultures of Empire: Colonizers in Britain and the Empire in the Nineteenth and Twentieth Centuries*, Manchester University Press, Manchester, 2000

Cannadine, David, 'The making of the British upper classes', in his *Aristocracy: Grandeur and Decline in Modern Britain*, Yale University Press, New Haven/London, 1994

——— , *Ornamentalism: How the British Saw their Empire*, Penguin, London, 2002

Christie, Ian R, 'The Yorkshire Association 1780–1784: A study in political organization', *The Historical Journal*, 3(2), 1960, pp 144–61

Clark, CMH, *A History of Australia*, vol 2, *New South Wales and Van Diemen's Land 1822–1838*, Melbourne University Press, Melbourne, 1968

Clune, Frank and PR Stephenson, *The Viking of Van Diemen's Land: The Stormy Life of Jorgen Jorgensen*, Angus and Robertson, Sydney, 1954

Cochrane, Peter, *Colonial Ambition: Foundations of Australian Democracy*, Melbourne
University Press, Melbourne, 2006

Colley, Linda, *Britons: Forging the Nation 1707–1837*, Yale University Press, New
Haven/London, 1992

Davidoff, Leonore, *The Best Circles: Society, Etiquette and the Season*, Croom Helm,
London, 1973

Davidoff, Leonore and Catherine Hall, *Family Fortunes: Men and Women of the English
Middle Class 1780–1850*, Routledge, London, 1987

Davis, Natalie Zemon, *The Return of Martin Guerre*, Harvard University Press,
Cambridge, 1983

Denholm, DA, 'Port Arthur: the men and the myth', *Historical Studies*, 14(55), Oct
1970

Dolley, Michael, 'The murky career of 'Major Medallion', *The Numismatic Circular*,
87(7–8), 1979, pp 337–39

Duckham, Baron F, *A History of the Scottish Coal Industry*, vol 1, *1700–1815*, David &
Charles, Newton Abbot, 1970

Evans, Raymond, 'Creating 'an object of real terror': The tabling of the first Bigge
report', in Martin Crotty and David Andrew Roberts (eds), *Turning Points in
Australian History*, UNSW Press, Sydney, 2009

Fletcher, Anthony, *Gender, Sex and Subordination in England 1500–1800*, Yale
University Press, New Haven/London, 1995

Fletcher, Brian, *Ralph Darling: A Governor Maligned*, Oxford University Press,
Melbourne, 1984

Fraser, D, 'The life of Edward Baines: A filial biography of the "The Great Liar of
the North", *Northern History*, 31, 1995, p 209

Girouard, Mark, *Life in the English Country House: A Social and Architectural History*,
Yale University Press, New Haven, 1994

Gregory, Derek, *Regional Transformation and Industrial Revolution: A Geography of the
Yorkshire Woollen Industry*, Macmillan, London, 1982

Habakkuk, John, *Marriage, Debt, and the Estates System: English Landownership 1650–
1950*, Clarendon Press, Oxford, 1994

Hague, William, *William Pitt the Younger*, Harper Perennial, London, 2005

——— , *William Wilberforce: The Life of the Great Anti-Slave Trade Campaigner*, Harper
Perennial, London, 2008

Hall, Catherine, *Civilising Subjects: Colony and Metropole in the English Imagination
1830–1867*, Routlege, Chicago/London, 2002

Halttunen, Karen, *Confidence Men and Painted Women: A Study of Middle-Class Culture
in America 1830–1870*, Yale University Press, New Haven, 1982

Hamilton, Douglas. 'Private enterprise and public service: Naval contracting in
the Caribbean, c 1720–1750', *Journal of Maritime Research*, April 2004,
<www.jmr.nmm.ac.uk>

Harling, Philip, *The Waning of 'Old Corruption': The Politics of Economical Reform in
Britain 1779–1846*, Clarendon Press, Oxford, 1996

Hartwell, RM, *The Economic Development of Van Diemen's Land 1820–1850*, Melbourne
University Press, Melbourne, 1954

Hilton, Boyd, *A Mad, Bad and Dangerous People? England 1783–1846*, Oxford

University Press, Oxford, 2006

Hirst, John, *Convict Society and Its Enemies*, Allen & Unwin, Sydney, 1983

Howse, Geoffrey, *The Wentworths of Wentworth: The Fitzwilliam (Wentworth) Estates and the Wentworth Monuments*, Trustees of the Fitzwilliam Wentworth Amenity Trust, Wentworth, 2002

Hudson, Pat, 'Proto-industrialisation: The case of the West Riding wool textile industry in the 18th and early 19th centuries', *History Workshop Journal*, 12, 1981, pp 34–61

——— , *The Genesis of Industrial Capital: A Study of the West Riding Wool Textile Industry c 1750–1850*, Cambridge University Press, Cambridge, 1986

Hughes, Robert, *The Fatal Shore: A History of the Transportation of Convicts to Australia 1787–1868*, Collins, London, 1988

Hurl-Eamon, Jennine, 'The Westminster impostors: Impersonating law enforcement in early eighteenth-century London', *Eighteenth-Century Studies*, 38(3), 2005, pp 461–83

Ihde, Erin, *A Manifesto for New South Wales: Edward Smith Hall and the Sydney Monitor 1826–1840*, Australian Scholarly, Melbourne, 2004

Keene, Judith, 'Surviving the Peninsula War in Australia: Juan D'Arrieta ~ Spanish free settler and colonial gentleman', *Journal of the Royal Australian Historical Society*, 85, 1999

Kennedy, Carol, *Harewood: The Life and Times of an English Country House*, Hutchinson, London, 1982

Kercher, Bruce, *Outsiders: Tales from the Supreme Court of New South Wales 1824–1836*, Australian Scholarly, Melbourne, 2006

Kidd, Thomas, 'Passing as a pastor: Clerical imposture in the colonial Atlantic world', *Religion and American Culture*, 14(2), 2004, pp 149–74

King, Hazel, *Richard Bourke*, Oxford University Press, Melbourne, 1971

Kingston, A, *History of New South Wales*, Cambridge University Press, Cambridge, 2006

Laidlaw, Zoe, *Colonial Connections 1815–1845: Patronage, the Information Revolution and Colonial Government*, Manchester University Press, Manchester, 2005

Lambert, David and Alan Lester (eds), *Colonial Lives Across the British Empire: Imperial Careering in the Long Nineteenth Century*, Cambridge University Press, Cambridge, 2006

Larsen, Ruth, 'Dynastic domesticity: The role of elite women in the Yorkshire country house 1685–1858', PhD thesis, University of York, 2003

Lester, Alan, *Imperial Networks: Creating Identities in Nineteenth-Century South Africa and Britain*, Routledge, London, 2001

Lynch, Karen, 'Some Lascelles ladies', in Ruth Larsen (ed), *Maids & Mistresses: Celebrating 300 Years of Women and the Yorkshire Country House*, Yorkshire Country House Partnership, Yorkshire, 2004

Macintyre, Stuart, *A Concise History of Australia*, Cambridge University Press, Cambridge, 1999

Macintyre, Stuart and Anna Clark, *History Wars*, Melbourne University Press, Melbourne, 2003

Mandler, Peter, *Aristocratic Government in the Age of Reform: Whigs and Liberals 1830–*

References

1852, Clarendon Press, Oxford, 1990

——— , *The Fall and Rise of the Stately Home*, Yale University Press, New Haven/London, 1997

Marlow, Joyce, *The Peterloo Massacre*, Panther, London, 1969

Mauchline, Mary, *Harewood House*, David and Charles, London, 1974

Maxwell-Stewart, Hamish, 'The rise and fall of John Longworth: Work and punishment in early Port Arthur', *Tasmanian Historical Studies*, 6(2), 1999, pp 96–114

——— , *Closing Hell's Gates: The Death of a Convict Station*, Allen & Unwin, Sydney, 2008

Milliss, Roger, *Waterloo Creek: The Australia Day Mssacre of 1838, George Gibbs and the British Conquest of New South Wales*, UNSW Press, Sydney, 1994

Murray, Les, *A Working Forest*, Duffy and Snellgrove, Sydney, 1997

Neal, David, *The Rule of Law in a Penal Colony: Law and Power in Early New South Wales*, Cambridge University Press, Cambridge, 1991

O'Gorman, Frank, *Voters, Patrons, and Parties: The Unreformed Electoral System of Hanoverian England 1734–1832*, Clarendon Press, Oxford, 1989

Phillips, Diane, *An Eligible Situation: The Early History of George Town and Low Head*, Karuda Press, Canberra, 2004

Porter, Bernard, *Plots and Paranoia: A History of Political Espionage in Britain 1790–1988*, Routledge, London/New York, 1992

Pybus, Cassandra and Hamish Maxwell-Stewart, *American Citizens, British Slaves: Yankee Political Prisoners in an Australian Penal Colony 1839–1850*, Melbourne University Press, Melbourne, 2002

Raven, James, *Judging New Wealth: Popular Publishing and Responses to Commerce in England, 1750–1800*, Clarendon Press, Oxford, 1992

Reid, Kirsty, *Gender, Crime and Empire: Convicts, Settlers and the State in Early Colonial Australia*, Manchester University Press, Manchester, 2007

Reid, Robert, *The Peterloo Massacre*, Heinemann, London, 1989

Ritchie, John, *The Wentworths: Father and Son*, Melbourne University Press, Melbourne, 1997

Robson, Lloyd, *A History of Tasmania*, vol 1, Oxford University Press, Melbourne, 1983

Rubenhold, Haillie, *Lady Worsley's Whim: An Eighteenth-Century Tale of Sex, Scandal and Divorce*, Chatto & Windus, London, 2008

Shaw, AGL, *Convicts and the Colonies: A Study of Penal Transportation from Great Britain and Ireland to Australia and Other Parts of the British Empire*, Melbourne University Press, Melbourne, 1977

Shoemaker, Robert A, *Gender in English Society 1650–1850: The Emergence of Separate Spheres?* Longman, London, 1998

Smith, EA, 'The Yorkshire elections of 1806 and 1807: A study in electoral management', *Northern History*, 2, 1967, pp 62–90

——— , *Whig Principles and Party Politics: Earl Fitzwilliam and the Whig Party 1748–1833*, Manchester University Press, Manchester, 1975

——— , 'Earl Fitzwilliam and Malton: A proprietary borough in the early nineteenth century', *English Historical Review*, 80(314), 1965, pp 51–69

Smith, SD, *Slavery, Family and Gentry Capitalism in the British Atlantic: The World of the Lascelles, 1648–1834*, Cambridge University Press, Cambridge, 2006

Sprod, Dan, *The Usurper : Jorgen Jorgenson and his Turbulent Life in Iceland and Van Diemen's Land 1780–1841*, Blubber Head Press, Hobart, 2001

Stevens, John, *England's Last Revolution: Pentrich 1917*, Moorland Publishing, Buxton, 1977

Stone, Lawrence, *Road to Divorce: England 1530–1987*, Oxford Uniersity Press, Oxford, 1990

——— , *Family, Sex and Marriage in England 1500–1800*, Weidenfeld & Nicolson, London, 1977

Stone, Lawrence and Jeanne C Fawtier Stone, *An Open Elite? England 1540–1880*, Clarenden Press, Oxford, 1984

Stoppard, Tom, *Arcadia*, Faber & Faber, Boston/London, 1993

Thomas, David, 'The social origins of marriage partners of the British Peerage in the eighteenth and nineteenth centuries', *Population Studies* 26, 1972, pp 99–111

Thompson, EP, *The Making of the English Working Class*, Penguin, Harmondsworth, 1968

Tosh, John, 'The Old Adam and the New Man: Emerging themes in the history of English masculinities 1750–1850', in Tim Hitchcock and Michele Cohen (eds), *English Masculinities 1660–1800*, Longman, London and New York, 1999.

Trumbach, Randolph, *The Rise of the Egalitarian Family: Aristocratic Kinship and Domestic Relations in Eighteenth-Century England*, Academic Press, New York, 1978

Vernon, James, *Politics and the People: A Study in English Political Culture c 1815–1867*, Cambridge University Press, Cambridge, 1993

Vickery, Amanda, *The Gentleman's Daughter: Women's Lives in Georgian England*, Yale University Press, New Haven/London, 1998

Walker, RB, *The Newspaper Press in New South Wales*, Sydney University Press, Sydney, 1976

Walvin, James, 'Freedom and slavery and the shaping of Victorian Britain', *Slavery and Abolition*, 15(2), 1994, pp 246–59

Weidenhofer, Maggie, *Port Arthur: A Place of Misery*, Oxford University Press, Melbourne, 1981

Williams, Eric, *Capitalism and Slavery*, Deutsch, London, 1964

Wilson, Kathleen, *The Island Race: Englishness, Empire and Gender in the Eighteenth Century*, Routledge, London/New York, 2003

Wilson, RG, *Gentlemen Merchants: The Merchant Community in Leeds 1700–1830*, Manchester University Press, Manchester, 1971

Wood, W Allan, *Dawn in the Valley: The Story of Settlement in the Hunter River Valley to 1833*, Wentworth, Sydney, 1972.

References

INDEX

Index

A Swindler's Progress

A Swindler's Progress